Financial Statements.xls, 2nd Edition

A Step-by-Step Guide to Creating Financial Statements Using Microsoft Excel™

Financial Statements.xls, 2nd Edition

A Step-by-Step Guide to Creating Financial Statements Using Microsoft Excel

Written by: Joseph Rubin, CPA

Published by: Limelight Media Inc.
12207 Wilshire Blvd.
Los Angeles, CA USA 90025
sales@limelightmediainc.com
www.limelightmediainc.com

Distributed by: Limelight Media Inc.,

First edition printing: November 2003

Second edition printing: November 2004

Printed in the State of India

Library of Congress Control Number (LCCN): 2004097957

ISBN: 0-9746368-4-3

About The Author

Joseph Rubin, CPA, principal of **www.exceltip.com** (a leading Excel Web site) is the author of the very successful book, *F1 Get the Most out of Excel! The Ultimate Excel Tip Help Guide.*

Joseph Rubin has over 25 years of financial experience in the accounting industry. He has served as CFO, Controller and has run his own CPA practice for years. Joseph Rubin, CPA, is an independent consultant specializing in the development of applications using Microsoft Excel for the financial industry and has instructed thousands of professionals on Microsoft Excel.

Contact the author — jrubin@exceltip.com

This book is dedicated to my family, my wife, and my three children.

Joseph Rubin

Why I Wrote This Book

During the last eight years, I have been teaching thousands of finance professionals and heavy Excel users through a unique course I created specifically for the needs of finance professionals.

The experience gained in teaching, consulting and developing financial applications for finance professionals such as CPAs, controllers, economists, accountants and others provided me with an understanding of their experience with the Microsoft Excel spreadsheet program, as well as their needs, weak points, and competency level.

My conclusions:

Excel is widely used to create Financial Statements, as well as many other types of financial reports, such as Budget, Forecast, Cash Flow, Ratio Analysis, Financial models, business scenarios and various types of analysis reports that present the company's business performance. There is hardly any financial professional who does not create, prepare, print and/or send a variety of reports, while making extensive use of the Microsoft Excel application.

Most Excel users use the program inefficiently, creating too many workbooks and preparing complicated reports that contain too many links between workbooks while using formulas haphazardly. Extensive hours are then invested on updating and auditing.

In the books I have written, **F1 Get the Most out of Excel! The Ultimate Excel Tip Help Guide, Financial Statements.xls**, and **Mr Excel on Excel**, I focused on writing straightforward solutions for professionals that might help other Excel users to learn the best techniques needed to create financial reports and Financial Statements, with an in-depth explanation of the appropriate use of techniques for creating full, concise and smart financial documents.

Joseph Rubin, CPA

About This Book

This book contains two parts:

Part One: Creating the Financial Statements.xls Workbook

This part contains ten chapters. It starts with an explanation of what each worksheet in the **Financial Statements.xls** workbook contains, and then moves on to discussing adding and automatically updating adjustments to Trial Balance, updating the Trial Balances data worksheet and creating Financial Statements worksheets reports. It also provides information regarding automating Notes numbers, customizing the **Financial Statements.xls** workbook by adding custom menus for easier navigation, operating macros that print and mail the Financial Statements reports while protecting the financial data, and much more.

✦ **Chapter 1, Introducing Financial Statements.xls Worksheets**, introduces the structure of the **Financial Statements.xls** workbook and its worksheets.

✦ **Chapter 2, Adjusting the Trial Balance**, introduces techniques to add or update adjustments to the account balances in the Trial Balance worksheet, and prepare an audit-adjusted Trial Balance report to be used before preparing financial statements.

✦ **Chapter 3, Updating the Trial Balances Data Worksheet**, describes how to add the balances of the final Trial Balance to the appropriate column in worksheet *21 — Trial Balances Data*.

✦ **Chapter 4, Balance Sheet**, provides step-by-step instructions for creating a Balance Sheet report, which is the major report in the Financial Statement.

✦ **Chapter 5, Income Statement**, explains how to create the Income Statement report using Excel's worksheet.

✦ **Chapter 6, Cash Flow**, explains how to create Cash Flow reports using an Excel worksheet.

✦ **Chapter 7, Notes**, explains the **Notes** worksheet.

✦ **Chapter 8, Customizing the Financial Statements.xls Workbook and Presenting Information**, explains how to use various techniques to customize the **Financial Statements.xls** workbook according to your needs.

✦ **Chapter 9, Protecting Financial Data**, reviews all of the various options you can use to protect your financial information data and files.

✦ **Chapter 10, Printing and Mailing Financial Statements Reports**, discusses the techniques you need to print or mail full Financial Statements reports.

Part Two: Analyzing Financial Statements and Creating Management Financial Reports

This part contains five chapters. It provides detailed explanations regarding how to create and present five-year comparison Balance Sheet and Income Statement reports and prepare Income Statements for monthly or quarterly ending reporting periods while dealing with fiscal year-end reporting periods. It also discusses how to use PivotTable reports to prepare and analyze Income Statement reports by Profit Centers, and to prepare the ratio analysis figures for managements needs and decision makers, both inside and outside the firm.

✦ **Chapter 11, Balance Sheet Five-year Comparison Reports**, describes how to use the reports already created in previous chapters to create the Balance Sheet five-year comparison report.

✦ **Chapter 12, Income Statement Five-year and Quarterly Comparison Reports**, describes how to use the Income Statement report already created in *Chapter 5, Income Statement* to create the Income Statement five-year comparison report and quarterly comparison reports.

✦ **Chapter 13, Analyzing Financial Statements Using PivotTable and PivotChart Reports**, describes how to use **PivotTable** and **PivotChart** reports to analyze the company's Financial Statements.

✦ **Chapter 14, Analyzing Financial Statements and Calculating the Ratio Analysis**, introduces techniques for Financial Statement Analysis.

✦ **Chapter 15, Analyzing Profit Centers**, describes how to create the company's **Profit Centers'** Income Statement reports.

Contents at a Glance

Table of Contents

List of Figures

Part One: Creating the Financial Statements.xls Workbook

Chapter 1

Introducing Financial Statements.xls Worksheets

About This Chapter

This chapter introduces the structure of the **Financial Statements.xls** workbook and its worksheets, and includes the following sections:

✦ **Overview**, page 2, presents an overview of the worksheets' functionality.

✦ **Financial Statements.xls Worksheets**, page 3, describes the different categories into which the various worksheets are sorted, and provides details about each of them.

✦ **Installing the ChooseSheet.xla Add-in**, page 18, describes a downloadable add-in that enables you to easily find and select specific worksheets in the **Financial Statements.xls** workbook.

✦ **Sorting Worksheets in Ascending Order**, page 21, provides macros that enable you to sort the worksheets to organize them in ascending order in the **Financial Statements.xls** workbook.

Overview

This chapter introduces the structure of the **Financial Statements.xls** workbook, and discusses:

The name of each worksheet

The purpose of each worksheet

The descriptive information that can be entered and/or the calculations that can be performed in the worksheets' cells

The data flow between the worksheets

The relationships between the worksheets

Before Starting

To use the examples in this book, download the **Financial Statements.xls** sample workbook from www.exceltip.com/xls, or use the **Financial Statements.xls** sample workbook available in the companion CD-ROM.

Financial Statements.xls Worksheets

The **Financial Statements.xls** workbook contains 15 worksheets in four categories. The worksheets in the workbook are as follows:

✦ **Category 1: General, Parameters and Calculated Worksheets**, page 4
  ❖ 11 — General Details
  ❖ 12 — Worksheet List
  ❖ 13 — Parameters and Calculations
  ❖ 14 — Months List
  ❖ 15 — BS, IS Level
  ❖ 16 — Notes List

✦ **Category 2: Data Worksheets**, page 14
  ❖ 21 — Trial Balances Data

✦ **Category 3: Reports Worksheets**, page 17
  ❖ 31 — Balance Sheet
  ❖ 41 — Income Statement
  ❖ 51 — Cash Flow
  ❖ 61 — Notes

✦ **Category 4: Trial Balance and Adjustments Worksheets**, page 17
  ❖ 91 — Trial Balance (Original)
  ❖ 92 — Trial Balance Adjustments
  ❖ 93 — Final Trial Balance
  ❖ 94 — Trial Balance Audit

After creating the workbook and its worksheets, you can add more worksheets, as required. Adding prefix numbers while naming these additional worksheets enables you to easily move between the different worksheets to find the one you need, as well as conveniently organize them in ascending order. For more details regarding these capabilities, refer to *Installing the ChooseSheet.xla Add-in*, page 18, and *Sorting Worksheets in Ascending Order*, page 21.

Category 1: General, Parameters and Calculated Worksheets

There are six worksheets in this category. These contain general information, parameters and formulas, worksheets list, months list, Balance Sheet and Income Statement section levels list, and **Notes** list.

Worksheet 11 – General Details

In worksheet *11 — General Details* you define the company name and the ending date of the report.

In the **Financial Statements.xls** workbook's first worksheet, type the desired company name into cell **C2** (as shown below), and define the *Name* **CompanyName** to the cell.

➤ **To define a Name to a cell:**

1. Select cell **C2** and press **<Ctrl+F3>**.

2. In the **Name in workbook** box, type **CompanyName** and click **OK**.

By entering a linked formula into the range *Name* **CompanyName** in the four report worksheets (described in *Category 3: Reports Worksheets*, page 17), the company name will change automatically in each worksheet.

➢ **To set the report ending date:**

✦ After you have defined the company name, select the month of the report ending date from the **MonthsList** (the **Input range** inserted into the *Format Control* dialog box in the **Combo Box** object, as described on page 7). The formulas in the worksheets containing the reports are automatically updated based on the month selected.

Before adding a **Combo Box** object, you must define the names to be inserted into the *Format Control* dialog box of the **Combo Box** object.

➢ **To define the Months List Name:**

1. In worksheet *14 — Months List*, follow these steps to insert the months list into the cells in column **B**.

	Microsoft Excel - Financial Statements			
	File Edit View Insert Format Tools Data Window Help			
	MonthsList ▼ *fx* 1/31/1998			
	A	B	C	D
1	Month Number	Months List		
2	1	January 31, 1998		
3	2	February 28, 1998		
4	3	March 31, 1998		
5	4	April 30, 1998		
6	5	May 31, 1998		
7	6	June 30, 1998		
8	7	July 31, 1998		
9	8	August 31, 1998		
10	9	September 30, 1998		
11	10	October 31, 1998		

2. Select cell **B2** and enter the first date in the list (in this example, 1/1/1998) in the *Name* box (located at the left of the Formula Bar), then type **B109** and press **<Shift+Enter>**. Cells **B2:B109** have been selected.

3. From the *Edit* menu, select **Fill** and then **Series**. The *Series* dialog box appears.

4. In the **Type** group box, select the **Date** option button, and in the **Date Unit** group box, select the **Month** option button.

5. Click **OK**.

6. Press **<Ctrl+1>**. The *Format Cells* dialog box appears.

7. In **Number** tab displayed, select **Custom** and type **mmmm dd, yyyy** in the **Type** box.

8. Click **OK**.

9. With cells **B2:B109** still selected, press **<Ctrl+F3>** and type the *Name* **MonthsList** in the **Names in workbook** input box.

10. Click **OK**.

➢ **To define a Name for the Combo Box linked cell:**

✦ In worksheet *13 — Parameters & Calculations*, select cell **B2** and define the *Name* **MonthSelectionNumber** for the cell, as shown below.

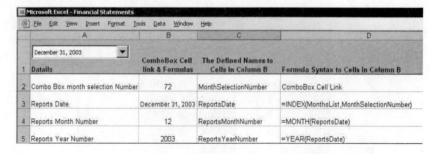

Details	ComboBox Cell link & Formulas	The Defined Names to Cells in Column B	Formula Syntax to Cells in Column B
2 Combo Box month selection Number	72	MonthSelectionNumber	ComboBox Cell Link
3 Reports Date	December 31, 2003	ReportsDate	=INDEX(MonthsList,MonthSelectionNumber)
4 Reports Month Number	12	ReportsMonthNumber	=MONTH(ReportsDate)
5 Reports Year Number	2003	ReportsYearNumber	=YEAR(ReportsDate)

Adding a Combo Box Object

➤ **To add a Combo Box object to the worksheet:**

1. In worksheet *11 — General Details,* place the cursor over any toolbar.

2. Right-click, and select **Forms** from the shortcut menu.

3. Click the **Combo Box** icon, as shown:

    The cursor changes into a cross when the **Combo Box** is copied.

4. Select a cell in the worksheet, and draw the shape of the **Combo Box**. When you are finished, a **Combo Box** appears.

➤ **To add a months list and cell link address to the Format Control dialog box in the Combo Box object:**

1. Select the **Combo Box** object and make sure you are in edit mode (as indicated by the small circles around the box).

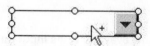

2. Right-click, and select **Format Control** from the shortcut menu.

3. Select the **Control** tab, as shown below.

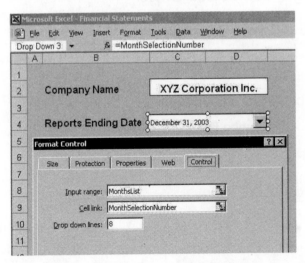

4. In the **Input range** text box, type the previously defined *Name*, **MonthsList**.

5. In the **Cell link** text box, type the defined *Name*, **MonthSelectionNumber**.

6. Select the **3-D shading** check box and click **OK**.

IMPORTANT:

The **<F3>** (**Paste Name**) shortcut is not available in the **Input range** and **Cell link** text boxes of the *Format Control* dialog box.

Worksheet 12 – Worksheet List

Worksheet *12 — Worksheet List* contains the list of worksheets in the workbook. You can update the worksheet list by using the **Update_WorksheetsList** macro, below, and entering it into a regular module. For more details on how to insert code lines into a regular Module, refer to page 121, *Chapter 8, Customizing the Financial Statements.xls Workbook and Presenting Information.*

NOTE:

The macro VBA code lines can be copied from http://www.excelforum.com/f96-s, the macro is also available in Chapter1.xls workbook at the companion CD-ROM.

```
Sub Update_WorksheetsList()

Dim I As Integer
On Error GoTo ErrorTrap:

'wList is the name defined to Range("A2") in 12-Worksheets List

Range(Range("wList"), Range("wList").End(xlDown)).ClearContents
For I = 1 To Sheets.Count
    Range("wList").Offset(I - 1, 0).Value = Sheets(I).Name
Next I

ErrorTrap:
Exit Sub

End Sub
```

Worksheet 13 – Parameters and Calculations

This worksheet stores the **Combo Box** cell link (cell **B2**) (as described in *Category 1: General, Parameters and Calculated Worksheets*, page 4) and formulas that calculate the Reports Date, Reports Month Number, and Reports Year Number (as shown in rows **3** through **5** in Figure 1-1). The resulting calculations are used to automatically change the titles' dates and year numbers in the reporting worksheets. For more details, refer to *Chapter 4, Balance Sheet, Chapter 5, Income Statement, Chapter 6, Cash Flow* and *Chapter 7, Notes.*

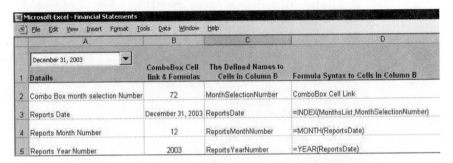

	A	B	C	D
		December 31, 2003 ▼		
1	**Details**	**ComboBox Cell link & Formulas**	**The Defined Names to Cells in Column B**	**Formula Syntax to Cells in Column B**
2	Combo Box month selection Number	72	MonthSelectionNumber	ComboBox Cell Link
3	Reports Date	December 31, 2003	ReportsDate	=INDEX(MonthsList,MonthSelectionNumber)
4	Reports Month Number	12	ReportsMonthNumber	=MONTH(ReportsDate)
5	Reports Year Number	2003	ReportsYearNumber	=YEAR(ReportsDate)

Figure 1-1: Worksheet 13 — Parameters and Calculations

✦ In cell **B3**, the *Name* defined to the cell is **ReportsDate**, with the formula:

=INDEX(MonthsList,MonthSelectionNumber)

This **Index** formula uses two arguments (the third argument is optional): **Array** and **Row Number**. The resulting calculation is the date in row **72** in the **MonthsList** (as shown on page 5).

✦ In cell **B4**, the *Name* defined to the cell is **ReportsMonthNumber**, with the formula:

=MONTH(ReportsDate)

This **Month** formula returns the month number from cell **B3** (**ReportsDate**).

✦ In cell **B5**, the *Name* defined to the cell is **ReportsYearNumber**, with the formula:

=YEAR(ReportsDate)

This **Year** formula returns the year number from cell **B4** (**ReportsMonthNumber**).

Worksheet 14 – Months List

For details regarding this worksheet, refer to *To define the Months List Name,* page 5.

Worksheet 15 – BS, IS Level

This worksheet contains lists of the three summary levels used in the Financial Statements reports, as shown in Figure 1-2 (the **BS** in the worksheet name stands for Balance Sheet; **IS** for Income Statement):

✦ **Account Category** level (level 1, column **A**).

✦ **Account Groups** level (level 2, column **B**).

✦ **Account Types** level (level 3, column **C**).

	A	B	C
	Level1	Level2	Level3
2	Assets	Current Assets	Cash
3	Assets	Current Assets	Accounts Receivable
4	Assets	Current Assets	Inventories
5	Assets	Current Assets	Other Current Assets
6	Assets	Current Assets	Prepaid Expenses
7	Assets	Property and Equipment (at Cost)	Land & Building
8	Assets	Property and Equipment (at Cost)	Machinery and Equipment
9	Assets	Property and Equipment (at Cost)	Furniture and Fixtures
10	Assets	Property and Equipment (at Cost)	Less: Accumulated Depreciation
11	Assets	Property and Equipment (at Cost)	Leasehold Improvements
12	Assets	Other Assets	Investment in Revenue Bond
13	Assets	Other Assets	Patents, Trademarks and Goodwill
14	Liabilities and Stockholder's Equity	Current liabilities	Line of Credit
15	Liabilities and Stockholder's Equity	Current liabilities	Current portion of long-term debt
16	Liabilities and Stockholder's Equity	Current liabilities	Accounts payable
17	Liabilities and Stockholder's Equity	Current liabilities	Accrued Expenses
18	Liabilities and Stockholder's Equity	Current liabilities	Other Payables

Figure 1-2: Worksheet 15 — BS, IS Level

The formulas inserted into cells in the Financial Statements worksheets reports will return data summarized by criteria, that is, a summary of each level. There are three summary levels in the Balance Sheet report (shown in Figure 1-3):

✦ **Level 1, Category:** Assets, Liabilities, Stockholder's Equity and Income Statements.

✦ **Level 2, Account Groups:** Under the Assets section — Current Assets, Property and Equipment (at Cost), Other Assets. Under the Liabilities and Stockholder's Equity section — Current Liabilities, Long-Term Liabilities, Stockholder's Equity.

✦ **Level 3, Account Types:** Under the Current Assets section (as an example) — Cash, Accounts Receivable, Inventories and Prepaid Expenses.

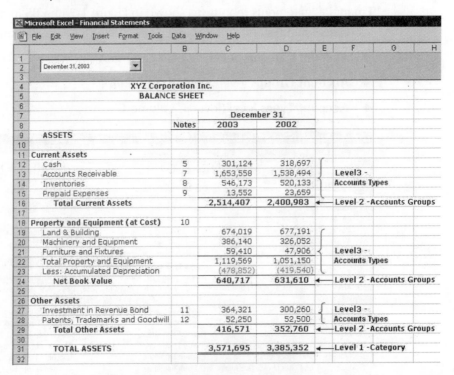

Figure 1-3: Balance Sheet Summary Levels

➢ **To define Names for the three column levels:**

1. Select column **A**, and press **<Ctrl+F3>**.

2. In the **Name in workbook** box, type **Level1**, and then click **OK**.

3. Repeat the steps above and define the *Names* for column **B** (**Level2**) and column **C** (**Level3**).

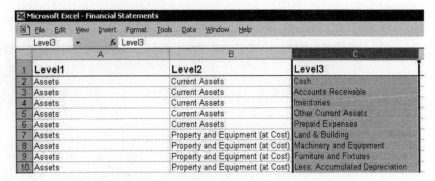

Figure 1-4: Defining a Name for Column C, Level3

Worksheet 16 – Notes List

This worksheet contains a list of **Notes** titles, details, and formulas.

The calculation of a **Note** number is automatically updated in worksheets containing reports in the **Financial Statements.xls** workbook. For more details, refer to *Chapter 7, Notes*.

Category 2: Data Worksheet

There is one worksheet in this category, in which the trial balances figures are stored.

Worksheet 21 – Trial Balances Data

Figure 1-5 shows an example of worksheet *21 — Trial Balances Data.*

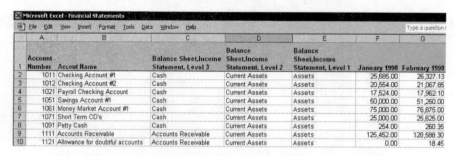

Figure 1-5: Worksheet 21 — Trial Balances Data

The worksheet is structured as follows:

✦ **Column A:** Account Number

✦ **Column B:** Account Name

✦ **Column C:** Account Types, Level 3, described on page 15

✦ **Column D:** Account Groups, Level 2, described on page 16

✦ **Column E:** Category, Level 1, described on page 16

✦ **Columns F and onwards:** Monthly Trial Balance figures, described on page 17

Column C: Account Types, Level 3

➤ **To add a Validation list for selecting an Account Type to column C:**

1. Select column **C**.

2. From the *Data* menu, select **Validation**, and then select the **Settings** tab.

3. From the **Allow** dropdown list, select **List**.

4. In the **Source** box, press **<F3>**, paste the *Name* **Level3**, and then click **OK**.

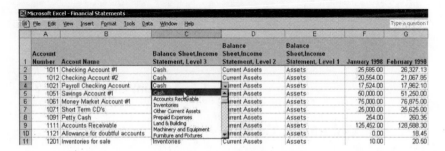

 TIP:

To open the **Validation** dropdown list in a cell in column **C**, select the cell and press **<Alt+Down Arrow>**.

Column D: Account Groups, Level 2

The formula in cell **D2** is:

=INDEX(BS_Level,MATCH(C2,Level3,0),2)

This **Index** formula returns the **Account Groups** for the **Account Types, Level 3** in column **C** from column **B** in worksheet *15 — BS, IS Level* (as described in *Worksheet 15 — BS, IS Level*, page 11).

	Microsoft Excel - Financial Statements				
	File Edit View Insert Format Tools Data Window Help				
	D2 ▼ *fx* =INDEX(BS_Level,MATCH(C2,Level3,0),2)				
	A	B	C	D	E	F
1	Account Number	Accout Name	Balance Sheet,Income Statement, Level 3	Balance Sheet,Income Statement, Level 2	Balance Sheet,Income Statement, Level 1	January 1998
2	1011	Checking Account #1	Cash	Current Assets	Assets	25,685.00
3	1012	Checking Account #2	Cash	Current Assets	Assets	20,554.00
4	1021	Payroll Checking Account	Cash	Current Assets	Assets	17,524.00
5	1051	Savings Account #1	Cash	Current Assets	Assets	50,000.00

Figure 1-6: Account Groups, Level 2

Column E: Category, Level 1

The formula in column **E** is:

=INDEX(BS_Level,MATCH(C2,Level3,0)0,1)

This formula returns the **Category** for the **Account Types, Level 3** in column **C** from column **A** in worksheet *15 — BS, IS Level* (as described in *Worksheet 15 — BS, IS Level*, page 11).

	Microsoft Excel - Financial Statements				
	File Edit View Insert Format Tools Data Window Help				
	E2 ▼ *fx* =INDEX(BS_Level,MATCH(C2,Level3,0),1)				
	A	B	C	D	E	F
1	Account Number	Accout Name	Balance Sheet,Income Statement, Level 3	Balance Sheet,Income Statement, Level 2	Balance Sheet,Income Statement, Level 1	January 1998
2	1011	Checking Account #1	Cash	Current Assets	Assets	25,685.00
3	1012	Checking Account #2	Cash	Current Assets	Assets	20,554.00
4	1021	Payroll Checking Account	Cash	Current Assets	Assets	17,524.00
5	1051	Savings Account #1	Cash	Current Assets	Assets	50,000.00
6	1061	Money Market Account #1	Cash	Current Assets	Assets	75,000.00
7	1071	Short Term CD's	Cash	Current Assets	Assets	25,000.00

Figure 1-7: Category, Level 1

Columns F and Onwards: Monthly Trial Balance

➢ **To enter the month names into the cells in row 1 from range F1 and onwards:**

1. Select and copy the months list in worksheet *14 — Months List.*

2. Select cell **F1**, and press **<Shift+F10>**,

   OR

   Right-click, and select **Paste Special** from the shortcut menu.

3. Change the paste direction from vertical to horizontal by selecting the **Transpose** check box and then clicking **OK**.

4. While range **F1** and onwards is selected, change the **Dates** format by pressing **<Ctrl+1>**, selecting the **Number** tab, and then selecting **Custom**.

5. In the **Type** box, type the format: **mmmm yyyy** and click **OK**.

Category 3: Reports Worksheets

This category has four worksheets.

✦ Worksheet *31 — Balance Sheet*, as described in *Chapter 4, Balance Sheet.*

✦ Worksheet *41 — Income Statement*, as described in *Chapter 5, Income Statement.*

✦ Worksheet *51 — Cash Flow*, as described in *Chapter 6, Cash Flow.*

✦ Worksheet *61 — Notes*, as described in *Chapter 7, Notes.*

Category 4: Trial Balance and Adjustments Worksheets

This category has four worksheets. For more details, refer to *Chapter 2, Adjusting the Trial Balance.*

Installing the ChooseSheet.xla Add-in

In a workbook containing multiple worksheets, moving between worksheets to select the one you need is not a convenient task. There are two techniques for selecting a worksheet you need:

✦ Press **<Ctrl+Page Down>** or **<Ctrl+Page Up>** to move to the next or previous worksheet.

✦ Right-click one of the arrows in the worksheet's horizontal scroll bars (in the leftmost lower corner) and select a worksheet from the displayed menu.

Selecting a worksheet from the worksheets menu is useful only if there are less than 10 to 15 worksheets in the workbook.

The **ChooseSheet.xla** add-in enables you to easily select a specific worksheet from a list of sorted worksheets in ascending order.

This add-in displays the list of worksheets in the active workbook (in this example it is **Financial Statements.xls**) in ascending order (as shown in Figure 1-8), and allows you to easily find and look into the worksheet before choosing it. Clicking a worksheet in the list displays a preview; clicking it again selects the worksheet itself. Worksheets can also be hidden and displayed, as required.

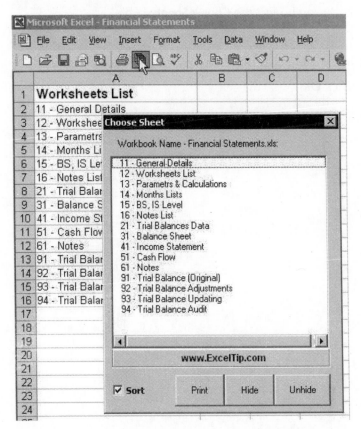

Figure 1-8: Choose Sheet Dialog Box

Figure 1-8 displays the *Choose Sheet* dialog box, which contains the list of worksheets. In the background, you can see the worksheets list in worksheet *12 — Worksheet List*. When the add-in has been installed, an icon is added to the regular toolbar, which can be clicked to display the *Choose Sheet* dialog box.

➢ **To install the add-in:**

1. Go to www.exceltip.com/xls and download the **Add-in**, or copy it from the companion CD-ROM.

2. Save the **ChooseSheet.xla Add-In** in any folder.

3. From the *Tools* menu, select **Add-Ins**, and click **Browse**.

4. Locate and select the **ChooseSheet.xla** file.

5. Click **OK**.

6. In the **Add-ins available** box, select the **ChooseSheet.xla** check box.

7. Click **OK**.

Sorting Worksheets in Ascending Order

When you have finished adding worksheets to the **Financial Statements.xls** workbook, it is recommended to arrange them in ascending order.

Type the macro **VBA** codes below into a regular Module. You can then either:

> Add a command button to execute the macro from worksheet *11— General Details,*
>
> OR
>
> Add the macro to a **Custom Menu**.

For more details, refer to page 121, *Chapter 8, Customizing the Financial Statements.xls Workbook and Presenting Information.*

 NOTE:

The macro VBA code lines can be copied from http://www.excelforum.com/f96-s, the macro is also available in Chapter1.xls workbook at the companion CD-ROM..

```
Sub SheetInABC_Order()

Dim I As Integer, J As Integer, ShNumber As Integer
ShNumber = Sheets.Count
On Error GoTo ErrorTrap:

For I = 1 To ShNumber - 1
    For J = I + 1 To ShNumber
        If Sheets(J).Name < Sheets(I).Name Then
        Sheets(J).Move Before:=Sheets(I)
        End If
    Next
Next

Sheets(1).Select

ErrorTrap:
Exit Sub

End Sub
```

You can also add a macro VBA code lines that both sort the worksheets in ascending order and update worksheet *12 — Worksheet List.* This macro runs the macro above, as well as the macro presented on page 9.

```
Sub SortAndUpdateShettsList()

    Call SheetInABC_Order
    Call Update_WorksheetsList

End Sub
```

Chapter 2

Adjusting the Trial Balance

About This Chapter

This chapter introduces techniques to add or update adjustments to the account balances of the General Ledger Trial Balance, and prepare a final adjusted Trial Balance to be used for preparing the financial statements. It includes the following sections:

Overview

A Trial Balance contains the account-balance figures that are calculated from journal-entry transactions posted into the General Ledger.

The Trial Balance is either imported or entered directly into an Excel worksheet's cells.

In most cases, the account balance figures in Trial Balance are not the final balances of the accounts from which the Financial Statements reports can be created.

In this chapter you will learn how to add and update adjustments to the account balances, and prepare an audit-adjusted Trial Balance to be used for preparation of the Financial Statements reports.

The **Financial Statements.xls** workbook contains four worksheets that deal with original Trial Balance, add /update Adjustments for a final adjusted Trial Balance:

✦ Worksheet *91 — Trial Balance (Original)*, described on page 25.

✦ Worksheet *92 — Trial Balance Adjustments*, described on page 29.

✦ Worksheet *93 — Final Trial Balance*, described on page 39.

✦ Worksheet *94 — Trial Balance Audit*, described on page 49.

Worksheet 91 – Trial Balance (Original)

Step 1: Entering and Saving the Trial Balance in an Excel Worksheet

➢ **To enter and save a trial balance:**

1. Select worksheet *91 — Trial Balance (Original)*.

2. Import the Trial Balance from the General Ledger application or type it directly into the worksheet, as shown below. When you have finished, save the **Financial Statements.xls** workbook.

	Account Number	Account Name	Debit	Credit
1				
2	1011	Checking Account #1	7,582.00	
3	1012	Checking Account #2	5,265.00	
4	1021	Payroll Checking Account	5,232.32	
5	1051	Savings Account #1	50,000.00	
6	1061	Money Market Account #1	20,000.00	
7	1071	Short Term CD's	15,000.00	
8	1091	Petty Cash	2,352.00	
9	1111	Accounts Receivable	275,652.00	
10	1121	Allowance for doubtful accounts		25,500.00
11	1201	Inventories for sale	98,565.00	
12	1211	Inventories for use	45,265.00	
13	1301	Prepaid expenses	6,582.00	
14	1501	Lease Deposits	12,565.00	
15	1571	Marketable Stocks	28,500.00	
16	1601	Loans	25,000.00	
17	1701	Loans to Employees	32,562.00	
18	1811	Land	125,252.00	
19	1821	Buildings	485,952.00	
20	1831	Tools & Equipment	45,265.00	
21	1841	Office Furninshings & Equip	33,651.00	
22	1891	Leasehold Improvements	19,567.00	
23	1921	Accumulated Depreciated Buildings	56,444.00	
24	1931	Accumulated Depreciated Tools/Equipment		15,652.00
25	1941	Accumulated Depreciated Office Equipment		12,666.00

The Trial Balance list (as shown in the figure on the previous page) is structured as follows:

✦ The table has a single title row with a text title at the top of each column.

✦ There are no empty rows between groups and/or subtotals.

✦ There are no totals at the bottom.

This structure has a number of advantages. A Trial Balance list entered into the worksheet's cells in list form enables extensive and efficient use of the various techniques offered by Excel, such as **Sorting**, **Filtering**, **Subtotaling**, **Consolidating**, creating **PivotTable** reports and easily using **Lookup & Reference**, and **SUMIF** formulas.

Step 2: Defining Names

After entering and saving the Trial Balance in worksheet *91 — Trial Balance (Original)*, define the *Names* of the columns and rows.

➢ **To define the Names of columns A through D:**

1. Select column **A**.

2. Press **<Ctrl+F3>** to open the *Define Name* dialog box.

3. In the **Names in workbook** box, type the *Name* **TB_Index** and click **OK**.

4. Repeat the above steps and define the *Names* of columns **B** through **D**, as follows:

   ✦ Column B: **TB_AccountName**

   ✦ Column C: **TB_Debit**

   ✦ Column D: **TB_Credit**

➢ **To define the Name for row 1:**

✦ Select row **1** in the worksheet, and follow the steps in the previous procedure to define the *Name* **TB_Row1** for the row.

➤ **To define a dynamic range name for the Trial Balance list:**

1. Select a cell in the data area of worksheet *91 — Trial Balance (Original)*, and press **<Ctrl+*>** (the * on the numeric keypad) or **<Ctrl+Shift+*>** (when using **Excel 2003**, press <Ctrl+A>instead).

2. Press **<Ctrl+F3>** to open the *Define Name* dialog box, as shown.

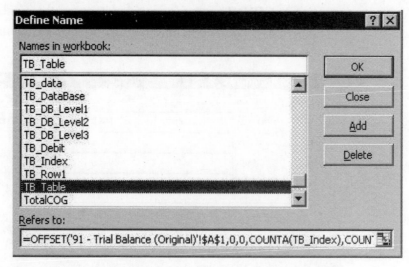

3. In the **Names in workbook** box, type the *Name* **TB_Table**.

4. In the **Refers to** box, type the following formula:

    =OFFSET('91 - Trial Balance
    (Original)'!$A$1,0,0,COUNTA(TB_Index),COUNTA(TB_Row1))

    This formula returns the size of the list by counting the non-empty cells in rows (Height) and columns (Width).

    The first **COUNTA** formula nested in it returns the number of non-empty cells in column **A**; the second returns the number of non-empty cells in row **1**.

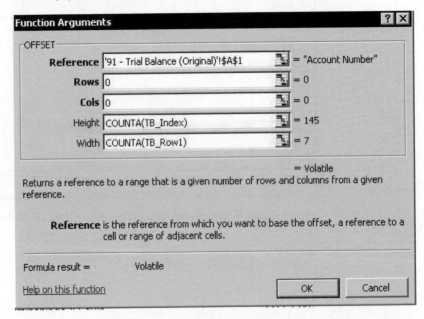

5. Click **OK**. The range *Name* **TB_Table** automatically updates its size without needing to be manually updated.

Step 3: Auditing

After you have completed the previous two steps, be sure to check that the Trial Balance Debit and Credit (columns **C** and **D**) totals entered match the totals of the original Trial Balance. For more details, refer to *Worksheet 94 — Trial Balance Audit*, page 49.

Worksheet 92 – Trial Balance Adjustments

In this section, you will learn how to add an unlimited number of new adjustments (up to a maximum of 65336 rows in a single worksheet).

The worksheet is structured as follows:

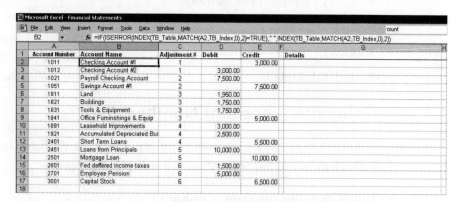

Figure 2-1: Worksheet 92 — Trial Balance Adjustments

✦ Adjustments are entered in columns **A** through **E**.

✦ Column **F** is an empty column, so there is a space between columns **E** and **G**.

✦ Column **G** is the Details column.

✦ Column **H** is an empty column, so there is a space between columns **G** and **I**.

✦ Columns **I** through **L** contain the audit formulas that return the balances for each adjustment number (to summarize the adjustments based on column **C**). For more details, refer to *Step 3: Auditing the Trial Balance Adjustment Balances*, page 35.

The following sections present step-by-step instructions for using worksheet *92 — Trial Balance Adjustments.*

Step 1: Entering Adjustments

Enter the new adjustments into cells in columns **A:G**.

The column titles (as shown in Figure 2-1) are as follows:

- ✦ Cell A1: **Account Number**
- ✦ Cell B1: **Account Name**
- ✦ Cell C1: **Adjustment Number**
- ✦ Cell D1: **Debit**
- ✦ Cell E1: **Credit**
- ✦ Cell G1: **Details**

Column A – Account Number

Column **A** contains the account numbers, which are validated by the **Validation** technique before they are entered into a cell.

➢ **To validate an account number:**

1. Select column **A**.
2. From the *Data* menu, select **Validation**, and then select the **Settings** tab.
3. From the **Allow** box, select **List**.
4. In the **Source** box, press **<F3>**, and paste the *Name* **TB_Index** (refer to step 2 of *To define the Names of columns A through D*, page 26).

5. Ensure that both the **Ignore blank** and **In-cell dropdown** check boxes are selected, as shown below.

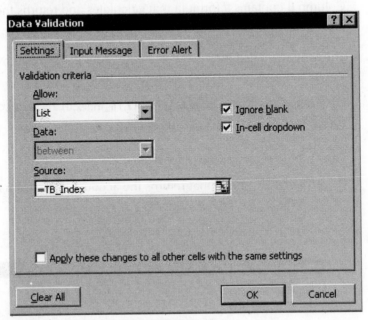

6. Select the **Input Message** tab.

7. In the **Title** box, type **Adjustments**.

8. In the **Input Message** text box, add an explanation.

9. Select the **Error Alert** tab and set the alert and control level from the **Style** dropdown list.

10. Add a title for the alert in the **Title** box and an error explanation in the **Error message** text box.

11. Click **OK**.

 TIP:
You can quickly select an item from a **Validation** dropdown list in a cell by selecting the cell and pressing **<Alt+Down Arrow>**.

Column B – Account Name

Column **B** contains a formula that calculates and returns the account name after entering the account number in column **A**.

The formula in cell **B2** as well as in the other cells in column **B** is (as shown in Figure 2-1):

**=IF(ISERROR(INDEX(TB_Table,MATCH(A2,TB_Index,0),2)=TRUE),"",
INDEX(TB_Table,MATCH(A2,TB_Index,0),2))**

The formula is composed of two parts:

✦ An **INDEX** formula that returns the account name from column **B** in worksheet *91 — Trial Balance*:

    =INDEX(TB_Table,MATCH(A2,TB_Index,0),2)

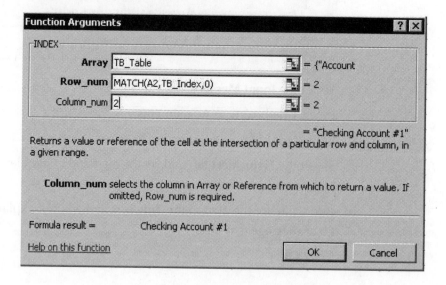

✦ An **IF** formula with a nested **ISERROR** formula to eliminate error messages. The formula's Logical_test (the first argument) checks for errors by calculating an **INDEX** formula. If the calculation returns an error, an empty cell is displayed.

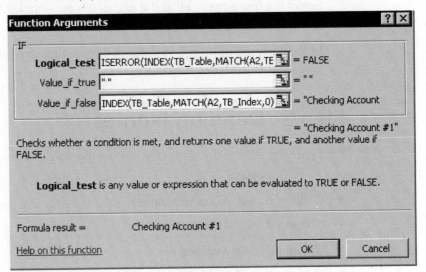

Adding a New Account Number and Name

While adding new adjustments, you might find (rarely) that a new account needs to be added to the Index list in the original Trial Balance.

➤ **To add a new account name and number to the original Trial Balance:**

1. Select worksheet *91 — Trial Balance*.

2. Select the first empty cell at the end of the account list in column **A**, and type the account number.

3. In the corresponding cell in column **B**, type the name of the new account.

Step 2: Defining Names

After carrying out the previous step, define the names of the columns and one row, as follows:

✦ Column A: **Adj_AccountNumber**

✦ Column B: **Adj_AccountName**

✦ Column C: **Adj_Number**

✦ Column D: **Adj_Debit**

✦ Column E: **Adj_Credit**

✦ Row 1: **Adj_Row1**

Refer to *Step 2: Defining Names*, page 26, for the naming procedure.

➤ **To define a dynamic range name for the Adjustment list:**

1. Select a cell in the Adjustments list, and press **<Ctrl+Shift+*>**.

2. Press **<Ctrl+F3>** to open the *Define Name* dialog box.

3. In the **Names in workbook** box, type the *Name* **Adj_Table**.

4. In the **Refers to** box, type the following formula:

   =OFFSET('92 - Trial Balance
   Adjustments'!F1,0,0,COUNTA(Adj_AccountNumber),COUNTA(Adj_Row1))

For an explanation of this formula, refer to *To define a dynamic range name for the Trial Balance list*, page 27.

Step 3: Auditing the Trial Balance Adjustment Balances

After adding the required adjustments to worksheet *92 — Trial Balance Adjustments,* you should make sure that they are balanced, and then update and correct those that are not.

This is done by:

✦ Adding a list containing formulas that sum the balances of the adjustments, as shown in Figure 2-2.

✦ Handling each unbalanced adjustment separately, as described on page 37.

✦ Using **Conditional Formattings** to color the unbalanced adjustments, as described on page 37.

Finding Unbalanced Adjustments

In columns **I** through **L**, you add formulas that calculate the totals of each adjustment number and find any unbalanced adjustment number.

	Adjustment #	Debit	Credit	Difference	M	N
1	Adjustment #	Debit	Credit	Difference		
2	1	3,000.00	3,000.00	0.00		
3	2	7,500.00	7,500.00	0.00		
4	3	5,450.00	5,000.00	450.00		
5	4	5,500.00	5,500.00	0.00		
6	5	10,000.00	10,000.00	0.00		
7	6	6,500.00	6,500.00	0.00		
8	7	0.00	0.00	0.00		
9	8	0.00	0.00	0.00		
10	9	0.00	0.00	0.00		
11	10	0.00	0.00	0.00		
12	11	0.00	0.00	0.00		
13	12	0.00	0.00	0.00		
14	13	0.00	0.00	0.00		
15	14	0.00	0.00	0.00		
16						

Microsoft Excel - Financial Statements

File   Edit   View   Insert   Format   Tools   Data   Window   Help

J2   =SUMIF(Adj_Number,I2,Adj_Debit)

Figure 2-2: Finding Unbalanced Adjustments

➤ **To find unbalanced adjustment numbers:**

1. Type the list of adjustment numbers into column **I** (as shown in Figure 2-2).

2. Type the following **SUMIF** formulas into columns **J** and **K**:

    ✦   Cell **J2**:

      =SUMIF(Adj_Number,I2,Adj_Debit)

    ✦   Cell **K2**:

      =SUMIF(Adj_Number,I2,Adj_Credit)

    The adjustment number in column **I** is the criteria used by the **SUMIF** formulas to sum each adjustment.

3. Type a formula calculating the difference between columns **J** and **K** into column **L**. The formula should return zero for each adjustment number.

    You can now use this column to find unbalanced adjustments, sort the list or filter it, as shown below.

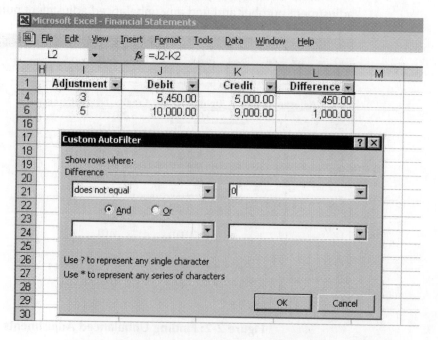

Correcting and Updating Unbalanced Adjustments

After you have found the unbalanced adjustments, you can use Excel's **AutoFilter** to make it easy to correct or update each one separately.

➤ **To correct and update unbalanced adjustments:**

1. Select cell **C1**.

2. From the *Data* menu, select **Filter** and then **AutoFilter**.

3. Filter the list based on your unbalanced adjustment number criteria, as shown.

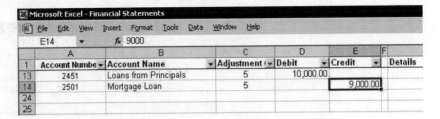

Coloring Rows Containing Unbalanced Adjustments

You can use **Conditional Formatting** to color cells in rows containing unbalanced adjustments, as described below.

➤ **To color rows with unbalanced adjustments:**

1. Select columns **A:E**.

2. From the *Format* menu, select **Conditional Formatting**.

3. From **Condition 1**, select **Formula Is** and type the following formula:

=SUMIF(Adj_Number,$C1,Adj_Credit)-SUMIF(Adj_Number,$C1,Adj_Debit)<>0)

4. Click **Format** and then select the **Patterns** tab.

5. Select a color and then click **OK**. Your screen should now look like this:

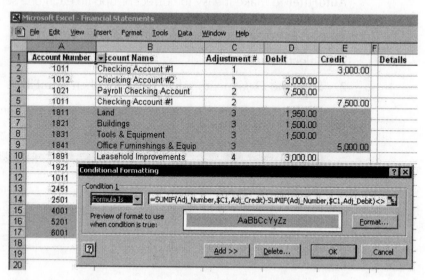

6. Click **OK** again to save the **Conditional Formatting**.

Each cell in the range (columns **A** through **E**) will check the result of the formula calculation in the parallel cell in the same column. When it does not equal zero, the cell pattern will be colored.

Worksheet 93 – Final Trial Balance

This worksheet consolidates the Trial Balance account figures with the Adjustment figures. There are two ways to consolidate the figures:

✦ Using a **SUMIF** formula, as described below.

✦ Using the **Consolidate** technique, as described on page 40.

Using a SUMIF Formula to Summarize Trial Balance Figures with Trial Balance Adjustment Figures

The **SUMIF** formula summarizes data based on certain criteria. In this example, the criterion is the account number.

➤ **To summarize the balance for each account, use the SUMIF formula:**

1. Select worksheet *91 — Trial Balance* (or use worksheet *93 — Final Trial Balance*).

2. Select cell **F2** and type the following formula:

   =SUMIF(TB_Index,A2,TB_Debit)+SUMIF(Adj_AccountNumber,A2,Adj_Debit)

3. Select cell **G2** and type the following formula:

   =SUMIF(TB_Index,A2,TB_Credit)+SUMIF(Adj_AccountNumber,A2,Adj_Credit)

4. Select cell **H2** and type the following formula:

   =G2-F2

5. Copy the formulas in cells **F2:H2** and paste them into cells in columns **F:H**.

6. Define a *Name* for column H by selecting it, pressing **<Ctrl+F3>**, typing the *Name* **TB_Adjusted**, and then pressing **OK**.

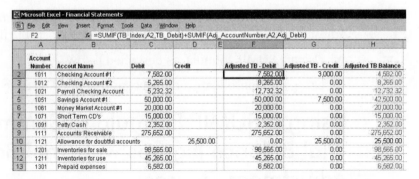

Using the Consolidate Technique to Summarize Trial Balance Figures with Trial Balance Adjustment Figures

The **Consolidate** technique has an important advantage over the **SUMIF** formula, as you can add links to the source data and then drill down to look at the list of adjustments entries to each account.

Technique 1: Consolidating Lists Without Links to the Source Data

Lists can be consolidated without linking it to the source data, if required.

➤ **To consolidate Lists without creating links to source data:**

1. Select worksheet *93 — Final Trial Balance*.

2. From the *Data* menu, select **Consolidate**.

3. In the *Consolidate* dialog box that appears, select **Sum** from the **Function** list box.

4. In the **Reference** box, press **<F3>**, select and paste the *Name* **TB_Table** (as described on page 27) and then click **Add**.

5. Repeat step 3 for the Trial Balance Adjustments list, select and paste the *Name* **Adj_Table** (as described on page 34) and then click **Add**.

The *Consolidate* dialog box should now look like this:

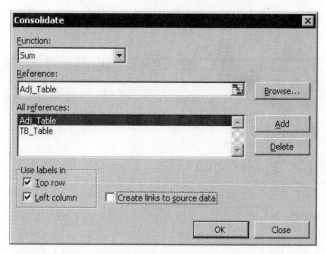

6. Ensure that the **Top row** and **Left column** check boxes in the **Use labels in** group box are selected, and that the **Create links to source data** check box is deselected.

7. Click **OK**.

8. Select cell **A2** and click the **Sort Ascending** ![icon] icon. The worksheet will be sorted automatically by Account Index number, as shown below.

	A	B	C	D	E	F	G
1		Account Name	Adjustment #	Accout Name	Debit	Credit	
2	1011		1		7,582.00	3,000.00	
3	1012		1		8,265.00		
4	1021		2		12,732.32		
5	1051		2		50,000.00	7,500.00	
6	1571				28,500.00		
7	1601				25,000.00		
8	1701				32,562.00		
9	1811		3		127,202.00		
10	1821		3		487,702.00		
11	1831		3		47,015.00		
12	1841		3		33,651.00	5,000.00	
13	1891		4		22,567.00		
14	1921		4		58,944.00		
15	1931					15,652.00	
16	1941					12,666.00	
17	1991					7,585.00	
18	2011					205,651.00	
19	2111					33,659.00	
20	2112					15,777.00	
21	2113					8,985.00	
22	2114					3,666.00	
23	2115					2,588.00	

Microsoft Excel - Financial Statements

File   Edit   View   Insert   Format   Tools   Data   Window   Help

> **To add a formula that returns the account balance after consolidating the figures:**

+ Type the formula into cell **G2**:

  =E2-F2

  and copy the formula to cells in column **G**.

Behind the Consolidating Lists Technique

The **Consolidate** technique consolidates figures from lists with similar structures, and summarizes the figures by cross-checking the text in the top row and leftmost column.

For example, **Consolidate** summarizes figures in the **Debit** column for the index account number 1011 (for example, cell **E2** in Figure 2-3).

	A	B	C	D	E	F	G
1		Account Name	Adjustment #	Accout Name	Debit	Credit	Balance
2	1011		1		7,582.00	3,000.00	4,582.00
3	1012		1		8,265.00		8,265.00
4	1021		2		12,732.32		12,732.32
5	1051		2		50,000.00	7,500.00	42,500.00
6	1571				28,500.00		28,500.00
7	1601				25,000.00		25,000.00
8	1701				32,562.00		32,562.00
9	1811		3		127,202.00		127,202.00
10	1821		3		487,702.00		487,702.00
11	1831		3		47,015.00		47,015.00
12	1841		3		33,651.00	5,000.00	28,651.00
13	1891		4		22,567.00		22,567.00

Microsoft Excel - Financial Statements — File Edit View Insert Format Tools Data Window Help — G2 fx =E2-F2

Figure 2-3: The Consolidated Lists

The inner area of the list is the area of consolidated figures. Note that the text is missing from column **B** (**Account Name**). This is because **Consolidate** uses functions that add figures via cross-checking identical text that appears in the top row and leftmost columns of the lists. Functions cannot consolidate text, however.

To get around this limitation, move the account name to the first column in both tables:

✦ In worksheets *91 — Trial Balance (Original)* and *92 — Trial Balance Adjustments*, switch columns **A** and **B** by moving column **B** (the account name) to column **A**, and vice versa.

✦ In worksheet *92 — Trial Balance Adjustments*, delete the account number column (do not forget to copy column **B** and paste it back as values).

The account number column has now been moved to the data area.

Why is it necessary to delete the Account Number column in worksheet 92 — Trial Balance Adjustments?

When using the **Consolidate** technique, account numbers are consolidated and the returned result figure is non-existing account numbers (for example, account number 1011 plus 1011 becomes 2022). The cell in column **B** with the account number in the first list (**TB_Table** in worksheet *91 — Trial Balance (Original)* is transferred to the consolidated list as is.

As can be seen in Figure 2-4, columns **A** through **D** show the results after switching between column **A** and **B**. Columns **F** through **I** are displayed after deleting the **Account Number** column.

	A	B Account Number	C Debit	D Credit	E	F	G Adjustme	H Debit	I Credit
1	Accout Name					Account Name			
2	Checking Account #1	1011	7,582.00			Checking Account #1	1		3,000.00
3	Checking Account #2	1012	5,265.00			Checking Account #2	1	3,000.00	
4	Payroll Checking Account	1021	5,232.32			Payroll Checking Account	2	7,500.00	
5	Savings Account #1	1051	50,000.00			Savings Account #1	2		7,500.00
6	Money Market Account #1	1061	20,000.00			Land	3	1,950.00	
7	Short Term CD's	1071	15,000.00			Buildings	3	1,750.00	
8	Petty Cash	1091	2,352.00			Tools & Equipment	3	1,750.00	
9	Accounts Receivable	1111	275,652.00			Office Furninshings & Equip	3		5,000.00
10	Allowance for doubtful acco	1121		25,500.00		Leasehold Improvements	4	3,000.00	
11	Inventories for sale	1201	98,565.00			Accumulated Depreciated Build	4	2,500.00	
12	Inventories for use	1211	45,265.00			Short Term Loans	4		5,500.00
13	Prepaid expenses	1301	6,582.00			Loans from Principals	5	10,000.00	
14	Lease Deposits	1501	12,565.00			Mortgage Loan	5		9,000.00
15	Marketable Stocks	1571	28,500.00			Fed deffered income taxes	6	1,500.00	
16	Loans	1601	25,000.00			Employee Pension	6	5,000.00	
17	Loans to Employees	1701	32,562.00			Capital Stock	6		6,500.00
18	Land	1811	125,252.00			Lease Deposits			
19	Buildings	1821	485,952.00						

Figure 2-4: Two Lists After Switching Columns and Deleting the Account Number Column from the Second List, Before Consolidating

The final result, after consolidating the lists, is shown in Figure 2-5:

	A	B	C	D	E	F
		Account Number	Adjustment #	Debit	Credit	Balance
2	Checking Account #1	1011	1	7,582.00	3,000.00	4,582.00
3	Checking Account #2	1012	1	8,265.00		8,265.00
4	Payroll Checking Account	1021	2	12,732.32		12,732.32
5	Savings Account #1	1051	2	50,000.00	7,500.00	42,500.00
6	Money Market Account #1	1061		20,000.00		20,000.00
7	Short Term CD's	1071		15,000.00		15,000.00
8	Petty Cash	1091		2,352.00		2,352.00
9	Accounts Receivable	1111		275,652.00		275,652.00
10	Allowance for doubtful accounts	1121			25,500.00	-25,500.00
11	Inventories for sale	1201		98,565.00		98,565.00
12	Inventories for use	1211		45,265.00		45,265.00
13	Prepaid expenses	1301		6,582.00		6,582.00
14	Lease Deposits	1501		12,565.00		12,565.00

Figure 2-5: Final Consolidated Trial Balance

The consolidation of the two lists results in worksheet *93 — Final Trial Balance* and a formula in column **F** that returns the final balances.

Technique 2: Consolidating Lists While Creating Links to Source Data

In the previous section, you learned how to consolidate lists without creating links to source data. This has the advantage of being more convenient and having fewer formulas; however, it has the following disadvantages as well:

✦ Adding new adjustments after you have completed the consolidation does not update the consolidated table.

✦ Account balances cannot by analyzed.

Consolidating and linking to the source data enables you to do both of these. Nevertheless, you will still have to perform **Consolidate** to add new adjustments to the worksheet. For this reason, it is recommended that you link to source data and perform **Consolidate** every time you add new records to the source lists.

➢ **To perform Consolidate after adding new records:**

1. Delete the data in worksheet *93 — Final Trial Balance* to delete the data along with the **Subtotal** levels buttons. To do this, select the **Select all Cells** button (in the top-left corner of rows and columns), press <**Shift+F10**>, and from the shortcut menu, select **Delete**.

2. Select cell **A1**.

3. From the *Data* menu, select **Consolidate**.

 NOTE:

The range *Names* are stored in the *Consolidate* dialog box so you do not have to paste them again.

4. Select the **Create links to source data** check box and click **OK**. The lists are now consolidated. Notice the **Subtotal** level numbers to the left of the row numbers.

Microsoft Excel - Financial Statements							
File Edit View Insert Format Tools Data Window Help							

1 2		A	B	C	D	E	F	G	H
	1			Account Name	Adjustment #	Accout Name	Debit	Credit	
+	6	1011			7		7,582.00	16,000.00	
+	9	1012			1		8,265.00		
+	12	1021			2		12,732.32		
+	14	1571					28,500.00		
+	16	1601					25,000.00		
+	18	1701					32,562.00		
+	21	1811			3		127,252.00		
+	24	1821			3		487,452.00		
+	27	1831			3		46,765.00		
+	30	1841			3		33,651.00	5,000.00	
+	33	1891			4		22,567.00		
+	36	1921			4		58,944.00		
+	38	1931						15,652.00	
+	40	1941						12,666.00	
+	42	1991						7,585.00	

Adding an Account Balance Calculation Column to Worksheet in Subtotal Mode

The procedure below describes how to add an account balance calculation column to the worksheet while it is in **Subtotal** mode.

➢ **To add an account balance calculation column to the worksheet in Subtotal mode:**

1. While the data is in **Subtotal** mode (as explained in the previous section), enter the following formula into cell **H2**:

    =F6-G6

2. Select the formula and press **<Ctrl+C>** to copy it.

3. Select the visible cells, and press **<F5>**. The *Go To* dialog box appears.

4. Click **Special**. The *Go To Special* dialog box appears.

5. Select the **Visible cells only** option button and click **OK**.

6. Press **<Enter>** to paste the formula into the visible cells in the range.

7. Select the **Level 2** button in the **Subtotal** levels (on the left side of the worksheet) and open the invisible rows. The worksheet should look like this:

	A	B	C	D	E	F	G	H	I
1			Account Name	Adjustment #	Accout Name	Debit	Credit	Balance	
2			Financial Statements	1			3,000.00		
3				2			7,500.00		
4				4			5,500.00		
5			Financial Statements			7,582.00			
6	1011			7		7,582.00	16,000.00	(8,418.00)	
7			Financial Statements	1		3,000.00			
8			Financial Statements			5,265.00			
9	1012			1		8,265.00		8,265.00	
10			Financial Statements	2		7,500.00			
11			Financial Statements			5,232.32			
12	1021			2		12,732.32		12,732.32	
13			Financial Statements			28,500.00			
14	1571					28,500.00		28,500.00	
15			Financial Statements			25,000.00			
16	1601					25,000.00		25,000.00	

Coloring the Subtotal Summary Rows

The procedure below describes how to color the **Subtotal** summary rows.

➢ **To color the Subtotal summary rows:**

1. Make sure that the **Subtotal** position is at **Level 2** (and all cells are visible).

2. Select cell **A1**, press **<Ctrl+Shift+*>** and select the current region.

3. From the *Format* menu, select **Conditional Formatting**.

4. From **Condition 1**, select **Formula Is** and type the following formula:

   =$A1<>0

5. Click **Format** and then select the **Patterns** tab.

6. Select a color and then click **OK**.

   Result: All rows in columns **A:H** where the cells in column **A** are not empty are colored.

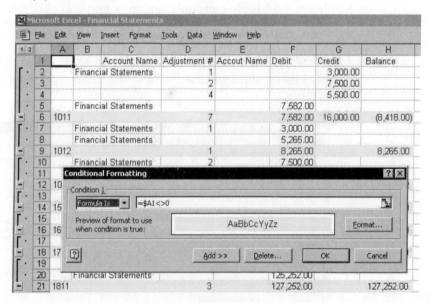

TIP:

You can use both **Consolidate** techniques (with and without source-data linking) in different worksheets and enjoy the advantages of both.

Worksheet 94 – Trial Balance Audit

In this worksheet, enter formulas that:

✦ Summarize the account balances of the original Trial Balance before new Adjustments were added.

✦ Summarize the new Adjustments to the accounts.

✦ Calculate the final adjusted balance accounts of the Trial Balance.

Figure 2-6 shows the worksheet and its formulas.

	A	B	C	D	E	F	G	H
			Trial Balance		Adjustments		Adjusted Trial Balance	
2			Debit	Credit	Debit	Credit	Debit	Credit
3		Total	3,381,488.32	3,392,150.00	37,500.00	37,500.00	3,418,988.32	3,429,650.00
4		Difference	10661.68	0.00	0	0.00	10661.68	0.00
5								
6		Totals Net Income Accounts	1,985,235.00	2,252,532.00	6,500.00	6,500.00	1,991,735.00	2,259,032.00
7		Net Income	0.00	267,297.00	0.00	0.00	0.00	267,297.00
8								
9								
10		**Formulas in Row 3**	=SUM(TB_Debit)	=SUM(TB_Credit)	=SUM(Adj_Debit)	=SUM(Adj_Credit)	=C3+E3	=D3+F3
11								
12			=SUMIF(TB_Index,">4000",TB_Debit)				=C6+E6	=D6+F6
13		**Formulas in Row 6**	=SUMIF(TB_Index,">4000",TB_Credit)					
14			=SUMIF(Adj_AccountNumber,">4000",Adj_Debit)					
15			=SUMIF(Adj_AccountNumber,">4000",Adj_Credit)					
16								

Figure 2-6: Worksheet 94 — Trial Balance Audit

Use the **SUMIF** formula to calculate the Net Income balance (refer to rows **6** and **7** in the figure above) based on the *Trial Balance* before and after new adjustments were added. This formula summarizes the figures by finding all the account numbers that are greater than 4000 (account numbers 4000 to 4999 represent sales and other income, while account numbers greater than 5000 are used for expenses).

Chapter 3

Updating the Trial Balances Data Worksheet

About This Chapter

This chapter describes how to add the account balances of the final Trial Balance (refer to *Chapter 2, Adjusting the Trial Balance*) to the appropriate column in worksheet *21 — Trial Balances Data*, and includes the following sections:

+ **Overview**, page 52, introduces worksheet *21 — Trial Balances Data* and describes how to add the account balances of the final Trial Balance to it.

+ **Finding and Adding New Account Details**, page 53, describes how to find and add new account detail information that appears in the final Trial Balance and is not in worksheet *21 — Trial Balances Data*.

+ **Entering Final Trial Balances to a New Column in Worksheet 21 — Trial Balances Data**, page 62, describes how to add the account balances of the new final Trial Balance to a new column in the worksheet.

Overview

In the previous chapter, *Chapter 2, Adjusting the Trial Balance*, you learned how to add adjustments to a General Ledger Trial Balance and prepare a final adjusted Trial Balance.

In this chapter, you will learn how to add the balances of the final adjusted Trial Balance to the appropriate column in worksheet *21 — Trial Balances Data*. If you correctly used the techniques described in the previous chapter, the balances of the final Trial Balance will be automatically added to the worksheet when you either add a new adjustment or update an existing one.

This chapter discusses two main issues:

✦ Finding and adding new account name and number information that appear in the final Trial Balance but not in the old Trial Balances stored in worksheet *21 — Trial Balances Data*, as described on page 53.

✦ Adding the balances of the new Trial Balance to a new column in the worksheet, as described on page 62.

Finding and Adding New Account Details

New accounts are added nearly every month in almost every accounting system. Finding the new account number and name information and adding them to column **A** of worksheet *21 — Trial Balances Data* is essential so that all of the balances of the new Trial Balance flow into the appropriate column in worksheet *21 — Trial Balances Data*.

To determine if there are any new accounts, and if so, to extract the list of new account names and numbers, you can use one of the following comparison techniques to compare lists:

✦ Using **Consolidate** (without using any formulas), as described on page 54.

✦ Using a **COUNTIF** formula, as described on page 58.

Using the Consolidate Technique to Compare Lists

The **Consolidate** technique uses formulas to consolidate lists. To learn how to use this technique, add two lists of account numbers to different columns and then consolidate them. The following example will make this idea clearer.

Figure 3-1 presents two lists. Column **A** (the first list) contains a list of account numbers from the old Trial Balance (stored in worksheet *21 — Trial Balances Data*). Column **D** (the second list) contains a list of account numbers from the new Trial Balance. The highlighted cells, **D4** and **D11** are new account numbers that are not listed in column A.

	A	B	C	D	E
1	Account Number List # 1			Account Number List # 2	
2	1011			1011	
3	1012			1012	
4	1021			1013	
5	1051			1021	
6	1061			1051	
7	1071			1061	
8	1091			1071	
9	1111			1091	
10	1121			1111	
11	1201			1112	
12	1211			1121	
13	1301			1201	
14	1501			1211	
15	1571			1301	

Figure 3-1: Two Lists of Numbers

The procedure below describes how to find the two new account numbers using the **Consolidate** technique.

➢ **To add a list number to column adjacent to the account numbers column:**

1. In cells **B1** and **E1**, type the text title **List Number** (ensure that the column title text is the same).

2. Type **1** into cell **B2**, copy cell **B2** and paste it to cells **B3:B12**.

3. Type **2** into cell **E2**, copy cell **E2** and paste it to cells **E3:E12**.

4. Define a *Name* for the first list by selecting cell **A1** in the first list and pressing **<Ctrl+Shift+*>**.

5. Press **<Ctrl+F3>** to open the *Define Name* dialog box.

6. In the **Names in workbook** box, type the *Name* **List1**, and then click **OK**.

7. Select cell **D1** in the second list, repeat steps 4 and 5, and define the *Name* **List2**. Your worksheet should now look like this.

	A	B	C	D	E
1	**Account Number List # 1**	**List Number**		**Account Number List # 2**	**List Number**
2	1011	1		1011	2
3	1012	1		1012	2
4	1021	1		1013	2
5	1051	1		1021	2
6	1061	1		1051	2
7	1071	1		1061	2
8	1091	1		1071	2
9	1111	1		1091	2
10	1121	1		1111	2
11	1201	1		1112	2
12	1211	1		1121	2

8. Select cell **G1**.

9. From the *Data* menu, select **Consolidate**.

10. From the **Function** drop-down box, select **Sum**.

11. In the **Reference** box, press **<F3>**, select and paste the *Name* **List1** and then click **Add** to add the *Name* to the **All references** box.

12. Repeat step 11 and add the *Name* **List2** to the **All references** box.

13. Select both check boxes in the **Use Label in** area, and then click **OK**. The *Consolidate* dialog box appears, as shown.

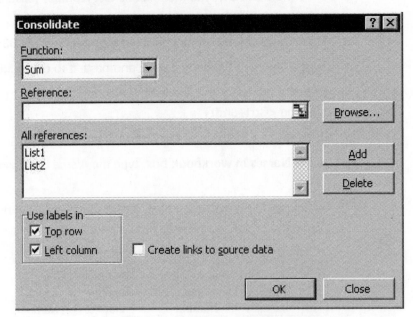

14. Select cell **H2** and click the **Sort Ascending** ▲↓ icon. When you are done, your worksheet should look like this (note columns **G** and **H**, as well as cells **G2** and **H2**):

	A	B	C	D	E	F	G	H
1	Account Number List # 1	List Number		Account Number List # 2	List Number			List Number
2	1011	1		1011	2		1013	2
3	1012	1		1012	2		1112	2
4	1021	1		1013	2		1011	3
5	1051	1		1021	2		1012	3
6	1061	1		1051	2		1021	3
7	1071	1		1061	2		1051	3
8	1091	1		1071	2		1061	3
9	1111	1		1091	2		1071	3
10	1121	1		1111	2		1091	3
11	1201	1		1112	2		1111	3
12	1211	1		1121	2		1121	3
13	1301	1		1201	2		1201	3
14	1501	1		1211	2		1211	3
15	1571	1		1301	2		1301	3
16			-	1501	2		1501	3
17				1571	2		1571	3

The **Consolidate** technique summarizes the lists by comparing and identifying texts in cells the top row and the leftmost column.

In the example presented here, list numbers 1 and 2 were summarized when the account number was identified in both lists. There are two new account numbers in the second list that do not appear in the first list. In the consolidated list, the numeral **2** is displayed next to each account number that does not appear in list 1.

Using the COUNTIF Formula to Compare Lists

A **COUNTIF** formula returns a calculation result that contains the number of counted occurrences according to the evaluated criteria.

The formula in cell **E2** in Figure 3-2 returns 0 (a new account number) if it cannot find the criteria (that is, the number in column **D**) in column **A**. If the calculated result equals 1, the account number already exists.

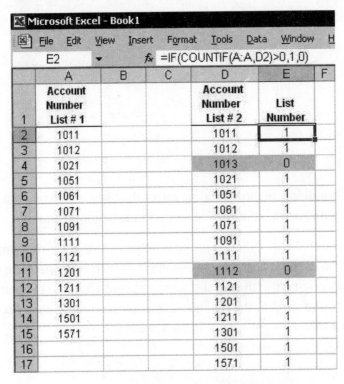

	A	B	C	D	E	F
1	Account Number List # 1			Account Number List # 2	List Number	
2	1011			1011	1	
3	1012			1012	1	
4	1021			1013	0	
5	1051			1021	1	
6	1061			1051	1	
7	1071			1061	1	
8	1091			1071	1	
9	1111			1091	1	
10	1121			1111	1	
11	1201			1112	0	
12	1211			1121	1	
13	1301			1201	1	
14	1501			1211	1	
15	1571			1301	1	
16				1501	1	
17				1571	1	

E2 = =IF(COUNTIF(A:A,D2)>0,1,0)

Figure 3-2: COUNTIF Formula

Adding New Account Details to Worksheet 21 – Trial Balances Data

The following sections provide step-by-step instructions for adding new account numbers and account names in worksheet *21 — Trial Balances Data*.

Step 1: Adding the Account Numbers

➢ **To add the account numbers to the Trial Balances Data worksheet:**

✦ Copy the new additional account numbers you find using the technique described in the previous section to worksheet *21 — Trial Balances Data* and paste them into column **A** after the last account number, as shown.

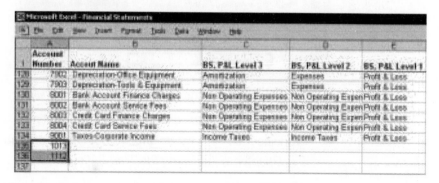

Step 2: Adding the Account Names

➢ **To add the account names to worksheet 21 – Trial Balances Data:**

1. Add the account names to the cells in column **B** by adding the formula:

    =INDEX(TB_table,MATCH(A135,TB_Index,0),2)

    to find and return the account names from worksheet *91 — Trial Balance (Original).*

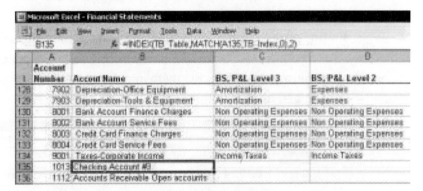

The formula contains the following *Name*s:

✦ **TB_table:** The *Name* defined for the Trial Balance data in worksheet *91 — Trial Balance (Original),* as described on page 27, *Chapter 2, Adjusting the Trial Balance.*

✦ **TB_Index:** The *Name* defined for the Account Number column (column **A**) in worksheet *91 — Trial Balance (Original),* as described on page 26, *Chapter 2, Adjusting the Trial Balance.*

2. Copy and paste the account names as values using **Paste Special, Values.**

💬 **TIP:**

Reduce the number of links to make the workbook smaller. In places where you entered formulas to retrieve text or numbers (where there is no need to save the formulas in the cells), you can delete the formulas by pasting the calculation results as values.

Step 3: Adding the Three Summary Levels of the Balance Sheet and Income Statement

➢ To add the summary levels to the Trial Balances Data worksheet:

1. Copy cells **C134:E134** (as shown in Figure 3-1) and paste them into the cells from **C135** onward.

2. Select an **Account Type** item from the **Validation** list in every cell from **C135** onwards.

   The cells in columns **D** through **E** contain formulas that return the text levels from worksheet *15 — BS, IS Level* (for more details about this worksheet, refer to page 11, *Chapter 1, Introducing Financial Statements.xls Worksheets*).

Step 4: Sorting the Trial Balances List

➢ To sort the trial balances list in worksheet *21 – Trial Balances Data*:

✦ After you have entered all of the new account names and numbers, as well as the formulas that return the financial statement's summary **Balance Sheet** and **Income Statement** levels, select a cell in column **A** and sort the complete list in ascending order by clicking the **Sort Ascending** ⬇ icon.

Entering Final Trial Balances to a New Column in Worksheet 21 – Trial Balances Data

This section discusses how to add the balances of the new final adjusted Trial Balance to a new column in the worksheet.

➤ **To add an account balance to the new month column:**

1. In worksheet *21 — Trial Balances Data*, add a **SUMIF** formula to the new month column (**BX**) you added to the worksheet, as shown below.

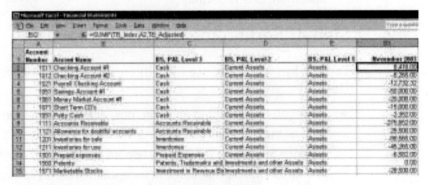

2. Type the following formula into cell **BX2**:

   = SUMIF(TB_Index,A2,TB_Adjusted)

   In the formula, the *Name* **TB_Index** has been defined for column **A** in worksheet *91 — Trial Balance (Original)* (as described on page 26, *Chapter 2, Adjusting the Trial Balance*), and the *Name* **TB_Adjusted** for column **H** (as described on page 39, *Chapter 2, Adjusting the Trial Balance*). The **SUMIF** formula summarizes the Trial Balance figures with the Trial Balance Adjustments figures (for more details, refer to page 39, *Chapter 2, Adjusting the Trial Balance*).

3. Copy the formula and paste it downward into the cells of column **BX** (as shown above).

Saving the Account Balances of the Trial Balance as Values

The formulas in worksheet *21 — Trial Balances Data* are saved until the Financial Statements reports are finalized. They are automatically updated either when a new adjustment is made, or when one or more adjustments is being updated (if you use the **SUMIF** formula technique explained on page 39, *Chapter 2, Adjusting the Trial Balance* or the **Consolidating** technique on page 40, *Chapter 2, Adjusting the Trial Balance*).

To delete the formulas after you have finalized the Financial Statements reports, return to worksheet *21 — Trial Balances Data*, copy column **BX** and then paste it back as values only into the same column.

Defining Names

Before creating Financial Statements reports, you must first define the *Names* you will use.

Defining a Dynamic Range Name

➢ **To define a Dynamic Range Name to Trial Balances Data:**

1. Select worksheet *21 — Trial Balances Data*, select cell **A1** and press **<Ctrl+Shift+*>** to select the Trial Balances data table.

2. Press **<Ctrl+F3>**.

3. In the **Names in wordbooks** box, enter **TB_DataBase**.

4. In the **Refers To** box, enter the following formula:

   =OFFSET(21 - Trial Balances Data!$A$1,0,0,COUNTA(21 - Trial Balances Data!$A:$A),COUNTA(21 - Trial Balances Data!$1:$1))

5. Click **OK**.

Advantages of Creating a Dynamic Range Name

A dynamic range *Name* automatically updates the size of a data table immediately after adding new data to rows or columns. This is very important, especially when using **PivotTable** reports (see page 237, *Chapter 13, Analyzing Financial Statements Using PivotTable and PivotChart Reports.*

Defining Names for Columns A:E in Worksheet 21 – Trial Balances Data:

✦ Column A: **TB_DB_AccountNumber**

✦ Column B: **TB_DB_AccountName**

✦ Column C: **TB_DB_Level1**

✦ Column D: **TB_DB_Level2**

✦ Column E: **TB_DB_Level3**

Chapter 4

Balance Sheet

About This Chapter

This chapter provides step-by-step instructions for creating a Balance Sheet report, which is the major report in the Financial Statement, and includes the following sections:

✦ **Overview**, page 66, introduces the Balance Sheet report, and describes the techniques used to create it in an Excel worksheet.

✦ **Creating a Balance Sheet Report in an Excel Worksheet**, page 68, provides step-by-step instructions for creating the Balance Sheet report using an Excel worksheet.

✦ **Presenting Two Different Periods**, page 85, describes how to add a **Combo Box** to the worksheet to enable comparing different periods.

✦ **Auditing the Balance Sheet Figures**, page 87, describes how to audit and balance the figures in the completed Balance Sheet.

Overview

The Balance Sheet, as well as many other components of a company's Financial Statements, is generated once every period. The figures presented in the Balance Sheet are the actual balances for the statement creation date, while the figures presented in the Income Statement and Cash Flow reports are the accumulated summarized balances for the report period.

Public companies and other types of companies publish full Financial Statements reports every quarter. Many companies or other types of entities prepare partial Financial Statements (usually only Income Statements) on a monthly, quarterly or semi-annual basis, and full Financial Statements annually, to be used internally for audit, decision-making and tax purposes.

This chapter provides step-by-step instructions for creating a Balance Sheet report (as shown in Figure 4-1, page 67) using an Excel worksheet. After creating the report, you can easily display and/or print the report at the end of selected month, quarter or calendar or fiscal year reporting period, prepare comparison reports, add charts, create PivotTable reports for analyzing the data, and so on.

In this chapter, you will learn the various Excel techniques you can use when creating Financial Statements and other types of financial reports, as well as how to combine them. These techniques include:

✦ Using a **Combo Box**.

✦ Using **Validation**.

✦ Using formulas that return and summarize data.

Balance Sheet formatting (including rounding to the thousands), printing, e-mailing, page-numbering methods, and so on, are described in subsequent chapters. Other important subjects, such as the common Balance Sheet and ratio analysis are discussed in the second part of this book, *Analyzing Financial Statements and Creating Management Financial Reports*.

			Microsoft Excel - Financial Statements

File   Edit   View   Insert   Format   Tools   Data   Window   Help

	A	B	C	D
1				
2	December 31, 2003 ▼			
3				
4	XYZ Corporation Inc.			
5	BALANCE SHEET			
6				
7			December 31	
8		Notes	2003	2002
9	ASSETS			
10				
11	**Current Assets**			
12	Cash	5	301,124	318,697
13	Accounts Receivable	7	1,653,558	1,538,494
14	Inventories	8	546,173	520,133
15	Prepaid Expenses	9	13,552	23,659
16	Total Current Assets		2,514,407	2,400,982
17				
18	**Property and Equipment (at Cost)**	10		
19	Land & Building		674,019	677,191
20	Machinery and Equipment		386,140	326,052
21	Furniture and Fixtures		59,410	47,906
22	Total Property and Equipment		1,119,569	1,051,150
23	Less: Accumulated Depreciation		(478,852)	(419,540)
24	Net Book Value		640,717	631,610
25				
26	**Other Assets**			
27	Investment in Revenue Bond	11	364,321	300,260
28	Patents, Trademarks and Goodwill	12	52,250	52,500
29	Total Other Assets		416,571	352,760
30				
31	TOTAL ASSETS		3,571,695	3,385,352
32				
33	LIABILITIES AND STOCKHOLDER'S EQUITY			
34				
35	**Current Liabilities**			
36	Line of Credit	6	476,783	500,834
37	Current Portion of Long-Term Debt		40,252	39,506
38	Accounts Payable	13	547,255	475,284
39	Accrued Expenses	14	234,296	221,291
40	Other Payables	15	19,250	26,937
41	Total Current Liabilities		1,317,837	1,263,851
42				
43	**Long-Term Liabilities**			
44	Note Payable	16	784,273	840,105
45	Equipment Leases Payable	17	185,459	224,965
46	Less: Current Portion Shown Above		(40,252)	(39,506)
47	Total Long-Term Liabilities		929,480	1,025,564
48				
49	TOTAL LIABILITIES		2,247,316	2,289,415
50				
51	**Stockholder's Equity**			
52	Capital Stock		151,897	152,623
53	Retained Earnings	19	1,172,482	943,314
54	Total Stockholder's Equity		1,324,379	1,095,937
55				
56	TOTAL LIABILITIES AND STOCKHOLDER'S EQUITY		3,571,695	3,385,352

Figure 4-1: Balance Sheet for the Year Ending December 31

Creating a Balance Sheet Report in an Excel Worksheet

The following sections provide step-by-step instructions for creating a Balance Sheet in worksheet *31 — Balance Sheet*.

Step 1: Defining Names

In order to ensure efficient and accurate work, you should use *Names* as range references in the worksheet. This is especially helpful for re-directioning in formulas, attaching lists to **Combo Boxes** and **Validation**, and for linking cells to a **Combo Box** object.

In worksheet *13 — Parameters & Calculations* (described in *Chapter 1, Introducing Financial Statements.xls Worksheets* and shown in Figure 4-2), you defined *Names* for cells used for a cell link to a **Combo Box**, and for cells that contain formulas that calculate the reporting date, month and year numbers. In worksheet *14 — Months Lists* (described on page 6, *Chapter 1, Introducing Financial Statements.xls Worksheets*), you defined a Name for the **MonthsList**. In worksheet *21 — Trial Balances Data* (described on page 63, *Chapter 3, Updating the Trial Balances Data Worksheet*), you defined *Names* to **TB_DataBase**, and so on.

	A	B	C	D
	Microsoft Excel - Financial Statements			
	File Edit View Insert Format Tools Data Window Help			
	MonthSelecti... ▼ *fx* 72			
1	December 31, 2003 ▼	ComboBox Link &	Name Defined in	
	Datails	**Formulas**	**Cells in Column B**	**Formula in Cells in Column B**
2	ComboBox month selection Number	72	MonthSelectionNumber	ComboBox Cell Link
3	Reports Date	December 31, 2003	ReportsDate	=INDEX(MonthsList,MonthSelectionNumber)
4	Reports Month Number	12	ReportsMonthNumber	=MONTH(ReportsDate)
5	Reports Year Number	2003	ReportsYearNumber	=YEAR(ReportsDate)

Figure 4-2: Worksheet 13 — Parameters & Calculations

Step 2: Adding a Combo Box

The **Combo Box** object enables you to select the reporting ending month for the Financial Statements. When you select one item (in this case, a month) from the **Combo Box** months list, the formulas in the worksheet summarize the data from the appropriate column in worksheet *21 — Trial Balance Data* where the Trial Balances data are stored.

➤ **To add a Combo Box to Worksheet 31 – Balance Sheet:**

1. Select worksheet *11 — General Details.*

2. Select and copy the **Combo Box**.

3. Select worksheet *31 — Balance Sheet* and paste the **Combo Box** object.

For more details on how to add a **Combo Box**, refer to *Chapter 1, Introducing Financial Statements.xls Worksheets.*

Step 3: Entering the Company Name

Add the company name to the Balance Sheet report.

➤ **To add the company name into the Balance Sheet report:**

1. Type the following formula into cell **A4** (see page 4, *Chapter 1, Introducing Financial Statements.xls Worksheets*):

   =CompanyName

2. Select cells **A4:D4** and click the **Merge and Center** icon, as shown below.

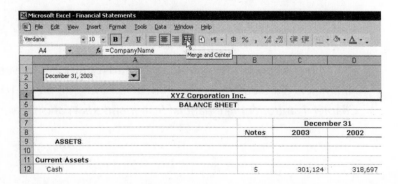

Step 4: Entering the Month Title and End-of-Year Numbers

The next step in creating a Balance Sheet report is adding the month title and the year numbers for the report.

➤ **To enter the month title and end-of-year numbers:**

1. Type the following formula into cell **C7**:

   =ReportsDate

   Select cells **C7:C8** and click the **Merge and Center** icon.

2. Type the following formula into cell **C8**:

   =ReportsYearNumber

3. Type the following formula into cell **D8**:

   =C8-1

   Your worksheet should look like this:

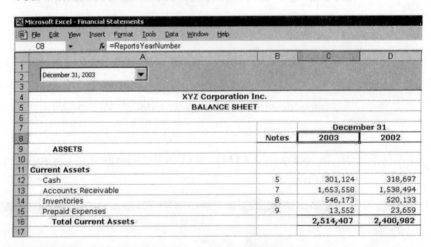

The *Names* **ReportsDate** and **ReportsYearNumber** are in worksheet *13 — Parameters & Calculations* (for more details, refer to pages 10 and 11, *Chapter 1, Introducing Financial Statements.xls Worksheets*).

Step 5: Formatting the Summary Levels

The Balance Sheet report contains three summary levels:

✦ **Level 1, Category:** Assets, Liabilities, Stockholder Equity.

✦ **Level 2, Account Groups:** Under the Assets section — Current Assets, Property and Equipment (at Cost), Other Assets. Under the Liabilities and Stockholder's Equity section — Current Liabilities, Long-Term Liabilities, Stockholder's Equity.

✦ **Level 3, Account Types:** Under the Current Assets section (as an example) — Cash, Accounts Receivable, Inventories, and Prepaid Expenses.

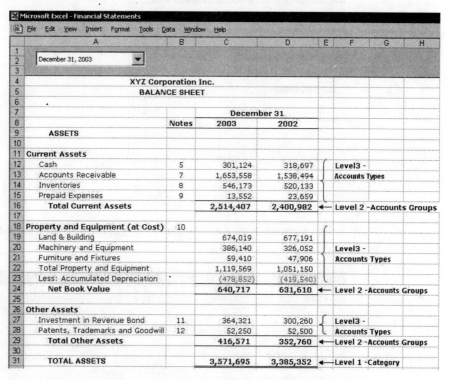

Figure 4-3: Balance Sheet Summary Levels

A professional Financial Statements report should keep the formatting of all reports, including Balance Sheet, Income Statement, and Cash Flow, identical. This is done by saving each **Style** as a separate and permanent **Style**. You can format cells in every report by selecting cells within any report and then selecting the desired **Style** from the **Style** Box, as explained in the following sections.

➤ **To create a Custom Format and save as a Style:**

1. Right-click one of the toolbars and select **Customize**. The *Customize* dialog box appears.

2. Select the **Commands** tab, as shown below.

3. Select **Format** from the **Categories** box, and drag the **Style** Box icon to the formatting toolbar.

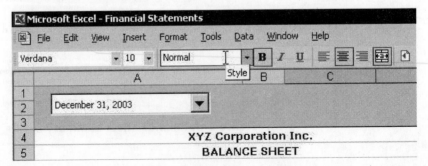

4. Click **Close**. The **Style** Box is now located on the Formatting toolbar.

5. Select cell **A12** (as shown in Figure 4-3, page 71).

6. Use the **Font Size** Box icon on the **Formatting** toolbar to set the font size to **10**. Ensure that it is not bolded or italicized.

7. Increase the indentation by two characters by either double-clicking the **Increase Indent** icon,

OR

Pressing **<Ctrl+1>** to open the *Format Cells* dialog box, and selecting the **Alignment** tab. In the **Indent** spin box, type **2**.

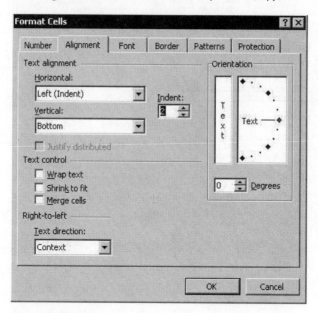

8. Press **<Alt+'>**,

OR

From the *Format* menu, select **Style**.

9. In the **Style** box, type **Level3** and then click **OK**. The Level 3 style has now been set.

10. Select cell **A11**, set the desired format and repeat steps 8 and 9 for **Level2**. The Level 2 style has now been set.

11. Select cell **A97**, set the desired format and repeat steps 8 and 9 for **Level1**. The Level 1 style has now been set.

12. Select the **Style** box icon and ensure that all three new styles (**Level1**, **Level2**, and **Level3**) have been added to it.

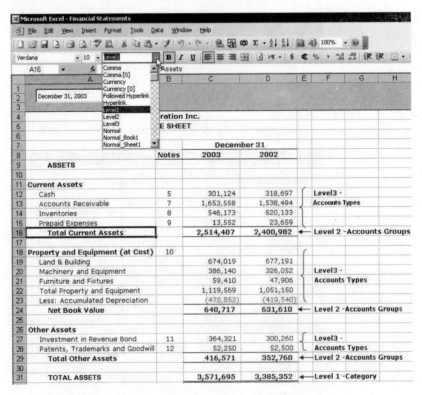

You can add and modify all **Styles**, as required.

➢ To add and modify a style:

1. From the *Format* menu, select **Style**.

2. In the *Style* dialog box, select a style from the **Style Name** box.

3. To add a new **Style**, type the **Style Name** into the **Style Name** box.

4. Click **Add**.

5. In the *Format Cells* dialog box, change to the desired format and click **OK**.

6. To modify a style, choose the **Style** from **Style Name**, and click **Modify**.

7. In the *Format Cells* dialog box, change to the desired format and click **OK**.

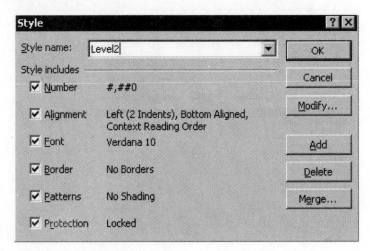

NOTE:

Editing and modifying a **Style** enables you to update all cells in the workbook with the same **Style** simultaneously.

Step 6: Choosing Account Type Items from a List Using Validation

Selecting an Account Type item from a list of Account Types using **Validation** (column **A** in Figure 4-4) enables formulas entered into cells in columns **C** and **D** to identify the text (**Account Type item — Level 3**) and returns the summary results from the Level 3 criteria (column **C** in worksheet *15 — BS, IS Level*, as described in *Chapter 1, Introducing Financial Statements.xls Worksheets*) for the reporting month selected from the **Combo Box** months list in worksheet *31 — Balance Sheet*.

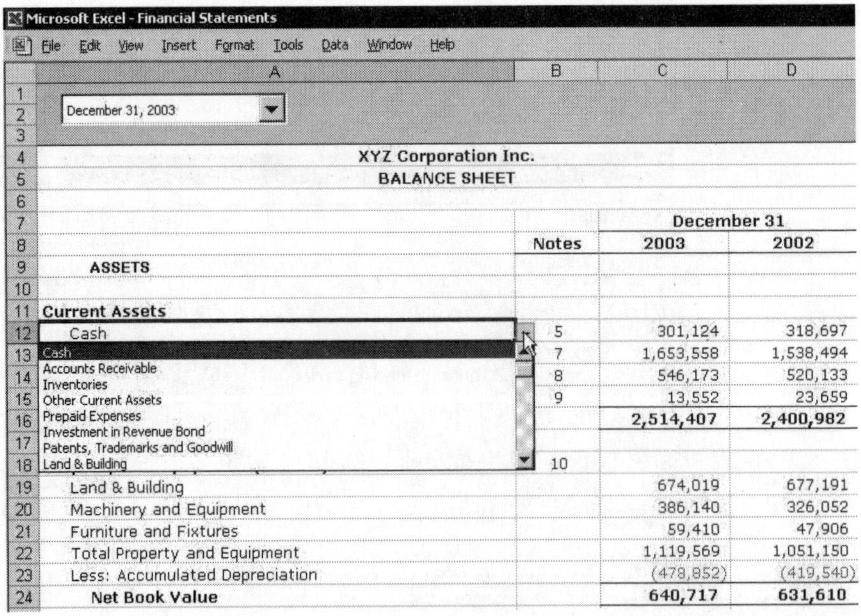

Figure 4-4: Choosing an Account Types Item from Validation List

The *Name* **Level 3** is defined for column **C** in worksheet *15 — BS, IS Level*. For more details, refer to page 13, *Chapter 1, Introducing Financial Statements.xls Worksheets*.

Add the list of Account Types to the **Validation** technique for easier selection of an Account Type item.

➢ **To add the Account Types list to the Validation source box:**

1. Select cell **A12**.

2. From the *Data* menu, select **Validation**. The *Data Validation* dialog box appears.

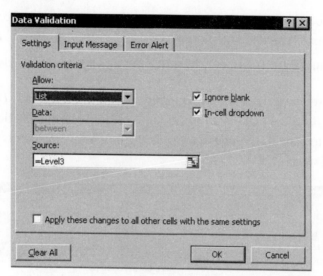

3. Select the **Settings** tab, and select **List** from the **Allow** Box.

4. In the **Source** box, press **<F3>**, select the *Name* **Level3**, and click **OK**.

5. Copy the cell and paste it to all cells in column **A** from which the Account Type items will be selected (see Figure 4-1).

Step 7: Entering Formulas That Return Summary Balances for Account Types (Level 3)

The formula in cell **C12** (and in the cells of column **C** that parallel an Account Type item in column A) is:

=SUMIF(TB_DB_Level3,A12,OFFSET(TB_DB_Level3,0,MonthSelectionNumber+2))

For the *Name* **TB_DB_Level3**, refer to page 64, *Chapter 3, Updating the Trial Balances Data Worksheet*; for the *Name* **MonthSelectionNumber**, refer to page 6, *Chapter 1, Introducing Financial Statements.xls Worksheets*.

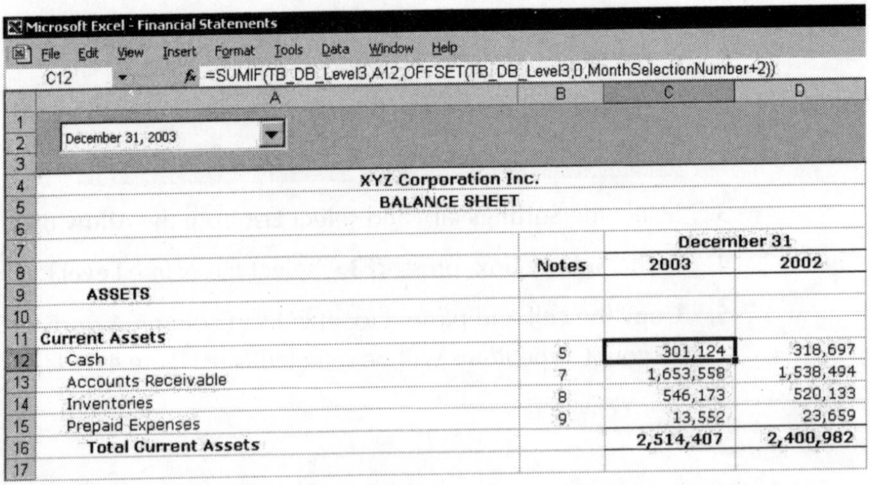

Figure 4-5: Formula Returning the Summary for an Account Type Item

The formula in cell **D12** (and in the cells of column **D** that parallel an Account Type item in column A) is:

=SUMIF(TB_DB_Level3,A12,OFFSET(TB_DB_Level3,0,MonthSelectionNumber+2-12))

	A	B	C	D
1				
2	December 31, 2003 ▼			
3				
4	XYZ Corporation Inc.			
5	BALANCE SHEET			
6				
7				December 31
8		Notes	2003	2002
9	ASSETS			
10				
11	Current Assets			
12	Cash	5	301,124	318,697
13	Accounts Receivable	7	1,653,558	1,538,494
14	Inventories	8	546,173	520,133
15	Prepaid Expenses	9	13,552	23,659
16	Total Current Assets		2,514,407	2,400,982
17				

Figure 4-6: Formula Returning a Summary for an Account Type Item for a Previous Reporting Ending Month

This **SUMIF** formula summarizes the data from the **December** month columns for the years **2002** and **2003** from worksheet *21 — Trial Balances Data*. The criterion the **SUMIF** formula uses is the Account Type item in column **A** (in worksheet *31— Balance Sheet*). The **SUMIF** formula has three arguments:

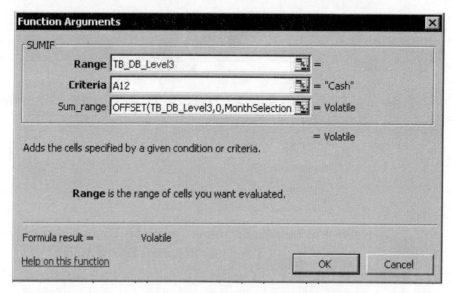

◆ **First argument:** The range to evaluate according to the criteria entered in the second argument of the **SUMIF** formula.

◆ **Second argument:** The criterion is the Account Type item chosen from the Level 3 **Validation** list.

◆ **Third argument:** The column from which the data will be summarized. The summary will be performed from the month column number selected in the **Combo Box** adjusted by the **OFFSET** formula. The **OFFSET** formula enables diversion to the column of the selected month from the base column (column **C**). The following section explains how the **OFFSET** formula diverts to the proper column.

The reference (first argument) in the **OFFSET** formula (as described on page 78) is column **C** in worksheet *21 — Trial Balances Data*.

	Account Number	Account Name	BS, P&L Level 3	BS, P&L Level 2	BS, P&L Level 1	January 1998	February 1998	March 1998
1								
2	1011	Checking Account #1	Cash	Current Assets	ASSETS	1	2	3
3	1012	Checking Account #2	Cash	Current Assets	ASSETS	2	4	6
4	1021	Payroll Checking Account	Cash	Current Assets	ASSETS	3	6	9
5	1051	Savings Account #1	Cash	Current Assets	ASSETS	4	8	12
6	1061	Money Market Account #1	Cash	Current Assets	ASSETS	5	10	15
7	1071	Short Term CD's	Cash	Current Assets	ASSETS	6	12	18
8	1091	Petty Cash	Cash	Current Assets	ASSETS	7	14	21
9	1111	Accounts Receivable	Accounts Receivable	Current Assets	ASSETS	8	16	24
10	1121	Allowance for doubtful accounts	Accounts Receivable	Current Assets	ASSETS	9	18	27

Figure 4-7: Account Types — Level 3

How the OFFSET Formula Operates

The section explains how the **OFFSET** formula diverts to the proper column.

Column **77** in Figure 4-8 is the column number for **December 2003** in worksheet *21 — Trial Balances Data* (to change the header title text to numbers, refer to page 82).

	1		2	3	4	5	65	77
1	Account Number	Account Name	BS, P&L Level 3		BS, P&L Level 2	BS, P&L Level 1	December 2002	December 2003
2	1011	Checking Account #1	Cash		Current Assets	ASSETS	51,606	50,446
3	1012	Checking Account #2	Cash		Current Assets	ASSETS	25,658	22,535
4	1021	Payroll Checking Account	Cash		Current Assets	ASSETS	15,998	17,558
5	1051	Savings Account #1	Cash		Current Assets	ASSETS	150,000	160,000
6	1061	Money Market Account #1	Cash		Current Assets	ASSETS	75,000	50,000
7	1091	Petty Cash	Cash		Current Assets	ASSETS	435	585
8	1111	Accounts Receivable	Accounts Receivable		Current Assets	ASSETS	1538493.6	1,653,558

Figure 4-8: Column Numbers in Worksheet 21 — Trial Balances Data

When **December 2003** is selected from the **MonthsList** in the **Combo Box** drop-down list, the month number in that list is **72** (this is calculated by determining the number of months between January 1978 to December 2003 -6 years * 12 months = 72), the linked cell to the **Combo Box** in worksheet *13 — Parameters & Calculations* receives the value of **72**, and the cell linked *Name* is **MonthSelectionNumber** (see page 6, *Chapter 1, Introducing Financial Statements.xls Worksheets*).

In worksheet *21 — Trial Balances Data,* column **3** (column **C**) is the base column where the **SUMIF** formula evaluates for the criteria in the second argument of the **SUMIF** formula. In this case, it is the difference between 77 and 3 (74).

In the third argument, the **Sum_range** should be 74 columns distant from the base column. The **OFFSET** formula returns the result of **74** and causes the **SUMIF** formula to summarize the figures from the **December 2003 Trial Balance** column.

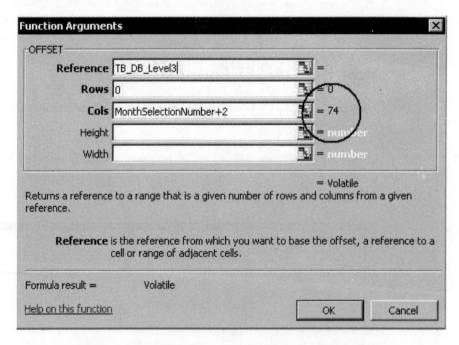

Figure 4-9: Offset Function Arguments Dialog Box

 TIP:
To turn the letters of the column title lines (**A**, **B**, **C**, and so on) into numbers while working in the worksheet:

1. From the *Tools* menu, select **Options**.

2. Select the **General** tab, and select the **R1C1 Reference Style** check box.

3. Click **OK**.

Step 8: Automatically Updating the Note Numbers

Worksheet *61 — Notes* contains a **Notes** list that you can update, add or delete (for more details, refer to *Chapter 7, Notes*).

The formula in the cells in column **B** in worksheet *31 — Balance Sheet* returns an updated **Note** number and prevents a situation where an incorrect **Note** number is displayed in the Balance Sheet.

The formula in cell **B12** (and all cells from **B12** to the last cell of the Balance Sheet report) is:

=IF(ISERROR(INDEX(NotesTable,MATCH(A12,NotesFSItem,0),1))=TRUE,"",
INDEX(NotesTable,MATCH(A12,NotesFSItem,0),1))

For more details about the *Names* **NotesTable** and **NoteFAItem**, refer to pages 109-110, *Chapter 7, Notes*.

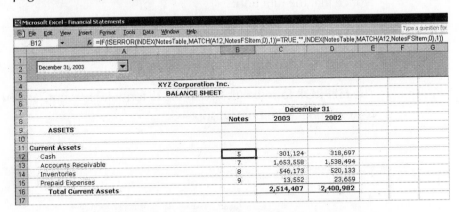

Figure 4-10: Formula Returning the Note Number

This formula returns an updated **Note** number from column **A** in worksheet *61 — Notes*, as shown below (for more details, refer to *Chapter 7, Notes*).

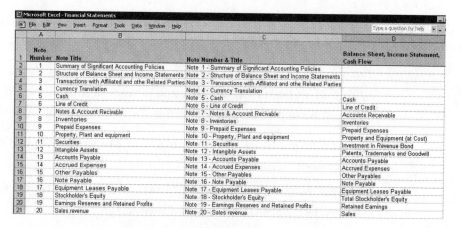

Figure 4-11: Worksheet 61 — Notes

Notice that the function:

=INDEX(NotesTable,MATCH(A12,NotesFSItem,0))

is nested twice in the formula in cell **B12**.

The **ISERROR** formula (nested in the **IF** formula) prevents an erroneous **Note** number from being displayed.

Presenting Two Different Periods

To present two periods by choosing each ending period separately, add a second **Combo Box** object to the worksheet.

Figure 4-12 shows two **Combo Boxes** at the top of each column.

	A	B	C	D
	Microsoft Excel - Financial Statements			
	File Edit View Insert Format Tools Data Window Help			
1				
2			April 30, 2003 ▼	December 31, 2002 ▼
3				
4		XYZ Corporation Inc.		
5		BALANCE SHEET		
6				
7			April 30	December 31
8		Notes	2003	2002
9	ASSETS			
10				
11	Current Assets			
12	Cash	5	269,506	318,697
13	Accounts Receivable	7	1,479,934	1,538,494
14	Inventories	8	488,825	520,133
15	Prepaid Expenses	9	12,129	23,659
16	Total Current Assets		2,250,394	2,400,982
17				
18	Property and Equipment (at Cost)	10		
19	Land & Building		603,247	677,191
20	Machinery and Equipment		345,595	326,052
21	Furniture and Fixtures		53,172	47,906
22	Total Property and Equipment		1,002,014	1,051,150
23	Less: Accumulated Depreciation		428,573	419,540
24	Net Book Value		573,441	631,610
25				
26	Other Assets			
27	Investment in Revenue Bond	12	326,068	300,260
28	Patents, Trademarks and Goodwill	13	46,764	52,500
29	Total Other Assets		372,831	352,760
30				
31	TOTAL ASSETS		3,196,667	3,385,352

Figure 4-12: Presenting Two Different Periods

➢ **To add a second Combo Box:**

1. Copy worksheet *31 — Balance Sheet* by selecting the worksheet's tab and dragging it to a different location while pressing **<Ctrl>**.

2. Select the **Combo Box** and press **<Ctrl+C>** to copy.

3. Select cell **D2** and press **<Ctrl+V>** to paste.

4. Select the new **Combo Box**, and from the shortcut menu, select **Format Control**, and then the **Control** tab.

5. In the **Cell Link** box, type **CompareMonthNumberBS**.

6. Select worksheet *13 — Parameters & Calculations* and define the *Name* **CompareMonthNumberBS** to cell **B10**.

7. Select the new worksheet you copied in step 1, and replace the *Name* in the third argument of the **OFFSET** formula in column **D** to **CompareMonthNumberBS** by using the keyboard shortcut **<Ctrl+H>**:

=SUMIF(TB_DB_Level3,A12,OFFSET(TB_DB_Level3,0,CompareMonthNumberBS+2))

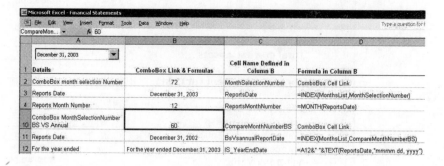

Auditing the Balance Sheet Figures

It is essential that the figures in the Balance Sheet be thoroughly checked before it can be presented or printed. This can be done by adding formulas that summarize the balances according to Level 2, **Account Groups**.

Microsoft Excel - Financial Statements

File Edit View Insert Format Tools Data Window Help

F16 =SUMIF(TB_DB_Level2,A11,OFFSET(TB_DB_Level2,0,MonthSelectionNumber+1))

December 31, 2003

	A	B	C	D	E	F	G
4	XYZ Corporation Inc.						
5	BALANCE SHEET						
7			December 31			Audit	
8		Notes	2003	2002		2003	2002
9	ASSETS						
11	Current Assets						
12	Cash	5	301,124	318,697			
13	Accounts Receivable	7	1,653,558	1,538,494			
14	Inventories	8	546,173	520,133			
15	Prepaid Expenses	9	13,552	23,659			
16	Total Current Assets		2,514,407	2,400,982		2,514,407	2,400,982
18	Property and Equipment (at Cost)	10					
19	Land & Building		674,019	677,191			
20	Machinery and Equipment		386,140	326,052			
21	Furniture and Fixtures		59,410	47,906			
22	Total Property and Equipment		1,119,569	1,051,150			
23	Less: Accumulated Depreciation		(478,852)	(419,540)			
24	Net Book Value		640,717	631,610		640,717	631,610
26	Other Assets						
27	Investment in Revenue Bond	11	364,321	300,260			
28	Patents, Trademarks and Goodwill	12	52,250	52,500			
29	Total Other Assets		416,571	352,760		416,571	352,760
31	TOTAL ASSETS		3,571,695	3,385,352		3,571,695	3,385,352

Figure 4-13: Auditing the Balance Sheet Figures

The formula in cell **F16** is (see page 64, *Chapter 3, Updating the Trial Balances Data Worksheet* for *Name* **TB_DB_Level2** and page 6, *Chapter 1, Introducing Financial Statements.xls Worksheets* for the *Name* **MonthSelectionNumber**):

=SUMIF(TB_DB_Level2,A11,OFFSET(TB_DB_Level2,0,MonthSelectionNumber+1))

This formula summarizes the totals in the **December 2003** column of worksheet *21 — Trial Balances Data* based on the **Current Assets** criteria (cell **A11** in Figure 4-13) in column **B** — Level 2.

Chapter 5

Income Statement

About This Chapter

This chapter explains how to create the Income Statement report using Excel's worksheet, and includes the following sections:

✦ **Overview**, page 90, introduces the concept of the Income Statement report.

✦ **Creating an Income Statement Report in an Excel Worksheet**, page 91, describes how to create the Income Statement report using Excel's worksheet.

✦ **Adding Unique Items to the Income Statement Report**, page 93, describes how to add the two unique items to the Income Statement report.

Overview

The Income Statement report presents the net result of a company's revenues, minus expenses, over a given period of time. In other words, the Income Statement bottom line is an indication of how much profit the company has made during the period.

In this chapter, you will learn how to create a regular Income Statement report using an Excel worksheet. In the second part of this book, *Analyzing Financial Statements and Creating Management Financial Reports*, you will learn how to:

◆ Interpret Income Statements.

◆ Analyze Income Statements.

◆ Create Income Statements that enable management to make business decisions.

◆ Generate monthly, quarterly or annual accumulated Income Statements based either on a calendar or on fiscal reporting periods.

◆ Analyze profit centers.

Creating an Income Statement Report in an Excel Worksheet

Figure 5-1 displays an example of an annual Income Statement report created in worksheet *41— Income Statement*.

	A	B	C	D
2	December 31, 2003			
3				
4	XYZ Corporation Inc.			
5	Income Statement			
6	For the year ended December, 31 2003			
7				
8		Notes	2003	2002
9	**Revenue**	20		
10	Sales		2,920,093	2,633,626
11	Services		955,214	725,458
12	Total Revenue		3,875,307	3,359,084
13				
14	**Cost of Goods Sold**			
15	Materials		854,521	733,352
16	Labor & Subcontractors Costs		602,125	536,645
17	Other Cost of goods sold		384,521	350,241
18	Increase / Decrease in Inventories	21	-26,040	-30,254
19	Total Cost of Goods Sold		1,815,127	1,589,984
20				
21	**Gross Income**		2,060,180	1,769,100
22				
23	**Operating Expenses**			
24	Selling		480,161	441,256
25	General & Administrative	22	758,542	675,992
26	Other Operating Expense	23	275,541	260,887
27	Depreciation		59,312	50,221
28	Total Operating Expenses		1,573,556	1,428,356
29				
30	**Net Income before Operations**		486,624	340,744
31				
32	**Operating Income (Loss)**			
33	Other income (expense)	24	32,512	-2,521
34	Interest expense		75,421	62,584
35	Total Operating Income		107,933	60,063
36				
37	**Income (Loss) Before Income Taxes**		378,691	280,681
38	Provision (benefit) for income taxes	25	149,523	133,251
39	**Net Income (Loss) for the year**		229,168	147,430
40	Retained Earnings beginning of the year	26	943,314	795,884
41	**Retained Earnings**		1,172,482	943,314

Figure 5-1: Income Statement Report

In *Chapter 4, Balance Sheet*, you learned how to create a Balance Sheet report using an Excel worksheet. The Income Statement report is created using similar techniques, including:

✦ Adding a **Combo Box** to select the ending-month reporting period.

✦ Entering the company name in the report's title.

✦ Using a **Validation** dropdown list to select an **Account Types** item (as described on page 12, *Chapter 1, Introducing Financial Statements.xls Worksheets*).

✦ Automatically calculating **Note** numbers in the **Notes** column.

✦ Calculating the report year's number in the comparison columns (columns **C** and **D** in Figure 5-1).

✦ Inserting formulas that return the total balance for each **Account Type** in the comparison columns (columns **C** and **D** below).

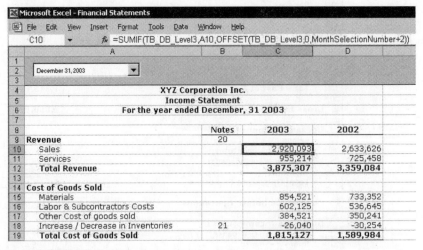

✦ Inserting auditing formulas to summarize the balance at the **Account Groups** level (for more details regarding the different types of levels, refer to page 12, *Chapter 1, Introducing Financial Statements.xls Worksheets*).

✦ Using **Styles** to apply the same format used in the Balance Sheet report (for more details, refer to page 71, *Chapter 4, Balance Sheet*).

Adding Unique Items to the Income Statement Report

The Balance Sheet, as well as many other components of a corporation's Financial Statements, is generated once every period. The figures presented in the Balance Sheet are the actual balances for the statement creation date, while the figures presented in the Income Statement and Cash Flow reports are the accumulated summarized balance figures for the report period.

There are two items that are unique to the Income Statement report compared to the Balance Sheet report:

✦ The year number of the report's year end.

✦ The retained earnings.

In this section, you will learn how to add these two items to worksheet *41 — Income Statement.*

Entering a Formula to Display the Ending Reporting Date

Account Types balances in the Balance Sheet are summarized for the date it is prepared (shown in cells **C7:D8** in Figure 5-2). **Account Types** balances in the Income Statement report are summarized for the reporting period, which can be monthly, quarterly or annually. The title in cell **A6** (in Figure 5-2) includes the reporting period and the creation date, as in this example for the year ending December 31, 2003.

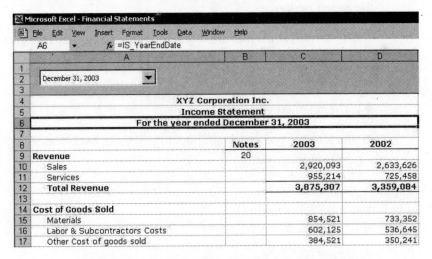

Figure 5-2: Income Statement Ending Period Date

➤ **To create and insert the formula that returns the income statement period and ending date:**

1. In cell **A6**, type the following formula:

   =IS_YearEndDate

   This formula returns the period (that is, the year the report ended) and the report end date (December 31, 2003) from cell **B12** in worksheet *13 — Parameters & Calculations* (shown on page 95) and places it in cell **A6** (**IS_YearEndDate**) of the Income Statement worksheet.

The formula in cell **B12** in *13 — Parameters & Calculations* is:

=A12&" "&TEXT(ReportsDate,"mmmm dd, yyyy")

which merges the text in cell **A12** with the calculated formatted date in cell **B3**, as shown:

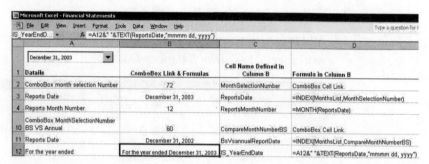

2. In the Income Statement worksheet, select cells **A6:D6** and click the

    Merge and Center icon. The report period and end date is displayed, as shown:

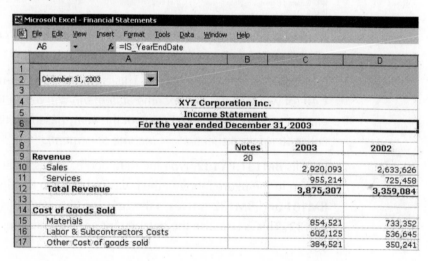

Adding the Retained Earnings Balances

Add Retained Earnings balances for previous years to the Income Statement report, as described in this section.

➤ **To add previous Year Retained Earnings balances:**

1. Add two new rows (rows **131** and **132**, in the figure below) to worksheet *21 — Trial Balances Data*.

	C	D	E	BM	BY
	BS, P&L Level 3	BS, P&L Level 2	BS, P&L Level 1	December 2002	December 2003
122	Other Operating Expense	Operating Expenses	Profit & Loss	0	0
123	Other Operating Expense	Operating Expenses	Profit & Loss	0	0
124	Other Operating Expense	Operating Expenses	Profit & Loss	0	0
125	Other Operating Expense	Operating Expenses	Profit & Loss	0	0
126	Other Operating Expense	Operating Expenses	Profit & Loss	0	0
127	Amortization	Operating Expenses	Profit & Loss	-50,221	-59,312
128	Interest expense	Operating Income (Loss)	Profit & Loss	-62,584	-75,421
129	Interest expense	Operating Income (Loss)	Profit & Loss	0	0
130	Provision (benefit) for income taxes	Income Taxes	Profit & Loss	-133,251	-149,523
131	Retained Earnings beginning of the year	Net Income (Loss) for the	Profit & Loss	795,884	943,314
132	Retained Earnings beginning year	Net Income (Loss) for the	Profit & Loss	-795,884	-943,314
133					

2. In row **A131**, type the exact text that should appear in cell **A40** of worksheet *41 — Income Statement* (Figure 5-1, page 91).

3. In cell **A132**, type different text. This is because the formula in cell **C40** (of worksheet *41 — Income Statement*) will return the retained earnings figure for the beginning of the year, based on the criteria in cell **A40** (of worksheet *41 — Income Statement*).

4. In cells **BM131:BY132**, type the Retained Earnings balances. As shown in the figure (above), the balance between the figures in cell **BM131** and **BM132** is 0, as is the balance between cells **BY131** and **BY132**. This is because the balance for each month must be kept at $0.

   The formula in cell **C40** in worksheet *41 — Income Statement* for the Retained Earnings is:

   =SUMIF(TB_DB_Level3,A40,OFFSET(TB_DB_Level3,0,MonthSelectionNumber+2))

   For more details regarding this formula, refer to page 79, *Chapter 4, Balance Sheet*.

Chapter 6

Cash Flow

About This Chapter

This chapter explains how to create a Cash Flow report using an Excel worksheet, and includes the following sections:

✦ **Overview**, page 98, introduces the concept of a Cash Flow report.

✦ **Sources and Uses of Cash**, page 99, presents the sources and uses of cash.

✦ **Creating a Cash Flow Report in an Excel Worksheet**, page 100, describes the steps needed to create a Cash Flow report using an Excel worksheet.

Overview

The Cash Flow report analyzes the movement of cash during the reporting period.

The Cash Flow report is different from the Income Statement report, as it analyzes the sources and uses of cash arising from both regular and non-regular operations. The reader of the Financial Statements will get information that he or she will not find in either the Balance Sheet or the Income Statement reports.

For example:

✦ Do Current Assets increase due to collecting Accounts Receivable balances or from slow Inventory sales?

✦ Has the company increased its Current Liabilities with short-term loans, which might result in a higher interest payment in the future?

The net Cash Flow is calculated by subtracting the uses of cash from the sources of cash.

Sources and Uses of Cash

Sources of cash include:

+ **Cash from Operating Activities:** The net income as calculated in the Income Statement report (after income taxes and before Retained Earnings as of the beginning of the year), adjusted by expenses not paid in cash during the reporting period, such as Depreciation and Amortization to Fixed and Other Assets.

+ **Decrease in Current Assets:** A decrease in Current Assets, except for Cash in bank.

+ **Selling of Fixed Assets.**

+ **Selling of Other Assets.**

+ **Increase in Current Liabilities.**

+ **Increase in Long Term Liabilities.**

+ **Money Paid by Stockholders for Capital.**

+ **Cash in Bank at the Beginning of the Year.**

Uses of cash include:

+ **Loss from operating activities:** The net loss as calculated in the Income Statement report (after income taxes and before Retained Earnings as of the beginning of the year), adjusted by expenses not paid in cash during the reporting period, such as Depreciation and Amortization to Fixed and Other Assets.

+ **Increase in Current Assets:** An increase in Current Assets, except for Cash in bank.

+ **Investments of Fixed Assets.**

+ **Investments of Other Assets.**

+ **Decrease of Current Liabilities.**

+ **Decrease of Long Term Liabilities.**

+ **Buying Stock Back from Stockholders.**

Creating a Cash Flow Report in an Excel Worksheet

After the Balance Sheet and Income Statement reports have been completed, the Cash Flow report can be created, as shown below:

Microsoft Excel - Financial Statements			
File Edit View Insert Format Tools Data Window Help			

	A	B	C	D
1				
2	December 31, 2003 ▼			
3				
4				
5	XYZ Corporation Inc.			
6	Cash Flow Report			
7	For the year ended December, 31 2003			
8				
9		Notes	2003	2002
10	Cash from Operating Activities			
11				
12	Net Income		229,168	147,430
13	Adjusted by:			
14	Depreciation		59,312	50,221
15	Net cash provided by operating activities		288,480	197,651
16				
17	Changes in Working Capital:			
18	(Increase) Decrease in Current Assets:			
19	Accounts receivable		-115,064	-210,824
20	Inventories		-26,040	-39,010
21	Prepaid expenses		10,107	-1,774
22	Increase (Decrease) in Current Liabilities:			
23	Line of Credit		-24,051	37,563
24	Current Portion of Long-Term Debt		746	2,963
25	Accounts Payable		71,971	35,646
26	Accrued Expenses		13,006	16,597
27	Other Payables		-7,687	2,020
28	Net changes in Working Capital		-77,012	-156,819
29				
30	Net cash provided before investments & financing activities		211,468	40,832
31				
32	Long Term Assets			
33	(Increase) Decrease in fixed assets		-68,419	-78,836
34	(Increase) Decrease in other assets		-63,811	-26,457
35	Cash used (from) Long Term Assets		-132,231	-105,293
36				
37	Long Term Liablilities			
38	Increase (Decrease) in long term debts		-96,085	76,917
39	Increase (Decrease) in capital		-726	11,447
40	Cash from (used) liablilities and capiatal		-96,810	88,364
41				
42	Net Increase (Decrease) in Cash		-17,573	23,903
43	Cash at the beginning of the year		318,697	294,795
44	Cash at the end of the year		301,124	318,697

Figure 6-1: Cash Flow Report

Before creating the Cash Flow report, copy worksheet *41 — Income Statement,* and change its name to *51 — Cash Flow.* Delete all text and formulas from row **10** downwards, and then change the text in cell **A6** to **Cash Flow Report**.

The following sections present step-by-step instructions for creating a Cash Flow report.

Step 1: Adding a Third Period Column to the Balance Sheet Report

To calculate the increase or decrease between the balances of two reporting periods, add a third period (that is, a third column) to a copied worksheet *31 — Balance Sheet* you created in *Chapter 4, Balance Sheet.*

➤ **To add a third period column:**

1. Copy worksheet *31 — Balance Sheet* by dragging and locating the *31 — Balance Sheet* tab after worksheet *51 — Cash Flow* while pressing **<Ctrl>**.

2. Rename it to *52 — BS ThreeYearColumns.*

3. Copy the formula from cell **D11** and paste it into cell **E11**, and change the third argument of the **SUMIF** formula number from 12 to 24, (the number 24 represents 24 columns/months/2 years before December 2003, which is December 2001 in worksheet *21 — Trial Balances Data*).

4. Copy the formula from cell **E11** to all appropriate cells in column **E**:

=SUMIF(TB_DB_Level3,A11,OFFSET(TB_DB_Level3,0,MonthSelectionNumber+2-24))

	A	B	C	D	E
1					
2	December 31, 2003				
3					
4		XYZ Corporation Inc.			
5		Balance Sheet			
6					
7				December 31	
8	ASSETS	Notes	2003	2002	2001
9					
10	**Current Assets**				
11	Cash	5	301,124	318,697	294,795
12	Accounts Receivable	7	1,653,558	1,538,494	1,327,670
13	Inventories	8	546,173	520,133	481,123
14	Prepaid Expenses	9	13,552	23,659	21,884
15	Total Current Assets		2,514,407	2,400,983	2,125,472
16					
17	**Property and Equipment (at Cost)**	10			
18	Land & Building		674,019	677,191	626,402
19	Machinery and Equipment		386,140	326,052	301,598
20	Furniture and Fixtures		59,410	47,906	44,313
21	Total Property and Equipment		1,119,569	1,051,150	972,314
22	Less: Accumulated Depreciation		(478,852)	(419,540)	(369,319)
23	Net Book Value		640,717	631,610	602,995
24					
25	**Other Assets**				
26	Investment in Revenue Bond	11	364,321	300,260	277,741
27	Patents, Trademarks and Goodwill	12	52,250	52,500	48,563
28	Total Other Assets		416,571	352,760	326,303
29					
30	TOTAL ASSETS		3,571,695	3,385,352	3,054,770

Step 2: Defining Names

The next step in creating a Cash Flow report is defining *Names*.

➢ **To define the cell Names in the new three-column balance sheet:**

✦ Define the cells' *Names* in column **C** (as shown in *Step 1: Adding a Third Period Column to the Balance Sheet Report*, page 101) using the text of the **Account Types** in column **A**, for example, **Cash** for cell **C11**, **AccountsReceivable** for cell **C12** and **Inventories** for cell **C13**.

➢ **To define cells' Names in a Income Statement report:**

✦ Define the *Name* **NetIncome** for cell **C39**, which contains the net income for the year, and define the *Name* **Depreciation** for cell **C27**, as shown in the figure below.

	Microsoft Excel - Financial Statements			
	File Edit View Insert Format Tools Data Window Help			
	A	B	C	D
1				
2	December 31, 2003			
3				
4	XYZ Corporation Inc.			
5	Income Statement			
6	For the year ended December, 31 2003			
7				
8		Notes	2003	2002
9	**Revenue**	20		
10	Sales		2,920,093	2,633,626
11	Services		955,214	725,458
12	**Total Revenue**		**3,875,307**	**3,359,084**
13				
14	**Cost of Goods Sold**			
15	Materials		854,521	733,352
16	Labor & Subcontractors Costs		602,125	536,645
17	Other Cost of goods sold		384,521	350,241
18	Increase / Decrease in Inventories	21	-26,040	-30,254
19	**Total Cost of Goods Sold**		**1,815,127**	**1,589,984**
20				
21	**Gross Income**		**2,060,180**	**1,769,100**
22				
23	**Operating Expenses**			
24	Selling		480,161	441,256
25	General & Administrative	22	758,542	675,992
26	Other Operating Expense	23	275,541	260,887
27	Depreciation		59,312	50,221
28	**Total Operating Expenses**		**1,573,556**	**1,428,356**
29				
30	**Net Income before Operations**		**486,624**	**340,744**
31				
32	**Operating Income (Loss)**			
33	Other income (expense)	24	32,512	-2,521
34	Interest expense		75,421	62,584
35	**Total Operating Income**		**107,933**	**60,063**
36				
37	**Income (Loss) Before Income Taxes**		378,691	280,681
38	Provision (benefit) for income taxes	25	149,523	133,251
39	Net Income (Loss) for the year		229,168	147,430
40	Retained Earnings beginning of the year	26	943,314	795,884
41	**Retained Earnings**		**1,172,482**	**943,314**

➤ **To define a Name:**

1. Select the cell, and then press **<Ctrl+F3>**.

2. In the **Names in workbook** box, type the desired text and click **OK**.

Step 3: Inserting Formulas into the Cash Flow Report

In this step, you will enter the formulas that return the balances from the Income Statement report.

➤ **To insert the Net Income link formula:**

1. Type the following formula into cell **C12**:

    =NetIncome

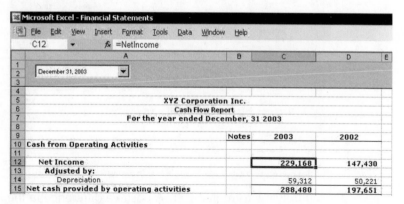

2. Type the following formula into cell **D12**:

    =OFFSET(NetIncome,0,1)

    This **OFFSET** formula diverts the cell address (cell *Name* **NetIncome**) from the reference address by a certain number of rows and columns, and returns the value from the diverted cell address. In this example, the value to be returned is the Net Income for the previous reporting year, which ends December 31, 2002.

3. Continue inserting formulas into cells **C14** and **D14** of the Cash Flow report using the *Name* **Depreciation** you defined in *Step 2: Defining Names*, page 102.

> ➢ **To insert formulas to calculate the increase or decrease in the Account Groups balances in the three-column Balance Sheet report:**

1. Type the following formula into cell **C19**:

   =(AccountsReceivable-OFFSET(AccountsReceivable,0,1))*-1

   This formula subtracts the Accounts Receivable balance at the end of the reporting period from the Accounts Receivable balance at the end of the previous reporting period.

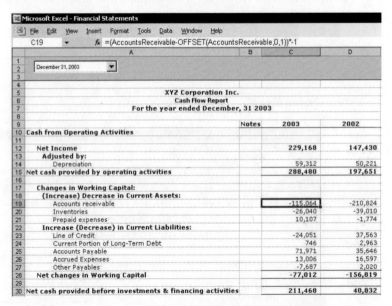

2. Multiply the formula by -1. A positive difference in the Accounts Receivable over the two periods indicates a decrease in cash (that is, less money has come in).

3. Type the following formula in cell **D19**:

   = (OFFSET(AccountsReceivable,0,1)-OFFSET(AccountsReceivable,0,2))*-1

   This formula returns the subtracted figure from the next two periods, columns **2** and **3** (columns **D** and **E** in the three-column balance sheet shown in *Step 1: Adding a Third Period Column to the Balance Sheet Report,* page 101).

4. Type the following formula in cell **C23**:

   =Line_of_Credit-OFFSET(Line_of_Credit,0,1)

5. Type the following formula in cell **D23**:

   =OFFSET(Line_of_Credit,0,1)-OFFSET(Line_of_Credit,0,2)

6. Type the following formula in cell **C43** (cash at the beginning of the year, which is the cash at the end of previous year):

   =OFFSET(Cash,0,1)

7. Type the following formula in cell **D43**:

   =OFFSET(Cash,0,2)

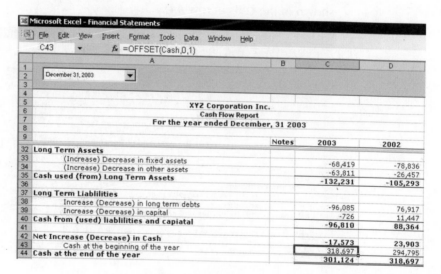

Step 4: Auditing the Net Cash Flow vs. Cash in the Bank Accounts

The final step in creating a Cash Flow report is auditing the **Cash at the end of the year** (the last line of the Cash Flow report) vs. the **Cash** in bank as it appears in the Balance Sheet report.

➤ **To audit the Cash Flow balance:**

✦ The figure in cell **C49** in the Cash Flow report (shown below) is the Cash balance that appears in the Balance Sheet report. These figures should be equal to the balance of the Cash Flow report in cell **C44** (as shown in the cells in row **44**).

Microsoft Excel - Financial Statements			
File Edit View Insert Format Tools Data Window Help			
C49 ▼ *fx* =Cash			

	A	B	C	D
1				
2	December 31, 2003 ▼			
3				
4				
5	XYZ Corporation Inc.			
6	Cash Flow Report			
7	For the year ended December, 31 2003			
8				
		Notes	2003	2002
9				
36				
37	**Long Term Liablilities**			
38	Increase (Decrease) in long term debts		-96,085	76,917
39	Increase (Decrease) in capital		-726	11,447
40	**Cash from (used) liablilities and capiatal**		-96,810	88,364
41				
42	**Net Increase (Decrease) in Cash**		-17,573	23,903
43	Cash at the beginning of the year		318,697	294,795
44	**Cash at the end of the year**		301,124	318,697
45				
46				
47				
48	Audit		301,124	318,697
49			=Cash	=OFFSET(Cash,0,1)
50	The Formulas in row 48			

Chapter 7

Notes

About This Chapter

This chapter explains the **Notes** worksheet, and includes the following sections:

✦ **Overview**, page 108, introduces the concept of **Notes** in the Financial Statements reports.

✦ **Creating the Notes Worksheet**, page 109, describes the steps needed to create and structure the **Notes** worksheet, as well as how to add or update **Notes**.

Overview

Financial Statements reports contain the Table of Contents, the Auditor Report, Balance Sheet, Income Statement, Cash Flow and Notes. **Notes** are an integral part of Financial Statements reports, as they contain essential and important information describing the company's business activities, as well as details of the major subjects in the Balance Sheet, Income Statement and Cash Flow reports.

A number of tasks must be carried out when preparing **Notes** reports using Excel worksheets and linking their numbers to other Financial Statements reports:

✦ The **Notes** numbers in column **B** in the Balance Sheet, Income Statement and Cash Flow reports must be automatically updated.

✦ The total figures in the **Notes** detailed pages must be equal to the figures that appear in these three major reports.

Creating the Notes Worksheet

Figure 7-1 presents worksheet *16 — Notes List*.

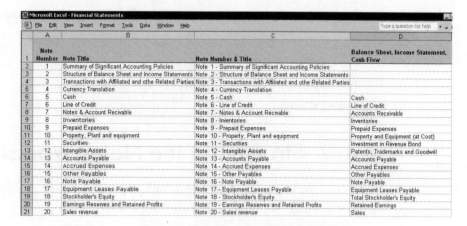

Figure 7-1: Notes List Worksheet

Step 1: Defining Names for the Notes Worksheet and Columns

The first step in creating the **Notes** worksheet is to define **Names** for the worksheet and for columns **A:D**.

➤ **To define a Name for the Notes worksheet:**

1. Select any cell in worksheet *16 — Notes List* and press **<Ctrl+A>** to select all the cells in the worksheet. When using **Excel 2003**, press **<Ctrl+A+A>** from a cell inside the Current Region area.

2. Press **<Ctrl+F3>**.

3. In the **Names in workbook** box, type **NotesTable**.

4. Click **OK**.

➢ **To define a Name for columns A:D:**

1. Select column **A**, and press **<Ctrl+F3>**.

2. In the **Names in workbook** box, type **NotesTable**.

3. Repeat steps 1 and 2 for column **B**, and define the *Name* **NoteTitle**.

4. Repeat steps 1 and 2 for column **C**, and define the *Name* **Note_Number_And_Title**.

5. Repeat steps 1 and 2 for column **D** and define the *Name* **NotesFSItem**.

Step 2: Structuring the Notes Worksheet

In this section, you will learn how to structure the columns in worksheet *16 — Notes List*, as shown in Figure 7-1, page 109.

➢ **To insert a formula into Column A – Note Number:**

✦ Type the following formula into cell **A2**:

=ROWS($A$2:A2)

This formula returns the number of rows between the first address (**$A$2**) with absolute reference mode and the second address (**A2**) with relative reference mode. Copy the formula to all the cells in column **A**, as necessary.

The formula in cell **A11**, for example,

=ROWS($A$2:A11)

returns the number 10, which is the number of rows between cell **A2** and cell **A11**.

When adding or deleting a row or rows, this formula enables the calculation result returned to always be in an automatic continuously ascending mode.

➢ **To insert the Note Title into Column B – Note Title:**

✦ Type the **Note Titles** in the cells in column **B**.

➢ **To concatenate a calculated number from cells in column A and a note title from column B into cells in Column C – Note Number and Title:**

1. Type the following formula into cell **C2**:

    ="Note "&" "& A2 &" - "& B2

    This formula concatenates the text **Note** with the number returned from the formula in cell **A2** and the text in cell **B2**. For example, the returned result for the first **Note** is:

    Note 1 — Summary of Significant Accounting Policies

2. Copy the formula to the cells in column **C**. When deleting or adding a **Note**, all **Notes** will be updated with the new calculation numbers returned from the formulas in column **A**.

➢ **To insert an Account Types list into cells in Column D:**

✦ Column **D** contains list of **Account Type** levels (as described on page 12, *Chapter 1, Introducing Financial Statements.xls Worksheets*) used in the three major reports: Balance Sheet, Income Statement and Cash Flow.

Formulas in Balance Sheets and Income Statements That Return the Note Number from Worksheet 16 – Notes List

Refer to page 84, *Chapter 4, Balance Sheet*, for details regarding how to automatically update the **Note** number in the **Notes** column. This is done via a formula that returns the **Note** number related to the **Account Type** level in column **A** in the Balance Sheet, Income Statement, and Cash Flow worksheets.

Step 3: Adding a Note to Worksheet 61 – Notes

After you have structured the columns in worksheet *16 — Notes List,* you can add **a Note** to worksheet *61 — Notes.*

➢ **To add a Note:**

1. Select worksheet *31 — Balance Sheet* and copy the first three rows.

2. Add a new worksheet by pressing **<Shift+F11>**.

3. Change the worksheet name to *61 — Notes.*

4. Select cell **A1** and paste the first three rows.

5. Select cell **E11**.

6. From the *Data* menu, choose **Validation**.

7. Select the **Settings** tab.

8. In the **Allow** box, select **List**.

9. Select the **Source** box, press **<F3>** and paste the *Name* **NoteTitle**.

10. Click **OK**.

11. Press **<Alt+Down Arrow>** to open the **Notes** list, as shown below.

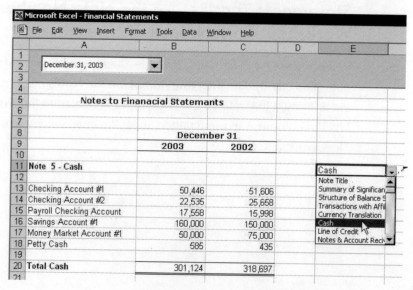

12. Type the following formula into cell **A11**, as shown below.

= INDEX(NotesTable,MATCH(E11,NoteTitle,0),3)

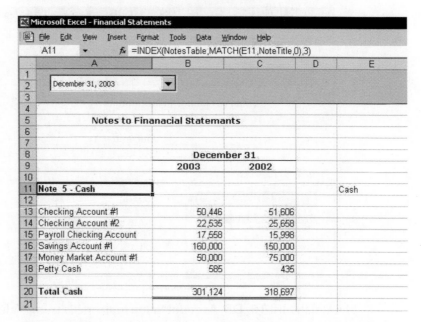

The formula returns the **Note** number combined with the **Note** title from column **C** in worksheet *16 — Notes List.*

13. Select cells in column **A** (for example, cells **A13:A18** in the figure below).

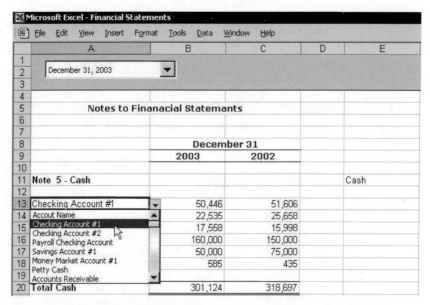

14. Add the list **TB_DB_AccountName** to the cells using **Validation** (to add a list to **Validation**, refer to steps 6 through 10), which is the list of **Account Names** from column **B** in worksheet *21 — Trial Balances Data.*

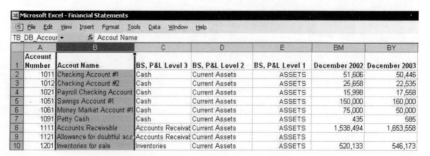

15. Type the following formula in cell **B13**:

=SUMIF(TB_DB_AccoutName,A13,OFFSET(TB_DB_AccoutName,0,
MonthSelectionNumber+3))

This formula returns the balance for the **Account Name** chosen from a cell in column **A** from the **December 2003** column in worksheet *21 — Trial Balances Data.*

The +3 in the formula represents the number of columns between columns **B** (as shown on page 114) and **F**, which is the first Trial Balance data column.

16. Type the following formula in cell **C13**:

    =SUMIF(TB_DB_AccoutName,A13,OFFSET(TB_DB_AccoutName,0, MonthSelectionNumber+3-12))

    This formula returns the balance for the **Account Name** chosen from a cell in column **A** from the **December 2002** column of worksheet *21 — Trial Balances Data*.

17. Copy the formulas from **B13** and **C13** downwards, as required. Worksheet *61 — Notes* should now look like this:

Step 4: Auditing the Totals

Cells **F11** and **G11** in worksheet *61 — Notes* contain formulas that are identical to those entered in the cells of worksheet *31 — Balance Sheet* (as described on page 79, *Chapter 4, Balance Sheet*).

The formulas return the **Cash** Account Type total balance from worksheet *21 — Trial Balances Data*. Cell **F20** displays the difference between the totals for **Cash** in cells **B20** and **F11**; cell **G20** displays it for **C20** and **G11**, as shown below.

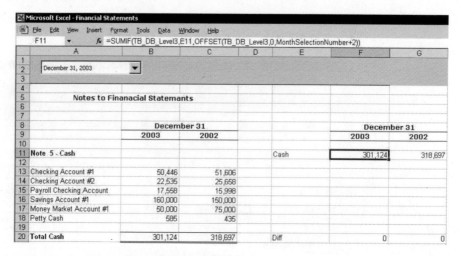

Figure 7-2: Auditing the Notes Figures

Chapter 8

Customizing the Financial Statements.xls Workbook and Presenting Information

About This Chapter

This chapter explains how to use various techniques to customize the **Financial Statements.xls** workbook according to your needs, and includes the following sections:

✦ **Overview**, page 118, introduces the various techniques you can use to customize your worksheets.

✦ **Creating a Custom Menu**, page 119, describes how to add **Custom Menus** to your worksheet.

✦ **Using Custom Views**, page 129, describes the advantages of using **Custom Views**.

✦ **Inserting the Workbook's File Path into the Title Bar**, page 131, describes how you can add the full path of the file to the title bar.

✦ **Using the Watch Window**, page 132, describes the new and exciting feature in Excel 2002 and higher that enables you to view cell location, formula, value or data in any cell in any open workbook, as well as move between cells in any open worksheet.

✦ **Using Comments to Save and Show Data and Charts**, page 134, describes how to add, delete and print **Comments** in your worksheet and use the **Camera** feature.

Overview

Over the course of the business day, whether in meetings or at your desk, you may be requested to quickly provide immediate answers and important information. In order to do this efficiently and correctly, it is crucial that you be able to rapidly move between worksheets and extract the appropriate answers required.

In previous chapters, you learned how to create a full **Financial Statements.xls** report in a single workbook. In this chapter, you will learn how to customize the workbook to suit your needs by:

✦ Adding a **Custom Menu** to display requested reports and select any worksheet, as well as to print or mail Financial Statements reports.

✦ Adding **Custom Views**.

✦ Inserting the workbook file's full name (including the path) into the title bar.

✦ Using the **Watch Window** to view data and information in cells, as well as move between them.

✦ Adding **Comments** to cells.

✦ Adding pictures to **Comments** and to the worksheet using the **Camera** feature.

Creating a Custom Menu

Figure 8-1 presents the **Custom Menu** created and added to the **Financial Statements.xls** workbook.

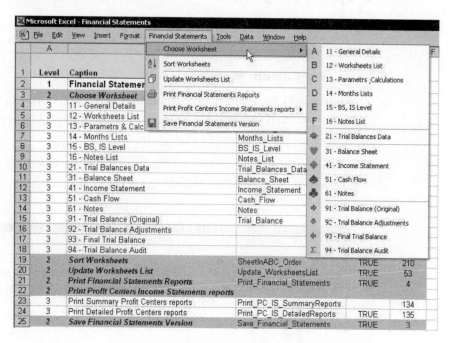

Figure 8-1: Custom Menu

The steps in this section will teach you how to create, modify, and delete a **Custom Menu**, even if you are not familiar with VBA macro language.

Creating a Custom Menu

Follow the steps below to create a **Custom Menu** for the workbook.

Step 1: Copying a Pre-existing Custom Menu

The first step you need to do when creating a **Custom Menu** is to copy a pre-existing one to the **Financial Statements.xls** workbook.

➢ **To copy a Custom Menu:**

1. Download John Walkenbach's **menumakr.xls** workbook from the following Web site: http://j-walk.com/ss/excel/tips/tip53.htm, or copy it from the companion CD-ROM.

2. Open the workbook, and select the *MenuSheet* worksheet, as shown below (the *MenuSheet* worksheet in the figure is shown after modifying).

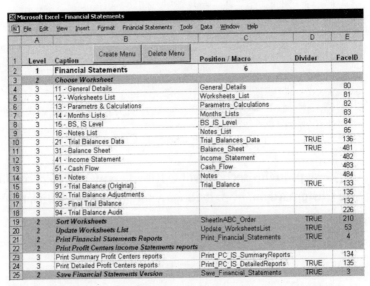

3. Right-click the *MenuSheet* worksheet tab and select **Move or Copy** from the shortcut menu displayed.

4. In the *Move or Copy* dialog box that opens, choose **Financial Statements.xls** from **To book**.

5. Select the **Create a copy** check box and click **OK**.

Step 2: Copying the Code Lines to a New Module

After you have copied the *MenuSheet* worksheet to the **Financial Statements.xls** workbook, copy the **Macros'** code lines to a new module within the workbook.

➤ **To copy the macros' code lines to a new module:**

1. Press **<Alt+F11>** to open the Visual Basic Editor.

2. In the *VBAProject* pane, double-click **Module1** in the **menumakr.xls** project to open it (if **Module1** is not visible, click the plus sign to the left of **Modules**, shown below, to expand the tree).

3. Move the cursor to any of the code lines in the rightmost pane, press **<Ctrl+A>** and then **<Ctrl+C>**.

4. In the *VBAProject* pane, select **Financial Statements.xls**.

5. From the *Insert* menu, select **Module**. A blank pane will appear on the right side of the window.

6. Click any place in the blank pane and press **<Ctrl+V>** to paste the code lines into the new module.

7. Change the **Module** name by selecting it in the *VBAProject* pane and pressing **<F4>**.

8. In the *Properties* dialog box that appears, type **Menu** in the **Name** text box and then close the dialog box.

IMPORTANT:
Ensure that the words `Option Explicit` are displayed only once at the top of the module. If necessary, delete the extra line.

9. Press **<Alt+F11>** to return to the Excel window.

10. Close the **menumakr.xls** workbook.

Step 3: Changing the Assigned Macro Links

The next step in creating a **Custom Menu** is changing the links of the macros assigned to the **Create Menu** and **Delete Menu** buttons in the *MenuSheet* worksheet (as shown in *Step 1: Copying a Pre-existing Custom Menu*, page 120).

➢ **To change the macro addresses:**

1. Select the **Create Menu** button, right-click and select **Assign Macro** from the shortcut menu.

2. In the *Assign Macro* dialog box that appears, select the **CreateMenu** macro from the list, as shown below, and click **OK**.

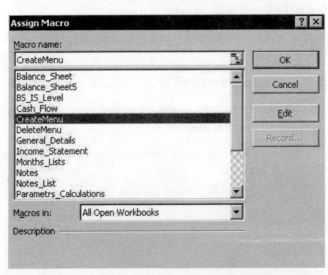

3. Repeat step 1 for the **Delete Menu** button.

4. In the *Assign Macro* dialog box, select the **DeleteMenu** macro from the list and click **OK**.

5. Save the **Financial Statements.xls** workbook.

6. Click the **Create Menu** button and check if a new menu has been added to the Excel menu bar.

7. Click the **Delete Menu** button and check if the new menu has been deleted.

Step 4: Modifying the Custom Menu

The next step in creating a **Custom Menu** is modifying it.

➤ **To modify the Custom Menu:**

✦ This technique uses a template table stored in the *MenuSheet* worksheet, as shown in the figure below. To modify the **Custom Menu**, simply modify the data in the template table.

	Level	Caption	Position / Macro	Divider	FaceID
1					
2	1	**Financial Statements**	6		
3	2	*Choose Worksheet*			
4	3	11 - General Details	General_Details		80
5	3	12 - Worksheets List	Worksheets_List		81
6	3	13 - Parametrs & Calculations	Parametrs_Calculations		82
7	3	14 - Months Lists	Months_Lists		83
8	3	15 - BS, IS Level	BS_IS_Level		84
9	3	16 - Notes List	Notes_List		85
10	3	21 - Trial Balances Data	Trial_Balances_Data	TRUE	136
11	3	31 - Balance Sheet	Balance_Sheet	TRUE	481
12	3	41 - Income Statement	Income_Statement		482
13	3	51 - Cash Flow	Cash_Flow		483
14	3	61 - Notes	Notes		484
15	3	91 - Trial Balance (Original)	Trial_Balance	TRUE	133
16	3	92 - Trial Balance Adjustments			135
17	3	93 - Final Trial Balance			132
18	3	94 - Trial Balance Audit			226
19	2	*Sort Worksheets*	SheetInABC_Order	TRUE	210
20	2	*Update Worksheets List*	Update_WorksheetsList	TRUE	53
21	2	*Print Financial Statements Reports*	Print_Financial_Statements	TRUE	4
22	2	*Print Profit Centers income Statements reports*			
23	3	Print Summary Profit Centers reports	Print_PC_IS_SummaryReports		134
24	3	Print Detailed Profit Centers reports	Print_PC_IS_DetailedReports	TRUE	135
25	2	*Save Financial Statements Version*	Save_Financial_Statements	TRUE	3

The template table contains five columns:

Level (column **A**): This is the level of the particular item. Valid values are 1, 2, and 3. A level of 1 is for a menu, 2 is for a menu item, and 3 is for a submenu item. In general, you will have one level 1 item, with level 2 items below it. A level 2 item may or may not have level 3 (submenus) items.

Caption (column **B**): This is the text that appears in the menu, menu item or submenu.

Position/Macro (column **C**): For level 1 items, this should be an integer that represents the position in the menu bar. For level 2 or level 3 items, this will be the macro executed when the item is selected. If a level 2 item has one or more level 3 items, the level 2 item may not have a macro associated with it.

Divider (column **D**): This displays **TRUE** if a divider should be placed before the menu or submenu items.

FaceID (column **E**): (Optional) This is a code number that represents the built-in graphic images displayed next to an item, as explained below. The **ShowFaceIDs** macro determines the FaceID code numbers.

 NOTE:

The macro VBA code lines can be copied from **menumakr.xls** workbook which is available in the companion CD-ROM.

➤ To determine FaceID code numbers:

1. Press **<Alt+F11>**, select the **Menu** module and look at the **ShowFaceIDs** macro below.

```
Sub ShowFaceIDs()
    Dim NewToolbar As CommandBar
    Dim NewButton As CommandBarButton
    Dim i As Integer, IDStart As Integer, IDStop As Integer

    ' Delete existing FaceIds toolbar if it exists
    On Error Resume Next
    Application.CommandBars("FaceIds").Delete
    On Error GoTo 0

    ' Add an empty toolbar
    Set NewToolbar = Application.CommandBars.Add _
        (Name:="FaceIds", temporary:=True)
    NewToolbar.Visible = True

    ' Change the following values to see different FaceIDs
    IDStart = 1
    IDStop = 250

    For i = IDStart To IDStop
        Set NewButton = NewToolbar.Controls.Add _
            (Type:=msoControlButton, ID:=2950)
        NewButton.FaceId = i
        NewButton.Caption = "FaceID = " & i
    Next i
    NewToolbar.Width = 600
End Sub
```

Excel has thousands of icons and each one has its own unique FaceID number; however, the limitations of the computer's memory do not allow them all to be displayed. Approximately 250 different icons can be displayed at any given time.

2. Change the **IDStart** and **IDStop** number after each execution of the macro to display more icons.

```
    ' Change the following values to see different FaceIDs
    IDStart = 1
    IDStop = 250
```

3. Execute the macro by pressing **<F5>** from inside the module. The following toolbar is displayed:

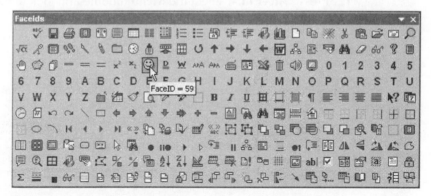

4. Place your cursor over an icon, and notice that a **FaceID** number appears. Write this number in column **E** of the *MenuSheet* worksheet.

Step 5: Adding the Macro's Name to the Custom Menu

The next step is to add the macro's names to the **Custom Menu**.

➢ **To add the macro name to the Custom Menu:**

1. Copy and paste the macro name to column **C**, **Position/Macro**, as shown in the template table, page 123.

2. To add macros to select a worksheet, simply write a macro based on one of the following three examples in a regular module, then copy the macro name and paste it into the appropriate cell in column **C**:

```
Sub General_Details()
Sheets("11 - General Details").Select
End Sub
```

```
Sub Worksheets_List()
Sheets("12 - Worksheets List").Select
End Sub
```

```
Sub Parametrs_Calculations()
Sheets("13 - Parametrs & Calculations").Select
End Sub
```

3. To add all other macros names, as shown in the template table on page 123, refer to the appropriate chapters, as follows:

   ✦ To **sort worksheets**, refer to page 21, *Chapter 1, Introducing Financial Statements.xls Worksheets.*

   ✦ To **update the worksheets list**, refer to page 9, *Chapter 1, Introducing Financial Statements.xls Worksheets.*

   ✦ To **print Financial Statements reports**, refer to page 185, *Chapter 10, Printing and Mailing Financial Statements Reports.*

   ✦ To **print profit center Income Statement reports**, refer to page 306, *Chapter 15, Analyzing Profit Centers.*

Step 6: Adding and Deleting Custom Menus Automatically

The final step is to add the **Custom Menu** automatically while the **Financial Statements.xls** workbook is being activated or opened, and to delete the **Custom Menu** while the **Financial Statements.xls** workbook is being deactivated or closed.

This is done by adding **Workbook_Activate** and **Workbook_Deactivate** events to the **ThisWorkbook** module, as described in the following procedure.

➤ **To add Workbook_Activate and Workbook_Deactivate events:**

1. Press **<Alt+F11>** to open the Visual Basic Editor.

2. In the *VBAProject* **pane**, at *VBAProject (Financial Statements.xls),* double-click the **ThisWorkbook** module to open it.

3. Two drop-down lists, **General** and **Declarations**, appear at the top of the module sheet (the right pane). From the **General** drop-down list, select **Workbook**.

4. From the drop-down list on the right, select **Activate**, as shown.

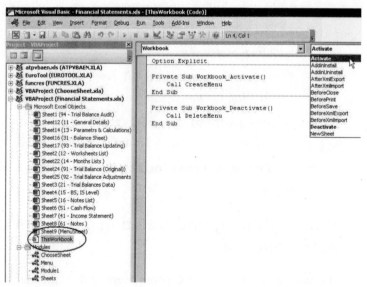

5. In the **ThisWorkbook** module sheet, type the following code:

```
Private Sub Workbook_Activate()
    Call CreateMenu
End Sub
```

6. From the drop-down list on the right, select **Deactivate**.

7. In the module sheet, type the following code:

```
Private Sub Workbook_Deactivate()
    Call DeleteMenu
End Sub
```

8. Save the **Financial Statements** workbook and then close it.

9. Reopen the workbook and check whether the **Financial Statements Custom Menu** appears in Excel's menu bar.

   The **Workbook_Activate** event is now activated when the workbook is opened, and the **Workbook_Deactivate** event deletes the **Custom Menu** while **Financial Statements.xls** is being deactivated or closed.

Using Custom Views

Custom Views can be used for two primary reasons:

✦ For display purposes. This is done by selecting a view from a list of previously saved views in **Custom Views**, as explained in this section.

✦ For saving the print settings for re-printing. For more details, refer to page 179, *Chapter 10, Printing and Mailing Financial Statements Reports.*

Adding the Custom Views Box Icon

The procedure below explains how to add the **Custom Views** box icon to the Excel menu.

➢ **To add the Custom Views box icon:**

1. Right-click one of the toolbars on the top of the worksheet and select **Customize**. The *Customize* dialog box appears.

2. Select the **Commands** tab, as shown below.

3. Select **View** from the **Categories** box, and drag the **Custom Views** box icon from the **Commands** box to the Excel menu.

4. Click **Close**. The **Custom Views** icon box is now located within the Excel menu.

Adding a Custom View

After you have added the **Custom Views** box icon to the Excel menu, add new **Custom View** to it.

➢ **To add a Custom View:**

1. Open worksheet *31 — Balance Sheet* and define the **Page Setup** options for the page to be printed.

2. Select the **Custom Views** box icon, type **Balance Sheet** into the box, and then press **<Enter>**. The *Add View* dialog box appears.

3. Click **OK**.

4. Repeat these steps for as many **Custom Views** as required.

5. After adding the **Custom Views**, you can select any View from **Custom Views** box icon as shown below:

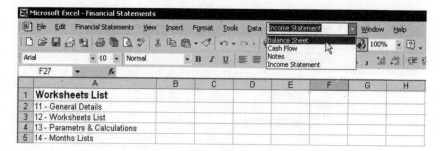

Inserting the Workbook's File Path into the Title Bar

When you open a workbook from a directory on the network, you may not always remember the path or name of the folder where it has been saved. To see this important information, it is recommended that you add the Path to the title bar (the colored line at the very top of the Excel window).

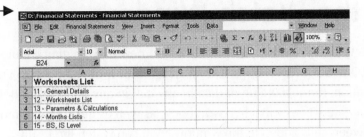

Figure 8-2: The Path Appears in the Title Bar

As can be seen from Figure 8-2, the Path where the workbook is stored, **D:\Financial Statements** is displayed before the workbook name **Financial Statements**.

➢ **To add the Path to the title bar:**

✦ Add the following code lines to the **Workbook_Activate** event in the **ThisWorkbook** module and to the **Workbook_Deactivate** event (described in *Step 5: Adding the Macro's Name to the Custom Menu*, page 126), while carefully avoiding duplication of the event's name.

```
Private Sub Workbook_Activate()
    Application.Caption = Path
    Call CreateMenu
End Sub


Private Sub Workbook_Deactivate()
    Application.Caption = ""
    Call DeleteMenu
End Sub
```

Using the Watch Window

The **Watch Window**, shown below, is a new and exciting feature in Excel 2002 and higher versions. The **Watch Window** enables you to view cell location, formula, value or data in any cell in any open workbook, in either an active or inactive workbook, as well as the ability to move between cells added to the window. You can watch the result calculations, formulas, links and the name defined for the cell.

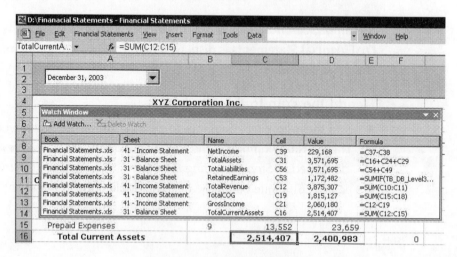

Figure 8-3: Watch Window

➢ **To open the Watch Window:**

✦ From the *Tools* menu, select **Formula Auditing**, and then **Show Watch Window**,

OR

Press **<Shift+F10>**,

OR

Right-click a cell, and select **Add Watch** from the shortcut menu.

➢ **To add a cell to the Watch Window:**

✦ With the **Watch Window** open, select the cell in the worksheet that you want to add and click **Add Watch** on the top left of the **Watch Window**.

➢ **To move between cells:**

✦ Double-click any row in the **Watch Window** to select the cell.

➢ **To toggle between the toolbars:**

✦ Double-click the caption bar of the **Watch Window** *(where the text Watch Window is)*. The **Watch Window** moves between the toolbars and the formula bar, as shown.

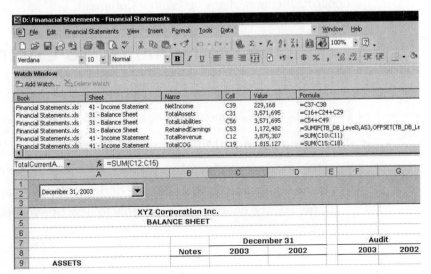

Using Comments to Save and Show Data and Charts

Excel lets you add a **Comment** to cells, which is a text box in which you can enter any text. Each **Comment** is limited in length to approximately 32,000 characters.

➤ **To add a Comment:**

1. Select a cell and press **<Shift+F2>**,

    OR

    Press **<Shift+F10>**,

    OR

    Right-click the cell and select **Insert Comment** from the shortcut menu.

2. In the **Comment** box, type the required text.

By default, Excel does not display **Comments**. The **Comment** is displayed only when you place the cursor over the **small red triangle** in the upper-right corner of any cell with a **Comment**.

Changing the Name of the Comment's Author

By default, each **Comment** includes the author's name.

➤ **To change or cancel the name of the author:**

1. From the *Tools* menu, select **Options** and select the **General** tab.

2. In the **User name** text box, change or delete the user name, as required. The change will only apply to new **Comments** that you insert.

Changing the Default Comment Format

Changes to the default **Comment** format are done from the *Display Properties* dialog box.

➤ **To change the default Comment format:**

1. Press <⊞+M> to minimize all open programs.

2. Right-click the desktop and select **Properties** from the displayed menu. The *Display Properties* dialog box appears.

3. Select the **Appearance** tab.

4. Click the **Advanced** button and from the **Item** drop-down list, select **ToolTip** and change the color, as required.

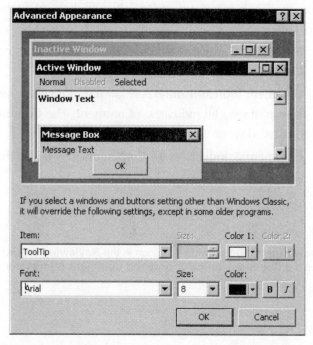

5. From the **Font** drop-down list, change the font, as required, and then change the font size and color.

6. Click **OK** to accept the new selection.

7. Click **OK** again at the bottom of the window to close it.

NOTE:

Changing the **ToolTip** format impacts all of the ToolTips in Excel, including those that appear below the toolbar icons.

Viewing Comments

You can decide how the **Comments** are displayed in the worksheet.

➢ **To set the Comment viewing properties:**

✦ From the *Tools* menu, select **Options** and then select the **View** tab. Excel offers three display options:

❖ **None:** The **Comment** indicator (red triangle) does not appear and **Comments** are not displayed.

❖ **Comment indicator only:** A small red triangle in the upper-right corner of the cell indicates a **Comment**. The **Comment** is displayed when the cell is selected.

❖ **Comment & indicator:** All **Comments** inserted in the worksheet are displayed.

NOTE:

The **Show/Hide All Comments** icon in the **Reviewing** toolbar toggles between the **Comment indicator only** and **Comment & indicator** options.

Displaying a Single Comment

You can display a single **Comment**, if necessary.

➢ **To display a single Comment:**

✦ Right-click a cell with a **Comment**, and select **Show Comment** from the displayed menu.

 TIP:

You can also use the **Validation** technique to add and display a single **Comment**:

1. Select a cell.

2. From the *Data* menu, choose **Validation**.

3. Select the **Input Message** tab, and select the **Show input message when cell is selected** check box.

4. Type the appropriate information in the **Title** and **Input Message** boxes, and click **OK**.

Changing a Comment's Location

If the **Comment** in your worksheet is covering up some of the data, you can change its location by dragging it to a place where it does not. You can only change the location of a **Comment** when the **Comment** is displayed.

Copying Comments to Different Cells

Follow the procedure below to copy **Comments** from one cell to another.

➢ **To copy a Comment to a different cell:**

1. Select a cell with a **Comment** and press <**Ctrl+C**> to copy it.

2. Select a different cell, and press <**Shift+F10**>,

   OR

   Right-click, and from the shortcut menu, select **Paste Special**.

3. Select the **Comments** option button and then click **OK**.

Deleting Comments

Comments can be deleted, as required.

➢ **To delete a Comment:**

✦ Select a cell with a **Comment**, and press **<Shift+F10>**,

OR

Right-click, and from the shortcut menu, select **Delete Comment**.

➢ **To delete all Comments in a worksheet:**

1. Press **<F5>**. The *Go To* dialog box appears.

2. Click **Special**. The *Go To Special* dialog box appears.

3. Select the **Comments** option button, and click **OK**.

4. Press **<Shift+F10>**,

OR

Right-click, and from the shortcut menu, select **Delete Comment**.

Printing Comments

To make them easier to review, **Comments** can be printed.

➢ **To print the Comments:**

✦ From the *File* menu, select **Page Setup** and then select the **Sheet** tab. Excel offers three options in the **Comments Combo Box:**

❖ **None: Comments** are not printed.

❖ **At end of sheet:** Prints the **Comments** on a separate page after printing the sheet.

❖ **As displayed on sheet:** Prints the **Comments** that are displayed.

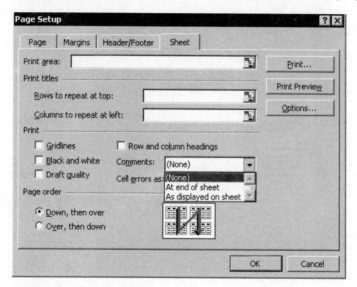

➢ **To print a single Comment:**

1. Select a cell containing a **Comment**.

2. From the *File* menu, select **Page Setup** and then select the **Sheet** tab.

3. In the **Comments** box, select **At end of sheet**, and then click **OK**.

4. From the *File* menu, select **Print**.

5. In the **Print what** box, select **Selection**, and then click **OK**.

Adding Pictures

You can use the **Paste picture** option (or the **Camera** icon) to add and paste a **Picture** that contains useful information.

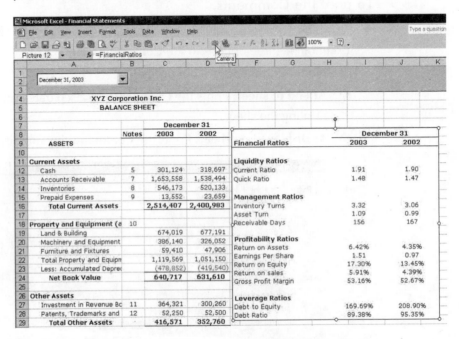

Figure 8-4: Viewing a Picture of a Range of Cells

➢ **To create links for viewing through a picture:**

1. Select the relevant cells in the worksheet, and then press **<Ctrl+C>** to copy them.

2. Select a cell in any worksheet.

3. Hold the **<Shift>** key, and from the *Edit* menu, select **Paste picture link**.

NOTE:

The *Paste Picture* sub-menu is added to the *Edit* menu after pressing **<Shift>**. The picture will show the value of the original cell as it changes.

➤ **To add the Camera icon:**

1. Right-click one of the toolbars on the top of the worksheet and select **Customize**. The *Customize* dialog box appears.

2. Select the **Commands** tab.

3. Select **Tools** from the **Categories** box, and drag the **Camera** icon to a toolbar.

4. Click **Close**. The **Camera** icon is now located on the toolbar.

NOTE:
Use of the **Camera** icon is limited, as you can only view calculation results or the data in one range of cells only.

Adding Pictures to Comments

You can add various pictures to **Comments**, for example, Financial Ratios, Charts and other useful comparable data.

➤ **To add a picture to a Comment:**

1. Select a cell that contains a **Comment**.

2. Right-click and select **Show Comment** from the displayed menu.

3. Click the edge of the **Comment** so that it is surrounded by dots (not slashes).

4. Right-click and select **Format Comment** from the displayed menu. The *Format Comment* dialog box appears.

5. Select the **Colors and Lines** tab.

6. In the **Fill** box, select the **Color** drop-down list, and then select **Fill Effects**.

7. Select the **Picture** tab, and click **Select Picture**.

8. Browse to the picture's location, select it, and then click **OK**.

Sending Information to Comments

You cannot link a **Comment** to a cell in Excel. This means that you cannot enter text or numerical data into a cell and then have it displayed in a **Comment**.

The solution is to add a macro. The following codes let you add and update text in **Comments**:

✦ To add a new **Comment** and add text to it:

```
Range("A1").AddComment Text:="Reviewed on " & Date
```

✦ To update or change text in a **Comment**:

```
Range("A1").Comment Text:="Change On " & Date
```

Chapter 9

Protecting Financial Data

About This Chapter

This chapter reviews all of the various options you can use to protect your financial information data and files, and includes the following sections:

✦ **Overview**, page 144, explains the need for protection and for higher security levels when using Excel worksheets to store financial data.

✦ **Security**, page 145, describes the new **Security** tab in Excel 2002 and later, as well as how to add a password or digital signature to a file.

✦ **Protecting Workbooks**, page 148, describes how to protect a workbook so that its structure cannot be changed, as well as how to hide worksheets.

✦ **Protecting Worksheets/Cells**, page 151, describes how to protect the content in cells from being changed, as well as hide the formulas in them from being viewed.

✦ **Protecting Cells That Contain Data**, page 156, describes how to protect only those cells in the workbook that contain text or formulas.

✦ **Allowing Multiple Users to Edit Ranges**, page 159, describes a new functionality in Excel 2002 and later, in which you can enable multiple users to update data in a well-defined and private area of the worksheet.

Overview

Protecting financial information is a critical issue in all organizations, as it is essential to ensure that financial information is kept confidential both internally and externally.

Consequently, it is of the utmost importance for you to be able to prevent intentional or inadvertent deletion of data by other users, as well as protect the data, formulas and calculations that you have worked hard on to prepare.

Security

A new **Security** tab, shown below, has been added to the *Options* dialog box in Excel 2002 and later. It contains a range of options that will help you secure and protect workbooks and the data they contain.

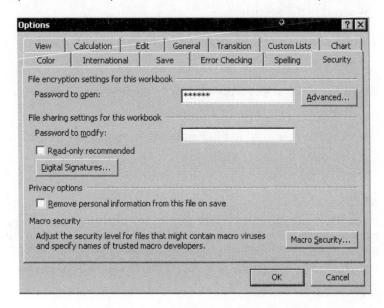

Figure 9-1: Security Tab

➢ **To open the Security tab:**

✦ From the *Tools* menu, select **Options**, and then select the **Security** tab.

Using a Password to Prevent Opening a Workbook

You can use a password to prevent opening a workbook. In Excel 2002 and later, you can also prevent the opening of a workbook by adding a password in the **Security** tab.

➢ **To use a password to prevent opening a workbook:**

1. From the *File* menu, select **Save as**.

2. In Excel 97, select **Options**. From Excel version 2000 and later, select **Tools** and then **General Options**.

3. Type the password in the **Password to open** text box and in **Password to modify** text box, and then click **OK**.

NOTE:

If you forget your password, do not despair. In exchange for a fee, there are a number of software manufacturers on the Web who can provide you with a password identification program (this will also cancel password protection).

Use any Internet search engine to search for the phrase Excel password, and click any of the results that appear.

Sending Password-protected Excel Workbooks

The procedure below explains how to send a password-protected Excel 2002 or Excel 2003 workbook to users of earlier Excel versions.

➢ **To send a password-protected workbook:**

1. From the *Tools* menu (in Excel 2002 and later), select **Options**, and then select the **Security** tab.

2. Click **Advanced**, and select **Office 97/2000 Compatible**.

Using a Digital Signature

A digital signature ensures a higher level of security when working with Excel workbooks on a network.

➤ **To set a digital signature:**

✦ From the *Tools* menu (in Excel 2002 and later), select **Options**, and then select the **Security** tab and add a digital signature.

Protecting Workbooks

Protecting a workbook prevents the structure from being changed. By assigning a password to a workbook, you prevent worksheets from being deleted, new worksheets from being inserted and hidden worksheets from being unhidden.

➤ **To protect a workbook:**

1. From the *Tools* menu, select **Protection**, and then **Protect Workbook**.

2. Type a password in the **Password** text box, and click **OK**. The *Confirm Password* dialog box appears.

3. Confirm the password in the appropriate text box and click **OK**.

➤ **To unprotect a workbook:**

1. From the *Tools* menu, select **Protection**, and then **Unprotect Workbook**.

2. Type the password in the **Password** text box, and click **OK**.

Hiding or Unhiding Worksheets

Excel allows you to hide or unhide worksheets, as required (one worksheet must remain unhidden). Hiding a worksheet or worksheets prevents others from viewing and/or changing data or formulas.

➤ **To hide/unhide worksheets:**

✦ Select the worksheet you want to hide/unhide and, from the *Format* menu, select **Sheet**, and then **Hide** or **Unhide**, as required.

You also can use the **ChooseSheet.xla** add-in to hide/unhide worksheets (for more information regarding **ChooseSheet.xla**, refer to page 18, *Chapter 1, Introducing Financial Statements.xls Worksheets*).

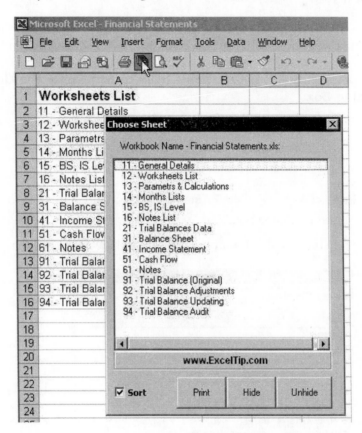

Figure 9-2: ChooseSheet.xla Add-in

Preventing Hidden Worksheets from Appearing

When a worksheet is hidden and the workbook is not protected, the list of hidden worksheets will still appear in the *Unhide* dialog box.

➢ **To prevent hidden worksheets from appearing in the Unhide dialog box:**

1. Press **<Alt+F11>** to open the Visual Basic Editor.

2. Under **VBA Project** in the top-left pane, select the worksheet for which you want to hide.

3. Press **<F4>** or click the **Properties** icon to open the worksheet's *Properties* dialog box.

4. From the **Visible** drop-down list, select **xlSheetVeryHidden**.

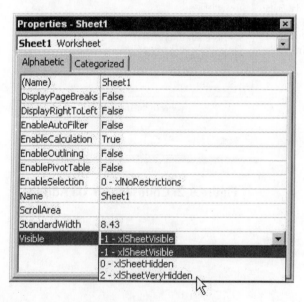

5. Close the *Properties* dialog box, and press **<Alt+F4>** to close the Visual Basic Editor and return to Excel.

Protecting Worksheets/Cells

You can protect the content in the cells from being changed, as well as hide the formulas in them from being viewed.

➢ **To lock or hide a cell:**

1. Open the *Format Cells* dialog box by either pressing **<Ctrl+1>** or by right-clicking the cell and selecting **Format Cells** from the shortcut menu.

2. Select the **Protection** tab. By default, Excel automatically selects the **Locked** check box and does not the **Hidden** check box. If you protect your worksheet, remember to unlock any cells you want to be unprotected.

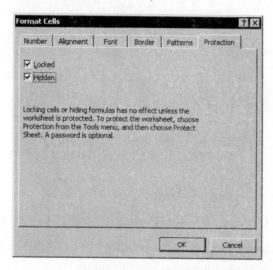

There are two conditions for protecting cells:

✦ The cell's **Locked** check box is selected.

✦ The worksheet is protected.

There are two conditions for hiding text and formulas in the Formula bar:

✦ The cell's **Hidden** check box is selected.

✦ The worksheet is protected.

Protecting a Worksheet

In Excel 2002 and later, the *Protect Sheet* dialog box (shown in Figure 9-3) enables you to select the operations you want users to be able to perform.

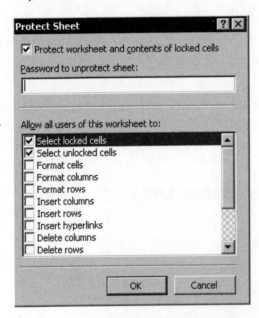

Figure 9-3: Protect Sheet Dialog Box

➢ **To protect a worksheet:**

1. From the *Tools* menu, select **Protection**, and then **Protect Sheet**.

2. In the **Allow all users of this worksheet to** text box, select the check boxes for the operations you want to protect.

In previous versions of Excel, all operations in the *Protect Sheet* dialog box were automatically protected, and you could not select them individually.

TIP:
To move between unprotected cells in a protected worksheet, press **<Tab>**.

Protecting Data by Hiding Rows and Columns

The restricted range of movement in the worksheet displayed in Figure 9-4 is **A1:E14**. Column **F** and onward, and row **15** and downward are hidden.

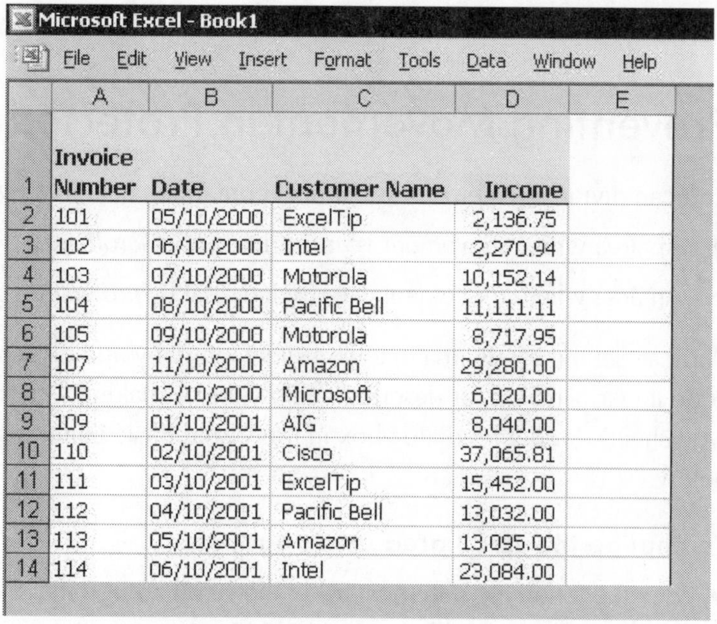

	A	B	C	D	E
1	Invoice Number	Date	Customer Name	Income	
2	101	05/10/2000	ExcelTip	2,136.75	
3	102	06/10/2000	Intel	2,270.94	
4	103	07/10/2000	Motorola	10,152.14	
5	104	08/10/2000	Pacific Bell	11,111.11	
6	105	09/10/2000	Motorola	8,717.95	
7	107	11/10/2000	Amazon	29,280.00	
8	108	12/10/2000	Microsoft	6,020.00	
9	109	01/10/2001	AIG	8,040.00	
10	110	02/10/2001	Cisco	37,065.81	
11	111	03/10/2001	ExcelTip	15,452.00	
12	112	04/10/2001	Pacific Bell	13,032.00	
13	113	05/10/2001	Amazon	13,095.00	
14	114	06/10/2001	Intel	23,084.00	

Figure 9-4: Worksheet with a Restricted Range of Movement

➤ To hide rows and columns:

1. Select column **F**.
2. Press **<Ctrl+Shift+Right Arrow>** and press <**Ctrl+0**> to hide the columns.
3. Select row **15**.
4. Press **<Ctrl+Shift+Down Arrow>** and press <**Ctrl+9**> to hide the rows.

➢ **To unhide rows and columns:**

1. Select row **14**.

2. Point the cursor at the row number, and then click and drag it slightly downward (this selects the hidden rows).

3. Press **<Ctrl+Shift+9>** to unhide the rows.

4. Select column **F**, repeat step 2 and press **<Ctrl+Shift+0>** to unhide the columns.

Preventing Movement in Protected Areas

You can divide the area of a worksheet containing data into two parts:

✦ An area where movement is unrestricted (the *scroll area*)

✦ An area where movement is restricted, that is, *protected*.

You can set the scroll area in a worksheet either by adding **Scroll Area** code line to a macro, as described below, or by making a change in the worksheet's *Properties* dialog box in the Visual Basic Editor, as described below.

➢ **To change the scroll area using a macro:**

✦ Use the following statement to set the scroll area so that the user cannot select any cells outside **A1:C15**:

```
Sheets(1).ScrollArea = "A1:C15"
```

To set scrolling back to normal, use the following statement:

```
Sheets(1).ScrollArea = ""
```

➢ **To change the scroll area using the Visual Basic Editor:**

1. Press **<Alt+F11>** to open the Visual Basic Editor.

2. Under **VBA Project** in the top-left pane, select the worksheet for which you want to change the scroll area.

3. Press **<F4>** or click the **Properties** icon to open the worksheet's *Properties* dialog box.

4. In the **ScrollArea** row, type the reference of the range you want to set as the scroll area (for example, **$A$1:$C$15**), as shown below.

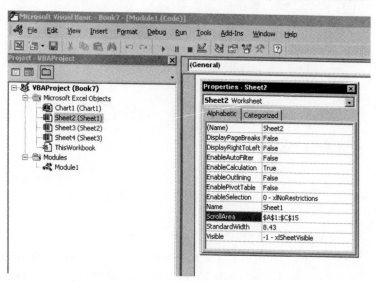

5. Press **<Alt+F4>** to close the Visual Basic Editor and return to Excel.

You can now perform any action in the range **A1:C15**. In the rest of the worksheet, however, you can view the cells, but not select, move or scroll between them.

Protecting Cells That Contain Data

Protecting formulas or text in cells requires isolating the cells from the rest of the worksheet, locking them and then protecting the worksheet, as explained in the following sections.

Step 1: Unlocking all Cells in the Worksheet

The first step in protecting cells containing formulas or text only is ensuring that all cells in the worksheet are unlocked.

➤ **To unlock all cells:**

1.   Select all the cells in the worksheet by pressing **<Ctrl+A>**. In Excel 2003, press **<Ctrl+A+A>** if the selected cell is inside the data area.

2.   Open the *Format Cells* dialog box by pressing **<Ctrl+1>**.

3.   Select the **Protection** tab.

4.   Deselect the **Locked** check box, and then click **OK**.

Step 2: Selecting Cells Containing Data

After you have unlocked all of the cells in the worksheet, select the cells containing data that you want to protect.

➢ **To select cells containing data:**

1. Press **<F5>**. The *Go To* dialog box appears.

2. Click **Special**. The *Go To Special* dialog box appears, as shown.

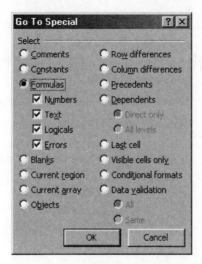

3. To choose cells containing formulas, select the **Formulas** option button; to choose cells containing text, select the **Constants** option button.

4. Click **OK**.

Step 3: Locking the Cells

To protect the cells containing data only, you must now re-lock them.

➤ **To lock the cells:**

1. With the cells containing data selected (as explained in the previous procedure), open the *Format Cells* dialog box by pressing **<Ctrl+1>**.

2. Select the **Protection** tab.

3. Select the **Locked** check box, and then click **OK**.

Step 4: Protecting the Worksheet

Locking cells has no effect unless the worksheet is protected as well.

➤ **To protect the worksheet:**

1. From the *Tools* menu, select **Protection** and then **Protect Sheet**. The *Protect Sheet* dialog box appears.

2. Click **OK** (a password is optional).

Allowing Multiple Users to Edit Ranges

Excel 2002 and later have an advanced option that enables multiple users (when working on a network, for example) to update data in a well-defined and private area. Each workbook user is allotted a range in the worksheet with a unique password.

➢ **To allow multiple users:**

✦ From the *Tools* menu, select **Protection** and then **Allow Users to Edit Ranges**. The following dialog box appears:

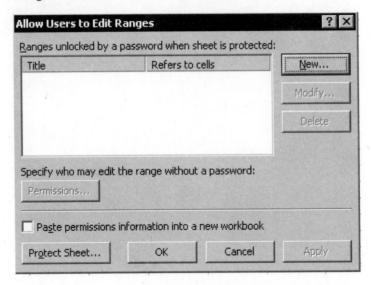

Chapter 10

Printing and Mailing Financial Statements Reports

About This Chapter

This chapter discusses the techniques you need to print or mail Financial Statements reports, and includes the following sections:

✦ **Overview**, page 163, introduces printing and mailing techniques.

✦ **Changing and Customizing the Default Settings in a Workbook**, page 164, describes various techniques you can use to customize your Excel workbook for printing purposes, for example, by adding the date and time into the header, adding a company logo and scaling the print out so that all columns appear on one page.

✦ **Other Important Printing Techniques**, page 170, describes other important techniques that may be useful when printing workbooks, for example, selecting a print area, printing **Comments** and hiding data.

✦ **Custom Views**, page 179, describes Excel's **Custom Views** technique, which enables you to save a set of print setup options that is unique for each print area in the worksheet, as well as create a menu of **Custom Views**.

✦ **Report Manager**, page 181, describes the **Report Manager** add-in, which lets you create and save as many reports as you need for future printing, as well as how to create an **Custom Report Manager** by adding a VBA macro.

✦ **Mailing Financial Statements Reports**, page 186, describes how to e-mail full Financial Statements reports from a new saved and formatted workbook.

Overview

Once you have completed the Financial Statements, you can then print or mail them, as required.

However, printing with Excel is can sometimes be difficult. The main problem is the size of a worksheet, which is 255 columns by 65536 rows — from this huge area you need to cut specific areas out, format them and change the row and column sizes in order to get a clear and well-formatted report in the proper style.

In this chapter you will learn how to print or mail full Financial Statements reports while learning to avoid the obstacles that may present themselves during the process.

Changing and Customizing the Default Settings in a Workbook

The default print-related settings for a standard Excel workbook may not always fit your needs. If they do not, certain items can be changed before printing and mailing.

Setting the Workbook to Black and White

While most printers print in black and white, this is not Excel's default setting for printing a workbook.

➢ **To change the black and white settings:**

1. Select **Page Setup** from the *File* menu, and then select the **Sheet** tab.

2. Select or deselect the **Black and white** check box, as appropriate.

Correcting the First Page Number

When using the **Report Manager** add-in (as described in *Report Manager*, page 181), a bug occurs in the automatic numbering for printing reports, and it is not possible to set the first page number or to number additional pages (for example, a page added from the Word program) so that they will print in the report. The first page that is printed will be numbered 1.

To solve this problem, you must insert an additional dummy **Custom View** or worksheet into the report (for example, reinsert the **Balance Sheet** view), and use the report with the correct number in the footer (you can later delete the extra pages with the incorrect numbers).

➤ **To set the first page number correctly:**

1. Select **Page Setup** from the *File* menu, and then select the **Page** tab.

2. In the **First page number** box, change the setting from **Auto** to **1** (or the appropriate number, as required).

3. Make this change in all the worksheets in the workbook.

Changing the Scaling

Scaling is used for precise printing, without blank extra pages and without a column or row wrapping onto an extra page. Scaling to one page wide by one page tall is necessary to avoid printing a blank page in addition to the page you printed.

➤ **To scale the worksheet:**

1. Select **Page Setup** from the *File* menu, and then select the **Page** tab.

2. In the **Scaling** area, select the **Fit to** option button, and then type **1** page(s) wide by **1** tall.

Another common problem during printing is a column being wrapped onto an extra page. For example, if you select a print area that includes columns **A** to **F**, column **F** may be printed on an extra page. For a report with many pages, in which you want to constrain the report to one page wide but allow it to span many pages in height, change step 2 to **1** page(s) wide by ___tall (leave the box blank).

Adding Information to Headers and Footers on All Printed Pages

Excel's default settings do not include printing the path where the workbook is saved, the name of the workbook, the name of the worksheet, or the date and time of printing.

➢ **To add the date, time, file name or worksheet name to the footer:**

1. Select **Page Setup** from the *File* menu, and then select the **Header/Footer** tab.

2. Click **Custom Footer**. The *Footer* dialog box appears.

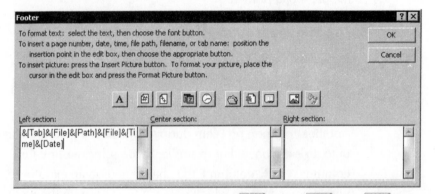

3. In the **Left section** area, click the **Date** , **Time** , **File** and **Tab** icons, as required.

4. Click **OK** to close the *Footer* dialog box, and then **OK** again.

In Excel 2002 and later, you can also add the file's Path (that is, where you saved the file on your computer or network).

➢ **To add the Path to the footer in Excel 2002 and later:**

✦ Follow steps 1 and 2 in the previous procedure, and click the **Add Path** icon.

Using a Macro to Add Information to Each Worksheet

In Excel 97 and 2000, you can add a macro that will automatically adds the relevant information, including the path, to appear on each worksheet as you print it from the workbook. When using this technique, the full path for where you saved the workbook will be printed.

➤ **To add the macro:**

1. Press **<Alt+F11>** to open the Visual Basic Editor.

2. In the **Project** pane, double-click the **ThisWorkbook** module to open it.

3. Two drop-down lists, **General** and **Declarations**, appear at the top of the module sheet (the right pane). From the **General** drop-down list, select **Workbook**.

4. From the drop-down list on the right, select **Workbook_BeforePrint**.

5. In the module sheet, type the following code:

```
Private Sub Workbook_BeforePrint (Cancel As Boolean)
    ActiveSheet.PageSetup.LeftFooter = _
        "&A&F&T&D " & ActiveWorkbook.Path
End Sub
```

The letters **A**, **F**, **T** and **D** are the worksheet name, workbook name, time and date, respectively.

In Excel 2002 and later, the middle line of code will be shorter:

```
"&A&F &Z&T&D"
```

6. Save the file.

Inserting the Company Logo in the Header

You can customize your worksheets by adding your company's logo (or any other picture) to the header. The procedure depends on which version of Excel you are using.

➢ **To insert a logo using Excel 2002 and later:**

1. Select **Page Setup** from the *File* menu, and then select the **Header/Footer** tab.

2. Click **Custom Header**. The *Header* dialog box appears.

3. In the **Left section** area, click the **Picture** icon (the second icon from right). The *Insert Picture* dialog box appears.

4. Search for and select the company logo or picture you want to add.

5. Click **Insert** and then click **OK**.

➢ **To insert the company logo using Excel 97 and 2000:**

1. Select cell **A1**.

2. From the *Insert* menu, select **Picture** and then **From File**.

3. Search for and select the company logo or picture you want to add, and then click **Insert**.

4. Adjust the picture to the height of the row.

5. Select **Page Setup** from the *File* menu, and then select the **Sheet** tab.

6. From **Print titles**, in the **Rows to repeat at top** text box, select ▦.

7. Select row **1**, and then press **<Enter>**. The range now appears in the **Rows to repeat at top** text box.

8. Click **OK**.

9. Repeat these steps for each worksheet in the workbook.

Changing the Default Settings for All Worksheets at Once

It is also possible to change the default settings of every worksheet in the workbook at one time.

➤ **To change the default settings of all worksheets:**

1. In the workbook, right-click any worksheet tab and select **Select All Sheets** from the displayed menu.

2. From the *File* menu, select **Page Setup**, and modify the settings, as described in the previous sections.

3. When you have finished, select the active worksheet again by right-clicking a worksheet tab and selecting **Ungroup Sheets** from the displayed menu.

Other Important Printing Techniques

This section will teach you a number of important techniques that may be useful when printing workbooks.

Printing the Page Number and the Running Page Number

Excel offers a number of options for printing a running page number:

✦ From the *Page Setup* dialog box, via the **Page** tab.

✦ Manually inserting the page number in a custom footer via the *Footer* dialog box.

✦ Printing a page number in portrait layout on a page, and the data in landscape layout (as described in *Printing Page Numbers in a Report Containing both Portrait and Landscape Layouts*, page 174).

✦ Utilizing **Report Manager** (as described in *Report Manager*, page 181).

Selecting the Print Area

An Excel worksheet has only one print area.

➢ **To define a contiguous print area:**

✦ Select a print area in the worksheet, and from the *File* menu, select **Print Area**, and then **Select Print Area**.

➢ **To define a non-contiguous print area:**

1. Select a range of cells in the worksheet, and then press **<Ctrl>** while selecting another range of cells.

2. From the *File* menu, select **Print Area**, and then **Set Print Area**.
   Each print area will be printed on a separate page.

In Excel 2000 and later, you can join non-continuous ranges to form a single contiguous range to print them as a single print area.

➢ **To add non-contiguous ranges to a single contiguous range for printing:**

1. Select a range of cells in the worksheet, and then press **<Ctrl>** while selecting another range of cells.

2. In Excel 2000, the **Paste All** icon appears on the **Clipboard** toolbar.
   In Excel 2002 and later, press **<Ctrl+C+C>** to open the **Clipboard** pane,
   OR
   From the *Edit* menu, select **Clipboard**.

3. Select a cell and click the **Paste All** icon. The ranges you copied are pasted in order.

4. Define these continuous ranges as a single print area, as described in *To define a contiguous print area*, previously.

NOTE:

In Excel 2002 and later, blank pages in the defined print area will not be printed.

Identifying and Selecting the Print Area in a Worksheet

Each worksheet has only one print area. When you select the print area, Excel creates a name for it, **Print_Area**. If you do not know what the print area is, select **Print_Area** from the **Name** box (to the left of the Formula bar).

Printing Comments

As discussed on page 139, *Chapter 8, Customizing the Financial Statements.xls Workbook and Presenting Information*, Excel lets you add **Comments** to cells, which are text boxes in which you can type free text. Refer to that chapter for information regarding printing **Comments** as well.

Hiding Data Before Printing

In general, only relevant data should be printed in a report, which means that irrelevant data must be hidden. There are number of ways of doing this:

✦ Hiding columns or rows before printing, as described in *Custom Views*, page 179.

✦ Changing the font color in cells whose data should not be printed to white, as described in *Hiding Errors in Formulas Before Printing*, page 173.

✦ Hiding parts of a worksheet by using a white text box without a border. This is done by using the **Text Box** icon on the **Drawing** toolbar.

Hiding Errors in Formulas Before Printing

Formulas that return errors should be hidden before a report is printed. This is done by changing the font color to white.

➤ **To hide errors in formulas:**

1. Select the **Print_Area** from the **Name** box, and from the *Format* menu, select **Conditional Formatting**. The *Conditional Formatting* dialog box appears.

2. From **Condition 1**, select **Formula Is**.

3. In the **Formula** text box, type:

   =ISERROR(A1)

4. Click **Format** and select the **Font** tab.

5. Under **Color**, select white and click **OK**.

6. Click **OK**.

In Excel 2002 and later, cell errors can be hidden by selecting **<blank>** from the **Cell errors as Combo Box** in the *Page Setup* dialog box's **Sheet** tab, as shown below.

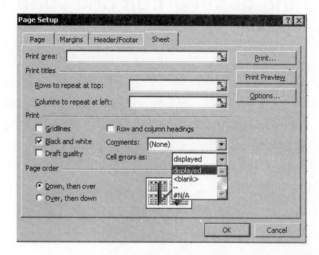

Figure 10-1: Cell Errors As Drop-down List

Copying Page Settings to Other Worksheets

Changing and updating page settings can take a long time, and it is much easier to copy them from one worksheet to another, even if you still need to change some of the parameters you have defined in the new worksheet.

➤ **To copy page settings to other worksheets:**

1. Select the worksheet whose print settings you want to copy.

2. Press **<Ctrl>** and click the worksheet tab of any worksheet you want to copy the page setup.

3. From the *File* menu, select **Page Setup**, and click **OK**. This will cause the page settings from the worksheet selected in step 1 to be copied to all of the selected worksheets.

4. When you have finished, select the active worksheet again by right-clicking a worksheet tab and selecting **Ungroup Sheets** from the displayed menu.

Printing Page Numbers in a Report Containing both Portrait and Landscape Layouts

What do you do if one of the pages in a report is set up in landscape layout, while all the other pages are set up in portrait layout? When all the pages are combined into a single report, the page number that should be at the bottom of the landscape page will not be printed at the bottom, but at the right side (that is, the footer of a page printed in landscape layout). In this case, you must print the page number from a cell in the worksheet, not in the footer.

For example, see the Balance Sheet report with 6 columns (**A:F**), as shown in Figure 10-2. It is part of a report with a large number of pages in portrait layout; however, it is in landscape layout. The procedure below explains how to solve this problem.

	A	B	C	D	E	F
1	December 31, 2003					
2						
3						
4	XYZ Corporation Inc.					
5						
6						
7			December 31			
8	ASSETS	2003	2002	2001	Year1-Year2	Year2-Year1
9						
10	**Current Assets**					
11	Cash	301,124	318,697	294,795	(17,573)	23,902
12	Accounts Receivable	1,653,558	1,538,494	1,327,670	115,064	210,824
13	Inventories	546,173	520,133	481,123	26,040	39,010
14	Prepaid Expenses	13,552	23,659	21,884	(10,107)	1,774
15	Total Current Assets	2,514,407	2,400,983	2,125,472	113,424	275,510
16						
17	**Property and Equipment (at Cost)**					
18	Land & Building	674,019	677,191	626,402	(3,172)	50,789
19	Machinery and Equipment	386,140	326,052	301,598	60,088	24,454
20	Furniture and Fixtures	59,410	47,906	44,313	11,504	3,593
21	(Increase) Decrease in fixed assets	1,119,569	1,051,150	972,314	68,419	78,836
22	Less: Accumulated Depreciation	(478,852)	(419,540)	(369,319)	(59,312)	(50,221)
23	Net Book Value	640,717	631,610	602,995	9,107	28,615
24						
25	**Other Assets**					
26	Investment in Revenue Bond	364,321	300,260	277,741	64,061	22,520
27	Patents, Trademarks and Goodwill	52,250	52,500	48,563	(250)	3,938
28	(Increase) Decrease in other assets	416,571	352,760	326,303	63,811	26,457
29						
30	TOTAL ASSETS	3,571,695	3,385,352	3,054,770	186,343	330,582

Figure 10-2: Balance Sheet

➤ **To print page numbers in a report containing both portrait and landscape layouts:**

1. Select column **A**.

2. Right-click and select **Insert** from the displayed menu. A new column is inserted.

3. In cell **A1**, type the page number of the report.

4. Select the range **A1:A30**.

5. Open the *Format Cells* dialog box by pressing **<Ctrl+1>**, and select the **Alignment** tab.

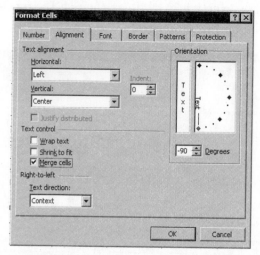

6. In the **Text alignment** area, select **Left** from the **Horizontal Combo Box**, and **Center** from the **Vertical Combo Box**.

7. In the **Text control** area, select the **Merge cells** check box.

8. In the **Orientation** area, change the text orientation to **-90** degrees (if the worksheet direction is right to left, text orientation should be +90 degrees).

9. Click **OK**.

10. Select **Page Setup** from the *File* menu, and then select the **Sheet** tab.

11. In the **Print area** box, change **B1** to **A1**. The new print area is new **A1:N30** (the print area includes the new column).

12. Select the **Margins** tab, and reduce the right margin to **0**, so that the page number appears at the bottom of the printed page.

13. Select the **Header/Footer** tab, and select **Custom Footer**.

14. If it appears in one of the sections, delete **& [Page]**, and click **OK**. The page number is now displayed horizontally and centered in column **A**.

Inserting a Watermark Behind the Text

Reports such as a company's Financial Statements are, by their very nature, confidential. It is therefore recommended that you insert the text **Confidential** as a **Watermark** behind the data in the report in such a way that it does not interfere with reading the report, as shown below.

Microsoft Excel - Financial Statements				
File Edit Financial Statements View Insert Format Tools Data Window Help				
	A	B	C	D
1				
2	December 31, 2003 ▼			
3				
4		XYZ Corporation Inc.		
5		BALANCE SHEET		
6				
7			December 31	
8		Notes	2003	2002
9	ASSETS			
10				
11	Current Assets			
12	Cash	5	301,124	318,697
13	Accounts Receivable	7	1,653,558	1,538,494
14	Inventories	8	546,173	520,133
15	Prepaid Expenses	9	13,552	23,659
16	Total Current Assets		2,514,407	2,400,983
17				
18	Property and Equipment (a	10		
19	Land & Building		674,019	677,191
20	Machinery and Equipment		386,140	326,052
21	Furniture and Fixtures		59,410	47,906
22	Total Property and Equipm		1,119,569	1,051,150
23	Less: Accumulated Deprec		(478,852)	(419,540)
24	Net Book Value		640,717	631,610
25				
26	Other Assets			
27	Investment in Revenue Bo	11	364,321	300,260
28	Patents, Trademarks and	12	52,250	52,500
29	Total Other Assets		416,571	352,760
30				
31	TOTAL ASSETS		3,571,695	3,385,352

Figure 10-3: Confidential Watermark

➢ **To insert a Watermark:**

1. Right-click a toolbar, and select the **WordArt** toolbar from the shortcut menu.

2. On the **WordArt** toolbar, click the **Insert WordArt** icon.

3. From the **WordArt Gallery**, select any example, and click **OK**.

4. In the *Edit WordArt Text* dialog box, type **Confidential** (or any other text), and select the font and the font size from the drop-down list.

5. Click **OK**.

6. Right click the **WordArt** in the worksheet and select Format **WordArt** from the shortcut menu. The *Format WordArt* dialog box appears.

7. Select the **Colors and Lines** tab and in the **Fill** box, select **Color**, and then **No Fill**.

8. In the **Line** box, select **Color**, and then select a color that is not too light.

9. Click **OK**.

10. Right-click the **WordArt** and select **Order**, and then **Send to Back**, from the shortcut menu.

11. Adjust the object's size and location to suit the worksheet.

Custom Views

A full report consists of a combination of individual worksheets, with different print options defined for each worksheet, and it is not worth the effort to begin re-defining print options for each of them. It is much more effective and efficient to save print options for repeated use.

Custom Views enable you to save a set of print options that is unique for each print area in the worksheet, as well as create a menu of **Custom Views** that lets you select a **Custom View** from any worksheet and print it without redefining the **Page Setup** options for the page.

Adding the Custom Views Icon Box

Refer to page 129, *Chapter 8, Customizing the Financial Statements.xls Workbook and Presenting Information*, for more details.

Adding a Custom View

Refer to page 130, *Chapter 8, Customizing the Financial Statements.xls Workbook and Presenting Information*, for more details, or use the procedure below.

➢ **To add a Custom View:**

1. Before defining the **Print_Area**, hide the rows and columns that you do not want to print.

2. Define the **Page Setup** options for the page to be printed, as described previously in this chapter.

3. From the *View* menu, select **Custom Views**. The *Custom Views* dialog box appears.

4. Click **Add**. The *Add View* dialog box appears.

5. Type the **Name** of the **Custom View** in the **Name** text box, and click **OK**.

Printing a Custom View

Custom Views can be printed, as required.

➢ **To print a Custom View:**

1. From the *View* menu, select **Custom Views**. The *Custom Views* dialog box appears.

2. Select the **Custom View** you want to print, as shown.

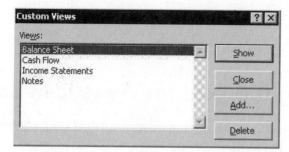

3. Click **Show**, and then click the **Print** icon on the toolbar.

Report Manager

Excel's **Report Manager** add-in lets you create and save reports for future printing.

Installing the Report Manager Add-in

If you use Office XP (2002) or later, your installation CD does not include the **Report Manager** add-in. To install it on your computer, you must download the add-in from the Microsoft Web site at http://office.microsoft.com/downloads/2002/rptmgr.aspx.

The Excel 97 and 2000 CDs include the add-in, named **Reports.xla**. If you have an earlier version of Excel, you can install the add-in in Excel 2002 and later without downloading the file from the Microsoft Web site. The add-in is the same for all versions of Excel.

➤ **To install the Report manager add-in:**

1. From the *Tools* menu, select **Add-ins**.

2. If the add-in **Report Manager** appears in the list of available add-ins, there is no need to install it. Go to step 5.

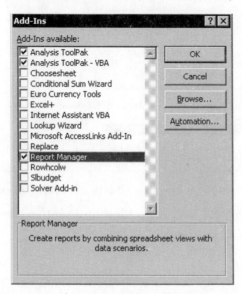

3. Click **Browse**.

4. Locate and select a file called **Reports.xla**, and then click **OK**. The **Report Manager** add-in will now appear in the **Add-Ins available** list.

5. Select the **Report Manager** check box, and click **OK**.

Adding and Saving a Report with Report Manager

Report Manager enables you to add and save reports, as required.

➢ **To add and save a report:**

1. From the *View* menu, select **Report Manager**, and click **Add**. The *Add Report* dialog box appears.

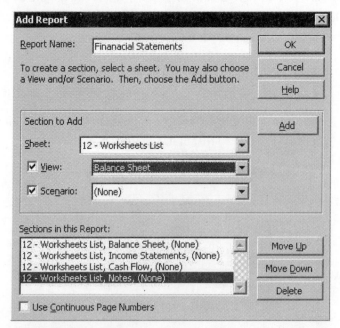

2. In the **Report Name** text box, type the name of the report.

3. In the **Section to Add** area, open **View** (or **Sheet**). It is recommended to print from **Custom Views**.

4. Select the first **Custom View** to add to the report, **Balance Sheet**.

5. Click **Add**. The **Balance Sheet Custom View** moves to the list at the bottom of the **Sections in this Report** area.

6. Repeat steps 2 through 5 to add other **Custom Views**, as required.

7. Select the **Use Continuous Page Number** check box if you want to print continuous numbers at the bottom of the page.

Advantages of Using Custom Views vs. Sheets when Adding a New Report

Choosing from **Views** (in the *Report Manager* dialog box) to add a new report using the **Report Manager** technique, instead of choosing from **Sheet**, is like buying an insurance policy for safe printing. The pages are printed according to the print page setup that were defined and saved earlier.

Printing, Editing or Deleting a Report

Reports can be printed, edited or deleted with **Report Manager**, as required.

➢ **To print a report:**

1. From the *View* menu, select **Report Manager**.

2. Select the report you want to print, and click **Print**.

➢ **To add pages, change the pages' printing order, to delete pages from the report or delete the entire report:**

1. From the *View* menu, select **Report Manager**.

2. Select the report you want to edit, and click **Edit**.

➢ **To delete a report:**

1. From the *View* menu, select **Report Manager**.

2. Select the report you want to delete, and click **Delete**.

Creating a Custom Report Manager

Rather than use the **Report Manager** to print the Financial Statements report, you can add a macro that will operate from a **Custom Menu** (shown in Figure 10-4, and described on page 119, *Chapter 8, Customizing the Financial Statements.xls Workbook and Presenting Information.*

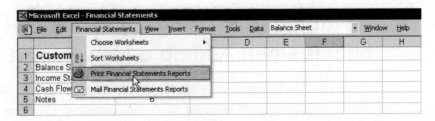

Figure 10-4: Print Financial Statements Reports in a Custom Menu

> ## To create and add a Custom Report Manager:

1. Press **<Alt+F11>** to open the Visual Basic Editor.

2. In the **Project** pane, double-click
    VBAProject(FinancialStatements.xls)

3. From the *Insert* menu, select **Module**.

4. Select the module, and press **<F4>**. The *Properties* dialog box
    appears.

5. In the **Name** row, change the module's name to **Printing**.

6. Type the code below into the module sheet:

```
Sub Print_Financial_Statements()
Dim NumberPages  As Integer, I As Integer
Dim ViewName As String

Application.ScreenUpdating = False
NumberPages = ActiveWorkbook.CustomViews.Count

For I = 1 To NumberPages
ViewName = ActiveWorkbook.CustomViews(I).Name
ActiveWorkbook.CustomViews(ViewName).Show
With ActiveSheet.PageSetup
    .CenterFooter = I
    .LeftFooter = ActiveWorkbook.FullName & "&A &T &D"
End With
ActiveSheet.PrintOut
Next I

Application.ScreenUpdating = True
End Sub
```

NOTE:

The macro VBA code lines can be copied from http://www.excelforum.com/f96-s,
the macro is also available in Chapter10.xls workbook at the companion CD-ROM.

Mailing Financial Statements Reports

It is simple and easy to send an entire workbook by e-mail. To do this, simply click the **E-Mail** icon (the fourth icon from the left) on the **Standard** toolbar and send the attachment workbook to the address you want.

To send selected worksheets from an entire workbook, however, is slightly more complex. If, for example, you want to send only worksheets that contain the Financial Statements reports, you should first save the **Custom Views** you created to a new workbook, and then send the entire workbook by mail, as described below.

➢ **To send selected worksheets from a workbook:**

1. Open a new worksheet, in this example, worksheet *17 — Printing*.

2. Type a list of **Custom Views** names into column **A** and the page number to add and print at the bottom of each page in column **B**, as shown.

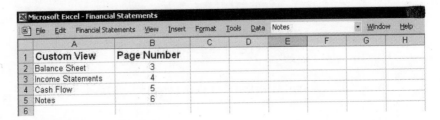

3. Add the following macro to any Module:

```
Sub Save_Financial_Statements()

Dim oSheet As Worksheet
Dim DateTimeStamp As String, CusViewName As String
Dim WB1 As String, WB2 As String, PH As String
Dim NumberCusViews As Integer, SheetsNum As Integer, I As Integer

Application.ScreenUpdating = False

'Create Date & Time Stamp
DateTimeStamp = Format(Now, "mmmm, dd yyyy HH-MM-SS")

WB1 = ActiveWorkbook.Name
NumberCusViews = ActiveWorkbook.CustomViews.Count
PH = ActiveWorkbook.Path

Workbooks.Add

'Save the new workbook at the same folder where the Financial Statements.xls
ActiveWorkbook.SaveAs Filename:=PH & "/" & "Financial Statements" & " " & "Saved at " & _
        DateTimeStamp & ".xls"

'Check the number of sheets included in the new workbook, add if necessary
SheetsNum = ActiveWorkbook.Sheets.Count
Do While SheetsNum < NumberCusViews
Sheets.Add
SheetsNum = ActiveWorkbook.Sheets.Count
Loop

WB2 = ActiveWorkbook.Name
Windows(WB1).Activate

 For I = 1 To NumberCusViews

    ActiveWorkbook.CustomViews(I).Show
    Selection.EntireColumn.Copy
    Windows(WB2).Activate
    Sheets(I).Select
    ActiveSheet.Paste
    Selection.Formula = Selection.Value
    ActiveSheet.DrawingObjects.Delete
    Rows("1:3").Delete
    Application.CutCopyMode = False
    Range("a1").Select

    Windows(WB1).Activate

 Next

Workbooks(WB2).Save
Windows(WB1).Activate

Application.ScreenUpdating = True
End Sub
```

NOTE:

The macro VBA code lines can be copied from http://www.excelforum.com/f96-s, the macro is also available in Chapter10.xls workbook at the companion CD-ROM.

This macro adds a new workbook, saves each one of the **Custom Views** based on the list in worksheet *17 — Printing* and then saves the new workbook (named *Financial Statements*) with the current date and time in the same folder as the previously saved *Financial Statement.xls* workbook. You can now mail the entire new saved workbook to any of your colleagues.

Part Two: Analyzing Financial Statements and Creating Management Financial Reports

Chapter 11

Balance Sheet Five-year Comparison Reports

About This Chapter

In this chapter, you will learn how to use the reports already created in the previous chapters to create the Balance Sheet five-year comparison report, and includes the following sections:

✦ **Overview**, page 190, presents the purpose of and need for creating a five-year Balance Sheet comparison report, to enables you to better see the long-term business activities.

✦ **Five-year Balance Sheet Comparison Report**, page 191, describes the five-year Balance Sheet comparison report, as well as how to round the numbers to the thousands and troubleshoot calculation errors due to the rounding.

Overview

In *Chapter 4, Balance Sheet*, you learned how to create a Balance Sheet report in the **Financial Statements.xls** workbook.

In addition to regular Financial Statements reports, you need to create and present comparable financial reports in different forms for management purposes, for fundraising from potential investors and for decision makers.

In this chapter, you will learn how to create a comparable Balance Sheet report to compare five years of business activity results, and how to present the figures rounded to the thousands.

Five-year Balance Sheet Comparison Report

After you have finished creating the five-year Balance Sheet comparison report, it will look like Figure 11-1:

	Notes	2003	2002	2001	2000	1999
XYZ Corporation Inc.						
BALANCE SHEET						
In Thousands						
				December 31		
ASSETS						
Current Assets						
Cash	5	301	319	295	434	673
Accounts Receivable	7	1,654	1,538	1,328	670	409
Inventories	8	546	520	481	434	265
Prepaid Expenses	9	14	24	22	473	289
Total Current Assets		**2,515**	**2,401**	**2,126**	**2,011**	**1,636**
Property and Equipment (at Cost)	10					
Land & Building		674	677	626	670	641
Machinery and Equipment		386	326	302	381	327
Furniture and Fixtures		59	48	44	53	42
Total Property and Equipment		1,119	1,051	972	1,104	1,010
Less: Accumulated Depreciation		-479	-420	-369	421	357
Net Book Value		**1,598**	**1,471**	**1,342**	**683**	**653**
Other Assets						
Investment in Revenue Bond	11	364	300	278	341	276
Patents, Trademarks and Goodwill	12	52	53	49	44	38
Total Other Assets		**417**	**353**	**326**	**384**	**314**
TOTAL ASSETS		**4,529**	**4,224**	**3,794**	**3,079**	**2,603**
LIABILITIES AND STOCKHOLDER'S EQUITY						
Current Liabilities						
Line of Credit	6	477	501	463	1,065	649
Current Portion of Long-Term Debt						
Accounts Payable	13	547	475	440	1,025	625
Accrued Expenses	14	234	221	205	1,143	697
Other Payables	15	19	27	25	1,341	818
Total Current Liabilities		**1,278**	**1,224**	**1,133**	**4,574**	**2,790**
Long-Term Liabilities						
Note Payable	16	784	840	777	1,735	1,058
Equipment Leases Payable	17	185	225	208	1,774	1,082
Less: Current Portion Shown Above		-40	-40	-37	1,656	1,010
Total Long-Term Liabilities		**929**	**1,026**	**949**	**5,165**	**3,150**
TOTAL LIABILITIES		**2,207**	**2,250**	**2,081**	**9,739**	**5,940**
Stockholder's Equity						
Capital Stock		152	153	141	1,853	1,130
Retained Earnings	19	1,172	943	796	3,824	2,333
Total Stockholder's Equity		**1,324**	**1,096**	**937**	**5,678**	**3,463**
TOTAL LIABILITIES AND STOCKHOLDER'S EQUITY		**3,531**	**3,346**	**3,018**	**15,416**	**9,403**

Figure 11-1: Five-year Balance Sheet Comparison Report

Creating a Five-year Balance Sheet Comparison Report

The first step in creating the five-year Balance Sheet comparison report is to add new worksheet. To do this, copy from worksheet *31 — Balance Sheet,* change the worksheet name and then add the needed formulas to three additional new columns.

➤ **To create a five-year Balance Sheet comparison report:**

1. Add new worksheet by pressing **<Shift+F11>**, and then rename it to *32 — Five-year Balance Sheet.*

2. Select worksheet *31 — Balance Sheet* and copy columns **A:D**.

3. Select worksheet *32 — Five-year Balance Sheet,* and press **<Enter>** to paste the columns.

4. Add the three additional year's number titles to cells **E8:G8** by typing the following formula to cell **E8**:

   =D8-1

   and then copying and pasting it to cells **F8:G8**.

NOTE:

For more details regarding the structure of the Balance Sheet report years' number titles, refer to page 70, *Chapter 4, Balance Sheet.*

5. Follow steps 6 through 12 below and add formulas to cells in columns **E: G** (from cell **E12**) that return the summaries for the **Account Type** items **(Level 3)** in column **A** from the appropriate month column in worksheet *21 — Trial Balances Data*.

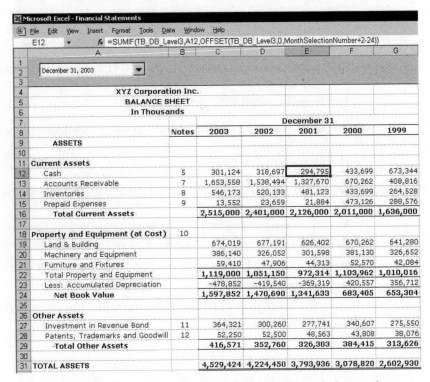

6. Select cell **D12**, then select the formula in the formula bar and press **<Ctrl+C>**.

7. Click either **Cancel** or **Enter** in the formula bar.

8. Select cell **E12** and press **<Ctrl+V>**, select cell **F12** and press **<Ctrl+V>**, and then select cell **G12** and press **<Ctrl+V>**.

9. Select cell **E12**, and in the last argument of the **Offset** formula, change the number from **12** to **24**.

10. In the formula in cell **F12**, change the number from **12** to **36**.

11. In the formula in cell **G12**, change the number from **12** to **48**.

12. Copy cells **E12:G12** and paste the formulas to all appropriate cells in columns **E:G**.

The **MonthSelectionNumber** is reduced by 12 in each formula in the cells from column **D** to column **G** (starting from cell **D12**, as shown in step 4). This parameter is the *Name* defined in worksheet *13 — Parameters & Calculations* for the **Combo Box** linked cell, as explained on page 6, *Chapter 1, Introducing Financial Statements.xls Worksheets.*

The formula in cell **C12** is:

=SUMIF(TB_DB_Level3,A12,OFFSET(TB_DB_Level3,0,MonthSelectionNumber+2))

The formula in cell **D12** is:

=SUMIF(TB_DB_Level3,A12,OFFSET(TB_DB_Level3,0,MonthSelectionNumber+2-12))

The formula in cell **E12** is:

=SUMIF(TB_DB_Level3,A12,OFFSET(TB_DB_Level3,0,MonthSelectionNumber+2-24))

As can be seen in Figure 11-1 on page 191, the third argument of the **OFFSET** function (the column number argument) is reduced by 12 (that is, twelve months or one year) in each year formula. As a result, the **SUMIF** formula summarizes from the appropriate column number in worksheet *21 — Trial Balances Data* based on the criteria in column **A**, which are **Account Type** items.

 NOTE:

The range *Names* pasted into the formulas above are defined on page 63, *Chapter 3, Updating the Trial Balances Data Worksheet.*

Presenting the Figures in the Five-year Balance Sheet Report in Thousands

It may be difficult to read the figures side-by-side in the five-year Balance Sheet comparison report if the numbers are not rounded to the thousands. In this section you will learn how to easily round the numbers to the thousands, as well as how to correct the display totals of the presented rounded numbers.

It is not convenient to use a **ROUND** formula to round numbers to the thousands, as it adds one more formula to the formulas already in the cells. It also makes auditing more complicated, uses more memory and expands the workbook size.

Instead, you should use **Custom Formatting** to round numbers to the thousands.

➤ **To format the numbers in column C:G:**

1. In the five-year Balance Sheet report shown in Figure 11-1, page 191, select the cells in columns **C: G** from cell **C12** onwards.

2. Press **<Ctrl+1>**, select the **Number** tab, and then select the **Custom** category.

3. In the **Type** box, type:

   #, ###, ;[Red](#, ###,);- ;

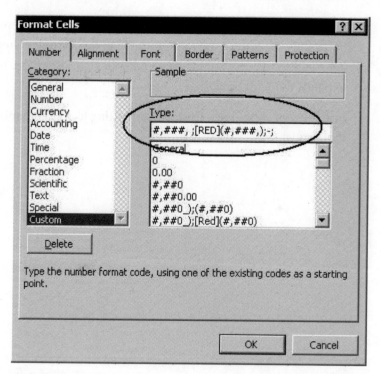

4. Click **OK**.

The **#** and **0** characters both display the digits entered into the cell. The difference between them, however, is that **#** does not display an irrelevant zero. For example, the zero-cents place in the figure **1112.50** will be displayed only if you type **0** (not **#**) in format's cents place. In other words, if the format is **#,##0.00**, the number displayed in the cell will be **1,112.50**; if it is **#,##0.0#**, the result displayed is **1,112.5**.

To round numbers to the thousands using the **Custom Format** technique, simply eliminate the **#** or **0** signs after the comma that separates the thousands from the hundreds, tens and ones, as shown:

#,###,;[Red]-#,###,

The left side of the formatting number up to the **;** sign presents the positive numbers, while the right side of the formatting number from the **;** **[Red]-#,###,**, presents the negative numbers (with or without parenthesis, as shown in the example on page 196).

Problem: The Summary of the Presented Numbers Is Unequal

It may sometimes occur that the summary of the displayed rounded numbers is incorrect. For example, the formula in cell **C16** returns **2,514** (as shown below). However, if you add the numbers up, the result is actually **2,515**.

	A	B	C	D	E	F	G
	Microsoft Excel - Financial Statements						
	File Edit View Insert Format Tools Data Window Help						
	C16 ▾ ƒ =SUM(C12:C15)						
1							
2	December 31, 2003 ▾						
3							
4	XYZ Corporation Inc.						
5	BALANCE SHEET						
6	In Thousands						
7					December 31		
8		Notes	2003	2002	2001	2000	1999
9	ASSETS						
10							
11	**Current Assets**						
12	Cash	5	301	319	295	434	673
13	Accounts Receivable	7	1,654	1,538	1,328	670	409
14	Inventories	8	546	520	481	434	265
15	Prepaid Expenses	9	14	24	22	473	289
16	Total Current Assets		2,514	2,401	2,125	2,011	1,635
17							
18	**Property and Equipment (at Cost)**	10					
19	Land & Building		674	677	626	670	641
20	Machinery and Equipment		386	326	302	381	327
21	Furniture and Fixtures		59	48	44	53	42
22	Total Property and Equipment		1,120	1,051	972	1,104	1,010
23	Less: Accumulated Depreciation		-479	-420	-369	421	357
24	Net Book Value		1,598	1,471	1,342	683	653

Figure 11-2: SUM Formula Returns Error Display Result

This error happens because the **SUM** formula calculates and returns the totals as they have been entered into the cells, not how they were formatted and displayed.

For example, the numbers **1,653,558 and 13,552**, shown in cells **C13** and **C15** of the five-year comparison report on page 193, will be rounded up and displayed as **1,654** and **14**, as shown in cells **C13** and **C15** in Figure 11-2, accordingly, and the total of **2,514,407** will be displayed as **2,514** after it is rounded to the thousands.

Applying a new format to cell **C16** does not change a calculation already performed or cause the formula in cell **C16** to run a new calculation. In other words, the formula is returned to the numbers in the cells, and not the numbers as displayed.

To solve this problem, you should use the **Array Formula** technique to return the totals of the rounded displayed numbers.

➢ **To make the SUM formula return the correct total of the displayed numbers:**

1. Type the following formula into cell **C16**:

    =SUM(ROUND(C12:C15,-3))

2. Ignore the **#VALUE** error, and select the cell.

3. Press **<F2>**.

4. Press **<Ctrl+Shift+Enter>** to call an **Array Formula**. The correct number will be shown.

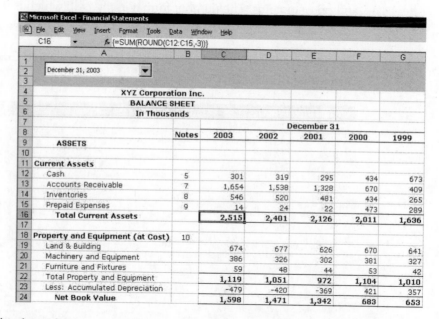

This formula returns the correct displayed numbers for two reasons:

✦ A **ROUND** formula plus the use of the rounded **Custom Format** to the thousands.

✦ An **Array Formula**.

Each of these reasons will be discussed in the following sections.

ROUND Formula and Rounding to the Thousands

The **ROUND** formula here is:

=ROUND(C12:C15,-3)

In the second argument of the **ROUND** formula, the value is **-3**, which rounds the number in cell **C12** (as an example) from **301124.065** to **301000**.

The **-3** in the second argument changes the three digits (hundreds, tens and ones) to zeros. The number format in the cell (which is **#,###,**) does not present the three digits after the comma, which are three zeros (000).

The final result from using both the **ROUND** formula and **Custom Formatting** displays **301** in the cell, as shown.

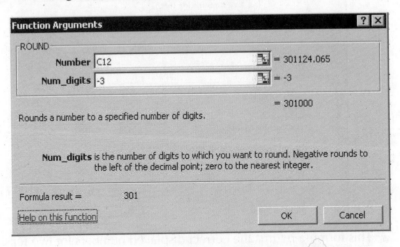

Figure 11-3: ROUND Formula Arguments

An Array Formula

Pressing **<Ctrl+Shift+Enter>** while the cell is in edit mode (by pressing **<F2>**) executes a macro that opens temporary cells in the memory to which the rounded numbers in the formula range are stored. The formula then returns the summary of the rounded numbers from the stored numbers and not the summary from the numbers displayed in the worksheet cells.

Chapter 12

Income Statement Five-year and Quarterly Comparison Reports

About This Chapter

In this chapter, you will learn how to use the Income Statement report already created in *Chapter 5, Income Statement* to create the Income Statement five-year comparison report and quarterly comparison reports, and includes the following sections:

✦ **Overview**, page 202, presents the purpose of and need for creating an *Income Statement* report that compares results from five years of business activities and compares results over the last four quarters.

✦ **Five-year Income Statement Comparison Report**, page 203, describes the creation of a five-year Income Statement report.

✦ **Quarterly Income Statement**, page 207, describes the creation of comparison quarterly Income Statements, as well as how to deal with the calendar or fiscal year end reporting period.

✦ **Creating Charts Easily and Quickly**, page 219, describes how to quickly create charts to display the comparison balances of the Income Statement report.

Overview

In *Chapter 5, Income Statement*, you learned how to create an Income Statement report in the **Financial Statements.xls** workbook.

In addition to regular Income Statement reports, you need to create and present Income Statement reports in different forms for analysis and management purposes, for fundraising from potential investors and for decision makers.

In this chapter, you will learn how to create different comparable Income Statement reports to compare the results between years and quarters of business activity results.

Five-year Income Statement Comparison Report

After you have finished creating the five-year Income Statement comparison report, it will look like Figure 12-1:

	A	B	C	D	E	F	G
	Microsoft Excel - Financial Statements						
	File Edit View Insert Format Tools Data Window Help						
1							
2	December 31, 2003						
3							
4	XYZ Corporation Inc.						
5	Income Statement						
6	For the year ended December 31, 2003						
7							
8		Notes	2003	2002	2001	2000	1999
9	**Revenue**	20					
10	Sales		2,920	2,634	2,436	2,175	2,002
11	Services		955	725	680	600	552
12	**Total Revenue**		**3,875**	**3,359**	**3,116**	**2,775**	**2,554**
13							
14	**Cost of Goods Sold**						
15	Materials		855	733	703	635	646
16	Labor & Subcontractors Costs		602	537	492	455	433
17	Other Cost of goods sold		385	350	333	300	276
18	Increase / Decrease in Inventories	21	-26	-30	12	-30	31
19	**Total Cost of Goods Sold**		**1,815**	**1,590**	**1,540**	**1,360**	**1,386**
20							
21	**Gross Income**		**2,060**	**1,769**	**1,576**	**1,416**	**1,169**
22							
23	**Operating Expenses**						
24	Selling		480	441	416	399	325
25	General & Administrative	22	759	676	628	555	500
26	Other Operating Expense	23	276	261	250	215	200
27	Amortization		59	50	46	41	39
28	**Total Operating Expenses**		**1,574**	**1,428**	**1,340**	**1,211**	**1,064**
29							
30	**Net Income before Operations**		**487**	**341**	**237**	**205**	**105**
31							
32	**Operating Income (Loss)**						
33	Other income (expense)	24	33	-3	23	15	-17
34	Interest expense		75	63	66	73	60
35	**Total Operating Income**		**108**	**60**	**89**	**88**	**43**
36							
37	**Income (Loss) Before Income Taxes**		**379**	**281**	**147**	**117**	**62**
38	Provision (benefit) for income taxes	25	150	133	75	46	49
39	**Net Income (Loss) for the year**		**229**	**148**	**72**	**71**	**13**
40	Retained Earnings beginning of the year	26	943	796	724	652	639
41	**Retained Earnings**		**1,172**	**944**	**796**	**723**	**652**

Figure 12-1: Five-year Income Statement Comparison Report

Creating a Five–year Income Statement Comparison Report

The first step in creating the five-year Income Statement comparison report is to add a new worksheet, rename it to 42 — *Five-year Income Statement*, copy the needed columns from worksheet *41 — Income Statement*, and then add the needed formulas to three additional new columns.

➢ **To create a five-year Income Statement comparison report:**

1. Add new worksheet by pressing **<Shift+F11>**, and then rename it to *42 — Five-year Income Statement*.

2. Select worksheet *41 — Income Statement*, copy columns **A:D**.

3. Select worksheet *42 — Five-year Income Statement* and press **<Enter>** to paste columns **A:D**.

4. Add the three additional years' number titles to cells **E8:G8** by typing the following formula to cell **E8**:

    =D8-1

    and then copying and pasting it to cells **F8:G8**.

 NOTE:

For more details regarding the structure of the Income Statement report years' number titles, refer to page 70, *Chapter 4, Balance Sheet*.

5. Follow steps 6 through 11 and add formulas to cells in columns **E: G** that return the summaries for the **Account Type** items **(Level 3)** in column **A** from the appropriate month column in worksheet *21 — Trial Balances Data.*

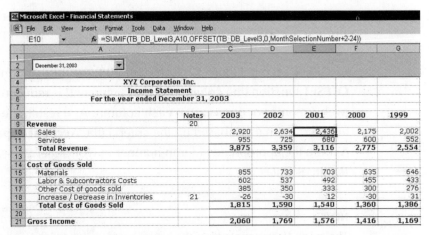

6. Select cell **D10**, then select the formula in the formula bar and press **<Ctrl+C>**.

7. Click either the **Cancel** or **Enter** sign in the formula bar.

8. Select cell **E10** and press **<Ctrl+V>**, select cell **F10** and press **<Ctrl+V>** and then select cell **G10** and press **<Ctrl+V>**.

9. Select cell **E10**, and in the last argument of the **OFFSET** formula, change the number from **12** to **24**.

10. In the formula in cell **F10**, change the number from **12** to **36**.

11. In the formula in cell **G10**, change the number from **12** to **48**.

12. Copy cells **E10:G10** and paste the formulas to all appropriate cells in columns **E: G**.

The **MonthSelectionNumber** is reduced by 12 in each formula in the cells from column **D** to column **G** (starting from cell **D10**). This parameter is the *Name* defined in worksheet *13 — Parameters & Calculations* for the **Combo Box** linked cell, as explained on page 6, *Chapter 1, Introducing Financial Statements.xls Worksheets.*

The formula in cell **C10** is:

=SUMIF(TB_DB_Level3,A10,OFFSET(TB_DB_Level3,0,MonthSelectionNumber+2))

The formula in cell **G10** is:

=SUMIF(TB_DB_Level3,A10,OFFSET(TB_DB_Level3,0,MonthSelectionNumber+2-48))

As can be seen in Figure 12-1 on page 203, the third argument of the **OFFSET** function (the column number argument) is reduced by 12 (that is, twelve months or one year) in each column. As a result, the **SUMIF** formula summarizes based on the criteria (the **Account Type** in column **A**) from the appropriate column number in worksheet *21 — Trial Balances Data*.

NOTE:

The range *Names* pasted into the formulas above are defined on page 63, *Chapter 3, Updating the Trial Balances Data Worksheet.*

Presenting the Figures in the Five-year Balance Sheet Report in Thousands

To present the figures in the five-year Income Statement report in thousands, refer to page 195, *Chapter 11, Balance Sheet Five-year Comparison Reports.*

Quarterly Income Statement

The Income Statement shown in Figure 12-1 displays the quarterly figures for the last four quarters (columns **B:E**), and the accumulated quarterly figures for the last four quarters (columns **F:I**).

The cells in row **2** of the worksheet contain the calculated quarter number based on a calendar year reporting period, as explained in the following sections.

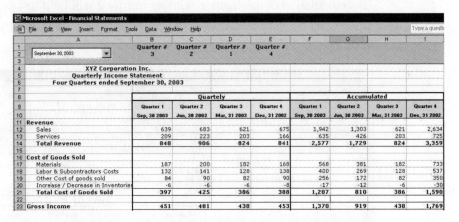

Figure 12-2: Quarterly Comparison Income Statement

Calculating the Quarter Number for a Calendar or Fiscal Year Reporting Period

Use worksheet *42 — Five-year Income Statement,* created in the previous section, to create an Income Statement report that compares the quarterly figures for the last four quarters.

Copy worksheet *42 — Five-year Income Statement* by selecting the worksheet tab and dragging it to a new location while pressing the **<Ctrl>** key. Then change the worksheet name to *43 — Four Quarters Income Statement.*

Start creating the Income Statement that compares the quarterly figures for the last four quarters by entering formulas that calculate the four quarter numbers.

In row **2** of Figure 12-3, three out of four quarters are from the same calendar year (2003) and the last quarter is from the previous year (2002). To display the quarterly balances only, you should calculate the difference between the accumulated balances of two consecutives quarters, except when the quarter is first quarter of the year.

This calculation of the quarter number in row **2** will help to calculate the differences between two consecutive quarters from the current year or from a previous year, as explained below.

	A	B	C	D	E
			Quarter #	**Quarter #**	**Quarter #**	**Quarter #**
1			**Quarter #**	**Quarter #**	**Quarter #**	**Quarter #**
2	September 30, 2003	3	2	1	4
3					
4	XYZ Corporation Inc.				
5	Quarterly Income Statement				
6	Four Quarters ended September 30, 2003				
7					
8			Quartely		
9		Quarter 1	Quarter 2	Quarter 3	Quarter 4
10		Sep. 30 2003	Jun. 30 2003	Mar, 31 2003	Dec, 31 2002
11	**Revenue**				
12	Sales	639	683	621	675
13	Services	209	223	203	166
14	**Total Revenue**	848	906	824	841
15					
16	**Cost of Goods Sold**				
17	Materials	187	200	182	168
18	Labor & Subcontractors Costs	132	141	128	138
19	Other Cost of goods sold	84	90	82	90
20	Increase / Decrease in Inventorie	-6	-6	-6	-8
21	**Total Cost of Goods Sold**	397	425	386	388
22					
23	**Gross Income**	451	481	438	453

The formula bar shows: B2 — =INDEX(MonthsTable,MonthSelectionNumber+1,5)

Figure 12-3: Formula for Calculating the Quarter Number

The formula in cell **B2** is:

=INDEX(MonthsTable,MonthSelectionNumber+1,5)

Two defined *Names* were pasted into the **INDEX** formulas in row **2**, **MonthTable** and **MonthSelectionNumber**, as explained in the next section.

Quarter Number Calculation Worksheet

Define a *Name* for columns **A:E** in worksheet *14 — Months Lists*. The *Name* to define is **MonthTable** (to define the *Name*, select columns **A:E**, press <**Ctrl+F3**>, type **MonthTable** in the **Name in workbook** text box, and then press **OK**).

Paste **MonthTable** into the first argument of the **INDEX** formula, as shown in Figure 12-3.

NOTE:
An explanation of the formulas entered into columns **C:E** is provided on page 210.

	Microsoft Excel - Financial Statements			
	File Edit View Insert Format Tools Data Window Help			
	A	B	C	D	E
1	Month Number	ComboBox, TB_Table Month List	Quarter Number Calendar year	Quarter Number Fiscal year	Quarter # - Calendar or Fiscal Year
2	1	January 31, 1998	1	1	1
3	2	February 28, 1998	1	1	1
4	3	March 31, 1998	1	1	1
5	4	April 30, 1998	2	2	2
6	5	May 31, 1998	2	2	2
7	6	June 30, 1998	2	2	2
8	7	July 31, 1998	3	3	3
9	8	August 31, 1998	3	3	3
10	9	September 30, 1998	3	3	3
11	10	October 31, 1998	4	4	4

Figure 12-4: Worksheet 14 — Months List

Cells from **B2** onwards contain the month list range. The *Name* defined for the range is **MonthsList**, which is the list entered in the **Combo Box** input box (as described on page 6, *Chapter 1, Introducing Financial Statements.xls Worksheets*.

When selecting the month-ending period, **September 2003** (in the example here), from the **Combo Box MonthsList**, the linked cell **MonthSelectionNumber** receives the number **69** (this is the month number, starting from January 1998).

In the **INDEX** formula's second argument, the row number of the selected months is **MonthSelectionNumber+1** (the sequence numbers in column **A** start from cell **A2**).

In the **INDEX** formula's third argument, the column number is column **5** (column **E** in the worksheet, as shown in Figure 12-4).

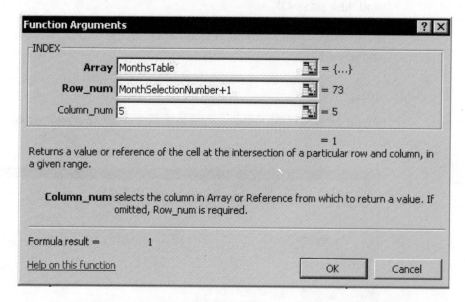

Figure 12-5: Index Formula That Returns the Quarter Number

The Formulas in Columns C:E of Worksheet 14 – Months List

Columns **C:E** in Figure 12-4 contain formulas that calculate the quarter numbers based on either a calendar or fiscal year reporting method:

✦ Cell **C2** contains a formula that calculates the calendar quarter number:

=INT((MONTH(B2)-1)/3)+1

✦ Cell **D2** contains a formula that calculates the fiscal quarter number, based on the month the fiscal year ended, as explained in the next section.

=MOD(CEILING(22+MONTH(B2)-FiscalYearMonthNumber-1,3)/3,4)+1

✦ Cell **E2** contains an **IF** formula that returns calculation results from cell **C2** or **D2** depending on the reporting year end period (either calendar or fiscal), as explained in the next section.

=IF(CalendarYear=True,C2,D2)

Selecting the Calendar or Fiscal Year Reporting Period

Add a **Check Box** to worksheet *11 — General Details* to choose the year-end reporting period, either calendar year or fiscal year, and add a **Scroll Box** to select the month year-end number (if the reporting year period is fiscal year), as shown in Figure 12-6.

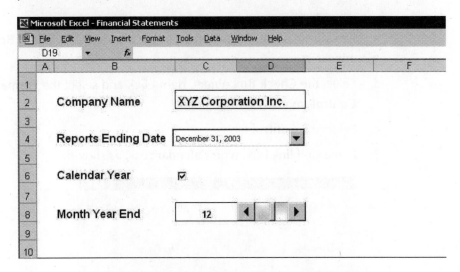

Figure 12-6: Worksheet 11-General Details

➢ **To add a Check Box:**

1. Define a *Name* by selecting cell **K6**, pressing **<Ctrl+F3>**, typing **CalendarYear** into the **Name in workbook** box, and then clicking **OK**.

2. Select one of the toolbars, right-click and then select the **Forms** toolbar from the shortcut menu.

3. Select the **Check Box** object, as shown.

4. Draw a small square anywhere in the worksheet. A **Check Box** appears.

5. Select the **Check Box** object, right-click and select the **Format Control** from the shortcut menu.

6. Select the **Control** tab.

7. In the **Cell link** box, type **CalendarYear**, as shown.

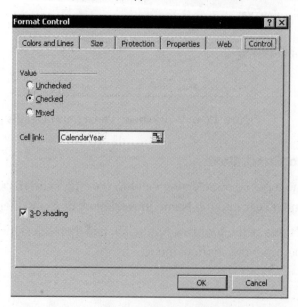

8. Click **OK**.

9. Press **<Esc>** to cancel edit mode.

10. Check the **Check Box**.

The value in cell **K6** is *True* when the **Check Box** is checked.

➢ **To add a Scroll Bar:**

1. Follow steps 1 through 3 in the previous procedure and define a *Name* for cell **C8** — **FiscalYearMonthNumber**

2. Select the **Scroll Bar** object, as shown.

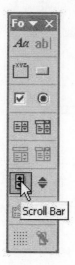

3. Draw a small square in cell **D8**. The **Scroll Bar** object appears.

4. Select the **Scroll Bar** object, right-click and select **Format Control** from the shortcut menu.

5. Select the **Control** tab.

6. Select **1** for the **Minimum value** and **12** for the **Maximum value**, as shown.

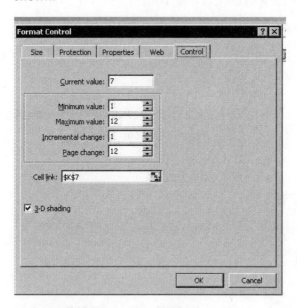

7. In the **Cell link** box, type **$K$7**.

8. Click **OK**.

9. Press **<Esc>** to cancel the edit mode.

10. Type the following formula into cell **C8 (FiscalYearMonthNumber)**:

    =IF(CalendarYear =TRUE,12,K7)

The formula will either return **12** if the reporting year-end period is based on the calendar year end, or the number from cell **K7** (the **Scroll Bar** cell link) chosen by using the **Scroll Bar**.

TIP:

To automatically fit the size of an object (**Combo Box**, **Check Box** or **Scroll Bar**) to the cell, press the **<Alt>** button while sizing the corner of the object to the cell borders.

Automatically Modifying the Quarter Column Titles

Select worksheet *43 — Four Quarters Income Statement* (as described in *Quarterly Income Statement*, page 207). The cells in row **10** from **B10** onwards (that is, the ending date of each quarter) contain an **INDEX** formula with two arguments, as shown in Figure 12-7. When choosing the reporting month from the **MonthsList Combo Box**, the formulas return the end date of each quarter.

Figure 12-7: Quarterly Comparison Income Statement

The formula in cell **B10** is:

=INDEX(MonthsList,MonthSelectionNumber)

The formula in cell **C10** is:

=INDEX(MonthsList,MonthSelectionNumber-3)

In worksheet *21 — Trial Balance Data*, the Trial Balances are stored on a monthly basis, one column for each month. The distance between the quarters is three columns. In the **INDEX** formula's second argument, the number in the **MonthSelectionNumber** cell is reduced by 3 (that is, in cell **D10** type **-6** instead of **3** and in cell **E10** type **-9** instead of 3).

Copy the formulas from cells **B10:E10** and paste them to cells **F10:I10**.

Summing the Quarterly Balances

Columns **F:I** and column **K** (from row **12**) contain formulas that return the accumulated balances for the **Account Types** in column **A** from the worksheet *21 — Trial Balances Data*. Column **K** contains the balances from the fifth quarter.

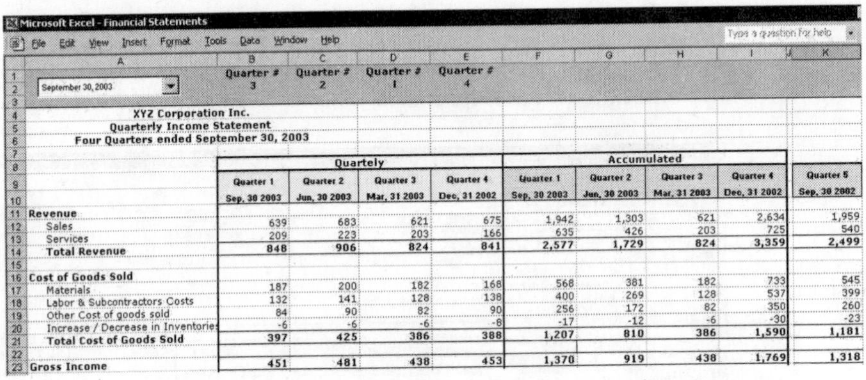

	Quartely				Accumulated				
	Quarter 1 Sep, 30 2003	Quarter 2 Jun, 30 2003	Quarter 3 Mar, 31 2003	Quarter 4 Dec, 31 2002	Quarter 1 Sep, 30 2003	Quarter 2 Jun, 30 2003	Quarter 3 Mar, 31 2003	Quarter 4 Dec, 31 2002	Quarter 5 Sep, 30 2002
Revenue									
Sales	639	683	621	675	1,942	1,303	621	2,634	1,959
Services	209	223	203	166	635	426	203	725	540
Total Revenue	**848**	**906**	**824**	**841**	**2,577**	**1,729**	**824**	**3,359**	**2,499**
Cost of Goods Sold									
Materials	187	200	182	168	568	381	182	733	545
Labor & Subcontractors Costs	132	141	128	138	400	269	128	537	399
Other Cost of goods sold	84	90	82	90	256	172	82	350	260
Increase / Decrease in Inventories	-6	-6	-6	-8	-17	-12	-6	-30	-23
Total Cost of Goods Sold	**397**	**425**	**386**	**388**	**1,207**	**810**	**386**	**1,590**	**1,181**
Gross Income	**451**	**481**	**438**	**453**	**1,370**	**919**	**438**	**1,769**	**1,318**

Figure 12-8: Summing Quarterly Figures

The formula in cell **F12** (the last quarter) is:

=SUMIF(TB_DB_Level3,A12,OFFSET(TB_DB_Level3,0,MonthSelectionNumber+3))

The formula in cell **K12** (the fifth quarter) is:

=SUMIF(TB_DB_Level3,A12,OFFSET(TB_DB_Level3,0,MonthSelectionNumber-9))

The formulas in columns **B:E** return the net balances for each quarter.

The formula in cell **B12** is:

=IF($B$2=1,F12,F12-G12)

The formula in cell **E12** is:

=IF($E$2=1,I12,I12-K12)

The **IF** formula's first argument checks the quarter number. If it is **1**, then in the second argument there is no need to subtract the accumulated quarterly figures from the previous accumulated quarterly figures.

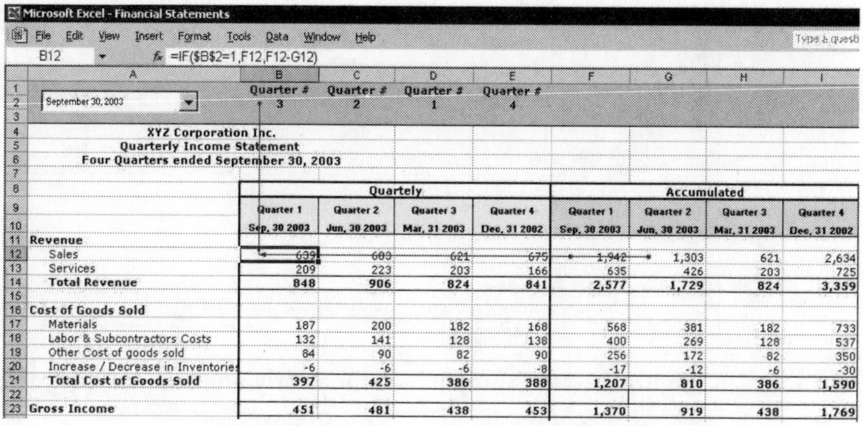

Figure 12-9: Using Trace Precedents to Audit Formula

Quarterly and Annual Income Statement Report Examples

Figure 12-10 shows the results of the last four quarters' activity and the annual results. To create the Income Statement report shown in the figure, hide columns **G:J** (as shown in Figure 12-8).

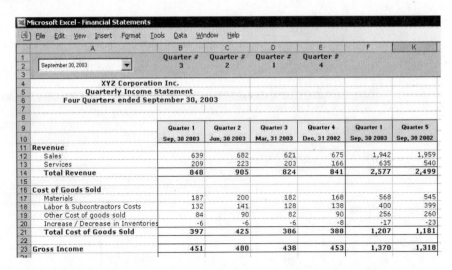

Figure 12-10: Example 1 — Quarterly and Annual Income Statement Report

Figure 12-11 shows the results of the last four quarters' activity, analyzed by percentage (sales = 100%) and annual results.

Microsoft Excel - Financial Statements										
	A	B	C	D	E	F	G	H	I	
1		Quarter #		Quarter #		Quarter #		Quarter #		
2	September 30, 2003	3		2		1		4		
3										
4	XYZ Corporation Inc.									
5	Quarterly Income Statements									
6	Four Quarters ended September 30, 2003									
7										
8										
9		Quarter 1		Quarter 2		Quarter 3		Quarter 4		
10		Sep, 30 2003	%	Jun, 30 2003	%	Mar, 31 2003	%	Dec, 31 2002	%	
11	Revenue									
12	Sales	639	75.35%	683	75.39%	621	75.36%	675	78.40%	
13	Services	209	24.65%	223	24.61%	203	24.64%	186	21.60%	
14	Total Revenue	848	100.00%	906	100.00%	824	100.00%	861	100.00%	
15										
16	Cost of Goods Sold									
17	Materials	187	22.05%	200	22.08%	182	22.09%	183	21.25%	
18	Labor & Subcontractors Costs	132	15.57%	141	15.56%	128	15.53%	138	16.03%	
19	Other Cost of goods sold	84	9.91%	90	9.93%	82	9.95%	90	10.45%	
20	Increase / Decrease in Inventorie	-	-0.59%	-	-0.55%	-	-0.73%	-	-0.93%	
21	Total Cost of Goods Sold	398	46.93%	426	47.02%	386	46.84%	403	46.81%	
22										
23	Gross Income	450	53.07%	480	52.98%	438	53.16%	458	53.19%	

Figure 12-11: Example 2 — Quarterly Income Statement Report, Analyzed by Percentage (Sales = 100%)

Creating Charts Easily and Quickly

After you have created a number of Income Statement reports that display the comparison balances for five years, or compare sales revenue and net income for the last four quarters, you may want to present the balances using **Charts** that provide the reader with a powerful tool for analyzing the figures.

Excel offers an excellent shortcut key (**<F11>**) that enables you to create **Charts** in a matter of seconds.

➢ **To create Charts with the shortcut key:**

1. Select worksheet *42 — Five-year Income Statement.*

2. Select non-adjacent cells by:

   ✦ Select the Sales figures by selecting cells **A12:G12**.

   ✦ Press **<Ctrl>** and select the Total Cost of Goods Sold by selecting cells **A19:G19**.

   ✦ Continue pressing **<Ctrl>** and select the Net Income by selecting cells **A39:G39**.

Your worksheet should now look like this:

	A	B	C	D	E	F	G
	Microsoft Excel - Financial Statements						
	File Edit View Insert Format Tools Data Window Help						
1							
2	December 31, 2003 ▼						
3							
4	XYZ Corporation Inc.						
5	Income Statement						
6	For the year ended December 31, 2003						
7							
8		Notes	2003	2002	2001	2000	1999
9	**Revenue**	20					
10	Sales		2,920	2,634	2,436	2,175	2,002
11	Services		955	725	680	600	552
12	**Total Revenue**		3,875	3,359	3,116	2,775	2,554
13							
14	**Cost of Goods Sold**						
15	Materials		855	733	703	635	646
16	Labor & Subcontractors Costs		602	537	492	455	433
17	Other Cost of goods sold		385	350	333	300	276
18	Increase / Decrease in Inventories	21	-26	-30	12	-30	31
19	**Total Cost of Goods Sold**		1,815	1,590	1,540	1,360	1,386
20							
21	**Gross Income**		2,060	1,769	1,576	1,416	1,169
22							
23	**Operating Expenses**						
24	Selling		480	441	416	399	325
25	General & Administrative	22	759	676	628	555	500
26	Other Operating Expense	23	276	261	250	215	200
27	Amortization		59	50	46	41	39
28	**Total Operating Expenses**		1,574	1,428	1,340	1,211	1,064
29							
30	**Net Income before Operations**		487	341	237	205	105
31							
32	**Operating Income (Loss)**						
33	Other income (expense)	24	33	-3	23	15	-17
34	Interest expense		75	63	66	73	60
35	**Total Operating Income**		108	60	89	88	43
36							
37	**Income (Loss) Before Income Taxes**		379	281	147	117	62
38	Provision (benefit) for income taxes	25	150	133	75	46	49
39	**Net Income (Loss) for the year**		229	148	72	71	13
40	Retained Earnings beginning of the year	26	943	796	724	652	639
41	**Retained Earnings**		1,172	944	796	723	652

3.   Press **<F11>**. A new **Chart** is created in a **Chart** worksheet:

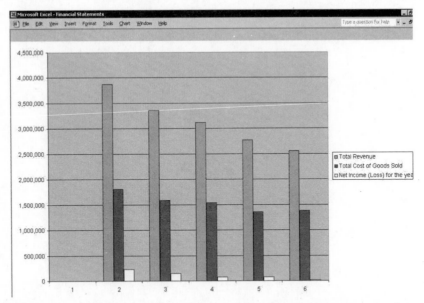

The same technique can be used to create a **Chart** that compares the balances in the Quarterly comparison report you have created, for example, a **Chart** that compares almost every subtotal item in the Quarterly Income Statement, as shown below.

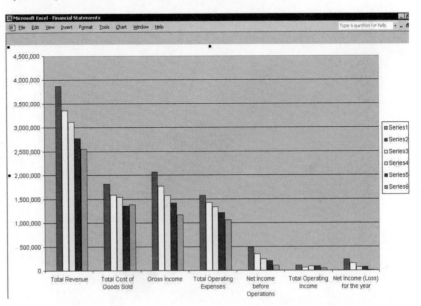

Chapter 13

Analyzing Financial Statements Using PivotTable and PivotChart Reports

About This Chapter

This chapter describes how to use **PivotTable and PivotChart** reports to analyze the company's Financial Statements. It contains examples and step-by-step instructions on how to create **PivotTable** and **PivotChart** reports, and then analyze them while summarizing the balances of the General Ledger Trial Balance accounts.

The following sections are included:

✦ **Overview**, page 225, provides an overview of the use of **PivotTable and PivotChart** reports to analyze financial reports and return summarized data to Financial Statements.

✦ **Saving Trial Balance Accumulated Balances in Different Structures**, page 225, describes how to create **PivotTable** reports from Trial Balances data stored in Excel worksheets, using two different storage structures.

✦ **Creating a PivotTable Report**, page 229, describes the steps required to create a new **PivotTable** report.

✦ **Using a PivotTable Report to Summarize Balances Used in Financial Statements Reports**, page 232, describes how to create and save a **PivotTable** report that retains a fixed structure of the **PivotTable Fields**, which is useful in preparing Financial Statements.

✦ **Using a PivotTable Report to Summarize Data According to Period**, page 238, describes how to use the **PivotTable** report to summarize the account balances of the accumulated Trial Balances by month, quarter and year.

✦ **Creating Monthly or Quarterly Income Statement Reports**, page 252, describes how to create a **PivotTable** to compare monthly Income Statement balances.

✦ **Creating a PivotChart Report to Compare Data Between Years**, page 252, describes how to create comparison reports quickly and easily using **PivotChart** reports.

✦ **Using PivotTable Reports to Create Common-size Balance Sheets**, page 255, describes how to analyze the Balance Sheet using a **PivotTable** report.

✦ **Summarizing Accumulated Trial Balance Account Balances Stored in Vertical Sequences in Adjacent Rows**, page 258, describes how to create **PivotTable** reports that use accumulated balances of the Trial Balance accounts stored in vertical sequences in adjacent rows.

✦ **Adding a Field to a PivotTable Report to Analyze the Balances by Fiscal Year-end Reporting Date**, page 266, describes how to deal with Financial reports when the ending reporting date is a fiscal year end.

Overview

In the previous chapters, you learned how to create Financial Statements using formulas combined with **Validation** lists and objects to summarize the balances of the General Ledger Trial Balances, which are stored in Excel worksheets.

In this chapter, you will learn how to use **PivotTable and PivotChart** reports to analyze financial figures and then return summarized figures to Financial Statements.

The **PivotTable and PivotChart** report technique, which analyzes data in Excel, is one of the quickest, most effective and amazing techniques provided by the Microsoft Excel program.

PivotTable and PivotChart reports enable you to summarize data, compare the summarized balances between months, quarters and years, summarize the balances from the source data by operating various functions and styles and create quick charts.

Saving Trial Balance Accumulated Balances in Different Structures

In this section, you will learn how to analyze the accumulated balances of the General Ledger Trial Balance accounts, which are stored in Excel worksheets in two different structures, using the power of **PivotTable and PivotChart** reports.

The two different structures that store the accumulated General Ledger Trial Balance account balances are described as:

✦ **Saving the accumulated balances of the Trial Balance accounts in adjacent columns** (for details, refer to page 14, *Chapter 1, Introducing Financial Statements.xls Worksheets*).

Account Number	Account Name	BS, P&L Level 3	BS, P&L Level 2	BS, P&L Level 1	January 1998	February 1998	March 1998
1011	Checking Account #1	Cash	Current Assets	Assets	1,483,475	1,667,426	1,668,093
1012	Checking Account #2	Cash	Current Assets	Assets	1,637,272	1,840,294	1,841,030
1021	Payroll Checking Accoun	Cash	Current Assets	Assets	1,032,983	1,161,073	1,161,537
1051	Savings Account #1	Cash	Current Assets	Assets	1,816,500	2,041,746	2,042,563
1061	Money Market Account #	Cash	Current Assets	Assets	2,119,250	2,382,037	2,382,990
1071	Short Term CD's	Cash	Current Assets	Assets	908,250	1,020,873	1,021,281
1091	Petty Cash	Cash	Current Assets	Assets	306,383	344,374	344,512
1111	Accounts Receivable	Accounts Receivable	Current Assets	Assets	3,102,582	3,487,302	3,488,697
1121	Allowance for doubtful ac	Accounts Receivable	Current Assets	Assets	-302,750	-340,291	-340,427
1201	Inventories for sale	Inventories	Current Assets	Assets	2,403,835	2,701,911	2,702,991
1211	Inventories for use	Inventories	Current Assets	Assets	3,493,735	3,926,958	3,928,529
1301	Prepaid expenses	Prepaid Expenses	Current Assets	Assets	345,135	387,932	388,087
1560	Patents	Patents, Trademarks and (	Investments and oth	Assets	1,211,000	1,361,164	1,361,708
1571	Marketable Stocks	Investment in Revenue Bor	Investments and oth	Assets	4,238,500	4,764,074	4,765,980
1811	Land	Land & Building	Fixed Assets	Assets	605,500	680,582	680,854
1821	Buildings	Land & Building	Fixed Assets	Assets	3,373,846	3,792,203	3,793,720
1831	Tools & Equipment	Machinery and Equipment	Fixed Assets	Assets	1,201,312	1,350,275	1,350,815
1841	Office Furninshings & Eq	Furniture and Fixtures	Fixed Assets	Assets	819,847	921,508	921,877
1891	Leasehold Improvements	Leasehold Improvements	Fixed Assets	Assets	284,585	319,874	320,001
1921	Accumulated Depreciate(	Less: Accumulated Deprec	Fixed Assets	Assets	26,642	29,946	29,958

Figure 13-1: Accumulated Balances of the Trial Balance Accounts in Adjacent Columns

+ **Saving the accumulated balances of the Trial Balance accounts in vertical sequence in adjacent rows** (for details, refer to *Summarizing Accumulated Trial Balance Account Balances Stored in Vertical Sequences in Adjacent Rows*, page 258).

	Account Number	Accout Name	BS, P&L Level 3	BS, P&L Level 2	BS, P&L Level 1	Month	Sum
2	1011	Checking Account #1	Cash	Current Assets	Assets	January 2002	1,483,475
3	1012	Checking Account #2	Cash	Current Assets	Assets	January 2002	1,637,272
4	1021	Payroll Checking Account	Cash	Current Assets	Assets	January 2002	1,032,983
5	1051	Savings Account #1	Cash	Current Assets	Assets	January 2002	1,816,500
6	1061	Money Market Account #1	Cash	Current Assets	Assets	January 2002	2,119,250
7	1071	Short Term CD's	Cash	Current Assets	Assets	January 2002	908,250
8	1091	Petty Cash	Cash	Current Assets	Assets	January 2002	306,383
9	1111	Accounts Receivable	Accounts Receivable	Current Assets	Assets	January 2002	3,102,582
10	1121	Allowance for doubtful accounts	Accounts Receivable	Current Assets	Assets	January 2002	-302,750
24	1011	Checking Account #1	Cash	Current Assets	Assets	February 2002	1,667,426
25	1012	Checking Account #2	Cash	Current Assets	Assets	February 2002	1,840,294
26	1021	Payroll Checking Account	Cash	Current Assets	Assets	February 2002	1,161,073
27	1051	Savings Account #1	Cash	Current Assets	Assets	February 2002	2,041,746
28	1061	Money Market Account #1	Cash	Current Assets	Assets	February 2002	2,382,037
29	1071	Short Term CD's	Cash	Current Assets	Assets	February 2002	1,020,873
30	1091	Petty Cash	Cash	Current Assets	Assets	February 2002	344,374
31	1111	Accounts Receivable	Accounts Receivable	Current Assets	Assets	February 2002	3,487,302
171	1011	Checking Account #1	Cash	Current Assets	Assets	March 2002	1,668,093
172	1012	Checking Account #2	Cash	Current Assets	Assets	March 2002	1,841,030
173	1021	Payroll Checking Account	Cash	Current Assets	Assets	March 2002	1,161,537
174	1051	Savings Account #1	Cash	Current Assets	Assets	March 2002	2,042,563
175	1061	Money Market Account #1	Cash	Current Assets	Assets	March 2002	2,382,990
176	1071	Short Term CD's	Cash	Current Assets	Assets	March 2002	1,021,281
177	1091	Petty Cash	Cash	Current Assets	Assets	March 2002	344,512
178	1111	Accounts Receivable	Accounts Receivable	Current Assets	Assets	March 2002	3,488,697
179	1121	Allowance for doubtful accounts	Accounts Receivable	Current Assets	Assets	March 2002	-340,427

Figure 13-2: Accumulated Balances of the Trial Balance Accounts in Vertical Sequence in Adjacent Rows

To learn more about saving and updating accumulated balances for the General Ledger Trial Balance accounts in Excel worksheets, refer to *Chapter 3, Updating the Trial Balance Data Worksheet*.

The essential difference between the two techniques described above is as follows:

+ The **Field** names in the **PivotTable** report (see the **Field** buttons on the right side of Figure 13-3 and Figure 13-4) are determined by the text entered in the top cells of each column in worksheet *21 — Trial Balances Data* (row **1** in Figure 13-2), which is the source data to create the **PivotTable** report.

The **PivotTable Fields** are divided into two categories:

❖ Data **Fields**

❖ Query, filtering and sorting **Fields**

An example of the **Fields** buttons for the second storing technique is shown in the two figures below.

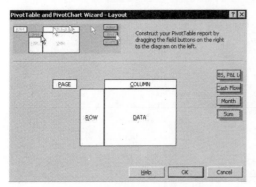

Figure 13-3: Before Field Layout   **Figure 13-4: After Field Layout**

When using the first technique to store the accumulated balances of the Trial Balance accounts in adjacent columns, the number of **Data Fields** in a **PivotTable** report equals the number of Trial Balance columns in the worksheet (the total number of data columns/fields is 72, from January 1998 to December 2003, 6 years * 12 months).

When using the second technique to store the accumulated balances of the Trial Balance accounts in vertical sequences in adjacent rows, the **PivotTable** report has only a single **Data Field** created from a single data column (the **Sum** column, as shown in Figure 13-2).

Each technique has its advantages and disadvantages. This chapter contains examples of **PivotTable** reports created using both techniques.

Creating a PivotTable Report

The technique to create a **PivotTable** report is similar for the two storing structure techniques described previously. Differences resulting from the structure used to store the Trial Balance will be described later.

Step 1: Defining a Dynamic Range Name for the Source Data Range

➢ **To define a Dynamic Range Name for the source data range:**

✦ Refer to page 63, *Chapter 3, Updating the Trial Balances Data Worksheet*.

The defined *Name* for this section is **TB_data**, which is the *Name* for the data stored using the second technique for storing the accumulated balances of the Trial Balance accounts in vertical sequences in adjacent rows (for more details, see *Using PivotTable Reports to Create Common-size Balance Sheets*, page 255).

Advantages of Creating a Dynamic Range Name

A dynamic range *Name* automatically updates the size of a data table immediately after adding new data to rows or columns, which is the first step when refreshing the PivotTable automatically (as described on page 237).

To learn more about defining a dynamic range *Name*, refer to page 27, *Chapter 2, Adjusting the Trial Balance*.

Step 2: Creating a PivotTable Report

➤ **To create a PivotTable report (in this example, the source data is created using the second (vertical) structure):**

1. Add a new worksheet by pressing **<Shift+F11>**, and change the worksheet name to *71 — PT Data In Vertical*.

2. Select worksheet *71 — PT Data In Vertical* and select cell **A1**.

3. From the *Data* menu, select **PivotTable and PivotChart Report**.

4. In the *Wizard Step 1 of 3*, ensure that the **Microsoft Excel list or database** box is checked.

5. Click **Next**.

6. In the *Wizard Step 2 of 3*, select the **Range** text box, press **<F3>**, select the *Name* **TB_data** and click **OK**.

7. Click **Next**.

8. In the *Wizard Step 3 of 3*, select cell **A1** and click **Finish**.

Step 3: Adding Fields to the PivotTable Report

➤ **To add fields to the PivotTable report:**

1. From the *PivotTable Field List* dialog box, drag the query **Fields** to **Page** (upper-left side). Query **Fields** are any **Fields** not defined as **Data Fields**, as shown below.

 NOTE:

The *PivotTable Field List* dialog box is new in Excel 2002 and later. In Excel 2000, drag a field from the **Fields** buttons at the bottom of the PivotTable toolbar; in Excel 97, drag the field in the *Layout* dialog box in Step 3 of the PivotTable Wizard.

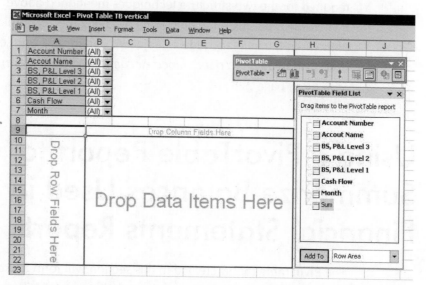

2. Drag the **Data Field** or **Data Fields** to the **Drop Data Items Here** area. The **Data Field** in the figure above is the **Sum Field**.

Using the PivotTable Report

The **PivotTable** report is a very powerful technique that has the ability to filter and summarize data quickly and easily. In this section, you will cover two subjects used by the **PivotTable** report:

✦ **Using the PivotTable report to summarize balances used in Financial Statement reports**, page 232, describes how to summarize the balances of the Trial Balance accounts to be used in the Financial Statements reports.

✦ **Use the PivotTable report to summarize data according to period**, page 238, describes how summary data can be used for data analysis, business decision making and immediate responses to queries.

In the next two sections, you will learn how to create **PivotTable** reports required for the two structure techniques mentioned above. The **PivotTable** report uses the technique of saving the accumulated balances of the Trial Balance accounts in adjacent columns as source data, as described in *Saving Trial Balance Accumulated Balances in Different Structures*, page 225.

Using a PivotTable Report to Summarize Balances Used in Financial Statements Reports

The **PivotTable** report created in this section will form a fixed structure of **Fields** while summarizing the account balances of the Trial Balance by levels.

This **PivotTable** report summarizes the figures from worksheet *21 — Trial Balances Data* to use in the Financial Statements report worksheets cells, and removes the need to use complicated formulas when creating Financial Statements reports.

	A	B	C	D	E	F	G
1				Data ▼			
2	BS, P&L Level ▼	BS, P&L Level 2 2 ▼	BS, P&L Level 3 2 ▼	Jan 2002	Feb 2002	Mar 2002	Apr 2002
3	Assets	Current Assets	Accounts Receivable	833	850	867	884
4			Cash	1372	1400	1428	1456
5			Inventories	1029	1050	1071	1092
6			Prepaid Expenses	588	600	612	624
7		Fixed Assets	Furniture and Fixtures	980	1000	1020	1040
8			Land & Building	1715	1750	1785	1820
9			Leasehold Improvements	1029	1050	1071	1092
10			Less: Accumulated Depreciation	4606	4700	4794	4888
11			Machinery and Equipment	931	950	969	988
12		Investments and other	Investment in Revenue Bond	686	700	714	728
13			Patents, Trademarks and Goodwill	637	650	663	676
14	Assets Total			14406	14700	14994	15288
15	Equity & Liabilities	Current liabilities	Accounts Payable	1274	1300	1326	1352
16			Accrued expenses - payroll	15435	15750	16065	16380
17			Current portion of long-term debt	2058	2100	2142	2184
18			Income taxes payable	3675	3750	3825	3900
19			Other accrued liabilities	2009	2050	2091	2132
20			Other current liabilities	5978	6100	6222	6344
21		Long-term Liabilities	Deferred tax liabilities	2205	2250	2295	2340
22			Loans from financial institutions	2156	2200	2244	2288
23			Pension fund loans	2254	2300	2346	2392
24		Shareholders' Equity	Common Stock	2303	2350	2397	2444
25			Paid in Capital	2352	2400	2448	2496
26			Retained earnings	2401	2450	2499	2548
27	Equity & Liabilities Total			44100	45000	45900	46800

Figure 13-5: Summary by Account Level Using a PivotTable Report

After creating the **PivotTable** report, as described in *Creating a PivotTable Report*, page 229, you should remove all unused **Fields** from the **PivotTable** report so that the table structure and **Field** position in the worksheet do not change when the **PivotTable** report is refreshed, particularly as a result of adding new **Fields** to the original source data.

Returning the Balances Summarized by the PivotTable Report to Financial Statements Report Worksheet Cells

Save the **PivotTable** worksheet in the structure described previously (as shown in Figure 13-5, page 233), and define the *Names* to be pasted into formulas in the Financial Statement worksheet cells.

➤ **To define the Names:**

1. Define a *Name* for worksheet *71 — PT Data In Vertical*, select the worksheet, and then press **<Ctrl+A>**.

2. Press **<Ctrl+F3>** and define the *Name* as **PT_data**.

3. Define the *Names* for the first three columns:

    ✦ Select column **A**, press **<Ctrl+F3>** and define the *Name* as **PT_Level1**.

    ✦ Select column **B**, press **<Ctrl+F3>** and define the *Name* as **PT_Level2**.

    ✦ Select column **C**, press **<Ctrl+F3>** and define the *Name* as **PT_Level3**.

4. Select row **2** (the title row above the columns), press **<Ctrl+F3>** and define the *Name* as **PT_Row2**.

Adding Formulas That Return the Summarized Balances from the PivotTable Report to the Balance Sheet Worksheet

In *Chapter 4, Balance Sheet*, you created a Balance Sheet report in worksheet *31 — Balance Sheet*. Copy this by dragging the worksheet tab while pressing the **<Ctrl>** key, and change the copied worksheet to *33 — Balance Sheet PT*.

For details about the structure and techniques used in worksheet *31 —
Balance Sheet*, refer to *Chapter 4, Balance Sheet*.

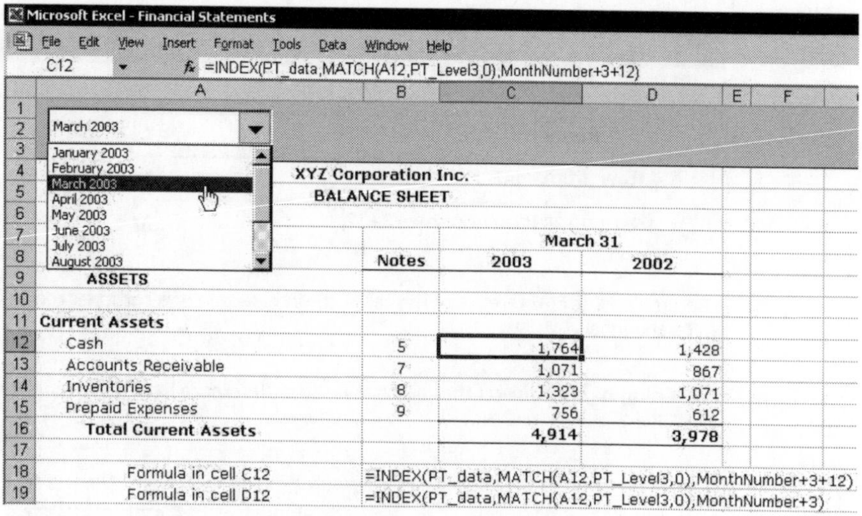

**Figure 13-6: INDEX Formula Returns Summarized Balances to Balance
Sheet Worksheet Cells**

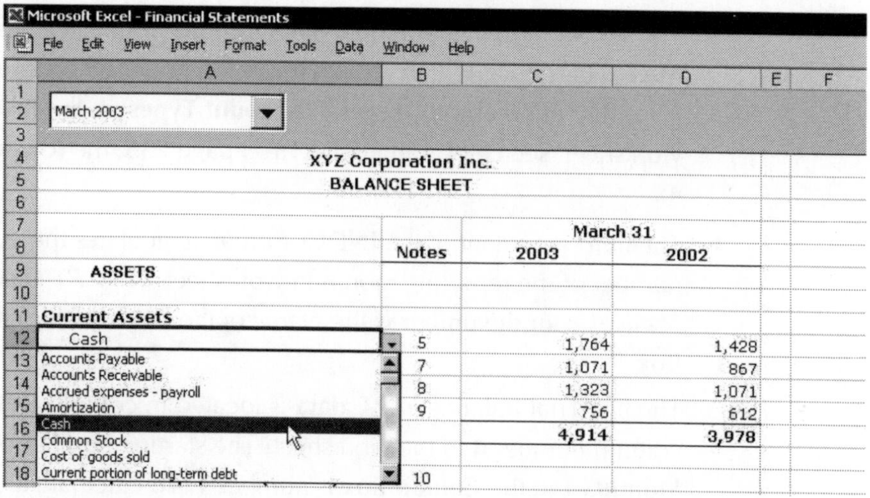

Figure 13-7: Choose an Account Type List Using Validation

The formula in cell **C12** (shown in Figure 13-6) is as follows:

=INDEX(PT_data,MATCH(A12,PT_Level3,0),MonthNumber+3+12)

The formula in cell **D12** is as follows:

=INDEX(PT_data,MATCH(A12,PT_Level3,0),MonthNumber+3)

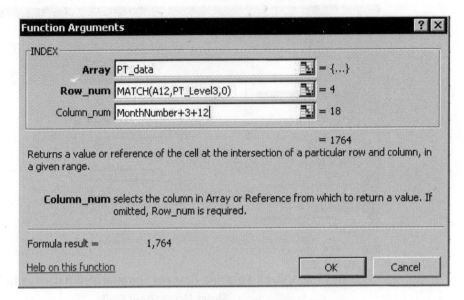

Figure 13-8: Index Function Arguments

✦   The second argument of the **INDEX** formula contains a nested
MATCH formula, which returns the cell number where the text **Cash**
is located in column **C** (**Level 3, Account Types**) in the **PivotTable**
worksheet (see cell **C4** in Figure 13-7, page 235; the row number is
4).

✦   The third argument of the **INDEX** formula calculates the column
number of the reporting month in worksheet *71 — PT Data In
Vertical*. **MonthNumber** is the *Name* of the linked cell to the **Combo
Box**.

The first Trial Balance in **PT_data** is located in column **D**, which is
column number **4** in the worksheet. The starting number of the
MonthList in the **Combo Box** is number **1**. To calculate the column
number in **PT_data**, add **3** to the number in the **MonthNumber** cell
and add **12** for the previous year (2002).

NOTE:

In this chapter, the *Name* **MonthNumber** replaces the *Name* **MonthSelectionNumber** that was defined on page 6, *Chapter 1, Introducing Financial Statements.xls Worksheets*. This is because the data used to create **PivotTable** report is **PT_data**, which has only 24 data columns (that is, 24 months starting from January 2002).

Refreshing the PivotTable Automatically

Updating the data source used by the **PivotTable** report is not automatic. You must refresh the **PivotTable** report to transfer any new or updated data from the source to the computer memory (cache). The **PivotTable** report is automatically updated from the cache memory.

To refresh the **PivotTable** report automatically add a dynamic range *Name* to the source data, see page 229 and add a **VBA** macro **Event** as explained here.

Add an **VBA** macro **Event** to worksheet *22 — TB In Vertical* that automatically refreshes the **PivotTable** report either when adding a new **Trial Balance** column to worksheet *21 —- Trial Balances Data*, or when updating the data in worksheet *22 — TB In Vertical*. The refresh option will be performed automatically when leaving worksheet *22 — TB In Vertical* by selecting a different worksheet in the workbook.

➢ **To add a VBA macro Event that refreshes the PivotTable report:**

1. Press **<Alt+F11>** to open the **VBE** (Visual Basic Editor).

2. In the **Project- VBAProject**, double-click worksheet *22 — TB In Vertical*.

3. From the left drop-down list above the **General** module sheet, select **Worksheet**.

4. From the drop-down list on the right above the module sheet, select **Deactivate Event**.

5. Enter the following code to the **Event**:

```
Private Sub Worksheet_Deactivate()
Sheets("22-TB In Vertical").PivotTables("PivotTable1").PivotCache.Refresh
End Sub
```

Using a PivotTable Report to Summarize Data According to Period

You can easily use the **PivotTable** report to summarize the accumulated balances of the Trial Balance accounts by months, quarters and years.

The **PivotTable** report allows the user to use a **Field** many times while changing the **Field** format and adding formulas to **Calculated Field**.

In Figure 13-9, all three columns from **B** to **D**, **2003** in column **B** (row **7**), **Running Balance 2003** in column **C**, and **% of Sales 2003** in column **D** were created from one data **Field** — **December 2003**. In columns **F:G**, the data **Field** is **December 2002**.

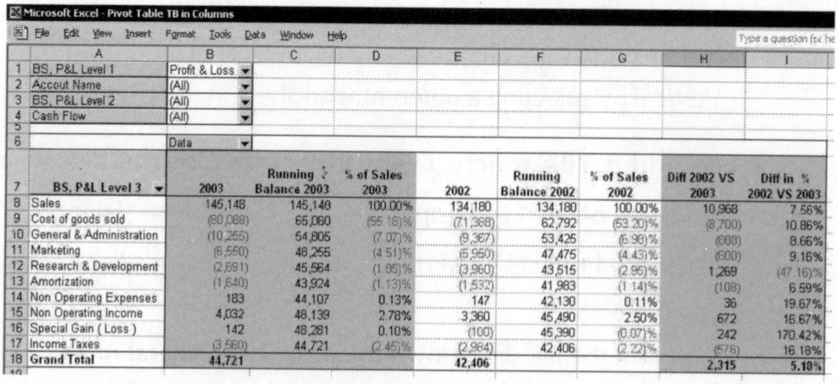

Microsoft Excel - Pivot Table TB in Columns

	A	B	C	D	E	F	G	H	I
1	BS, P&L Level 1	Profit & Loss							
2	Accout Name	(All)							
3	BS, P&L Level 2	(All)							
4	Cash Flow	(All)							
5									
6		Data							
7	BS, P&L Level 3	2003	Running Balance 2003	% of Sales 2003	2002	Running Balance 2002	% of Sales 2002	Diff 2002 VS 2003	Diff in % 2002 VS 2003
8	Sales	145,148	145,148	100.00%	134,180	134,180	100.00%	10,968	7.56%
9	Cost of goods sold	(80,088)	65,060	(55.18)%	(71,388)	62,792	(53.20)%	(8,700)	10.86%
10	General & Administration	(10,255)	54,805	(7.07)%	(9,367)	53,425	(6.98)%	(888)	8.66%
11	Marketing	(6,550)	48,255	(4.51)%	(5,950)	47,475	(4.43)%	(600)	9.16%
12	Research & Development	(2,681)	45,564	(1.85)%	(3,950)	43,515	(2.95)%	1,269	(47.16)%
13	Amortization	(1,640)	43,924	(1.13)%	(1,532)	41,983	(1.14)%	(108)	6.59%
14	Non Operating Expenses	183	44,107	0.13%	147	42,130	0.11%	36	19.67%
15	Non Operating Income	4,032	48,139	2.78%	3,360	45,490	2.50%	672	16.67%
16	Special Gain (Loss)	142	48,281	0.10%	(100)	45,390	(0.07)%	242	170.42%
17	Income Taxes	(3,560)	44,721	(2.45)%	(2,984)	42,406	(2.22)%	(576)	16.18%
18	Grand Total	44,721			42,406			2,315	5.18%

Figure 13-9: Analyzing a Comparison PivotTable Report

This is an exciting option, because it enables you to quickly and easily create a comparison report that compares two consecutive years, as shown in Figure 13-9.

In this section you will learn how to create similar report.

This **PivotTable** report contains eight columns in the data area, with each year having three data columns. This provides a total of six columns, plus two additional columns that calculate the increase (or decrease) between years.

The following steps describe how to create the **PivotTable** report to compare periods.

Step 1: Creating a PivotTable Report Containing Two Data Fields

➢ **To create a PivotTable report containing the two data Fields:**

✦ Create a **PivotTable** report in a new worksheet, *72 — PT Income Statement*, using the data in worksheet *21 — Trial balances Data* as the source data. The **PivotTable** report contains two data **Fields**, **December 2002** and **December 2003**, after formatting and modifying the **Field** names.

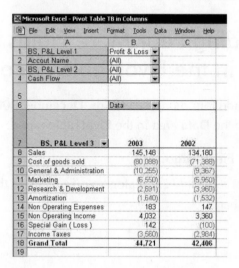

	A	B	C
	Microsoft Excel - Pivot Table TB in Columns		
	File Edit View Insert Format Tools Data Window Help		
1	BS, P&L Level 1	Profit & Loss ▼	
2	Accout Name	(All) ▼	
3	BS, P&L Level 2	(All) ▼	
4	Cash Flow	(All) ▼	
5			
6		Data ▼	
7	BS, P&L Level 3 ▼	2003	2002
8	Sales	145,148	134,180
9	Cost of goods sold	(80,088)	(71,388)
10	General & Administration	(10,255)	(9,367)
11	Marketing	(6,550)	(5,950)
12	Research & Development	(2,691)	(3,960)
13	Amortization	(1,640)	(1,532)
14	Non Operating Expenses	183	147
15	Non Operating Income	4,032	3,360
16	Special Gain (Loss)	142	(100)
17	Income Taxes	(3,560)	(2,984)
18	**Grand Total**	**44,721**	**42,406**
19			

NOTE:

Refer to *Creating a PivotTable Report*, page 229, for instructions on how to create a simple **PivotTable** report, structure and **Field** names.

➢ **To format and modify the Field name:**

1. Select a cell in the first Field data column, for example, select cell **B8** (as shown on page 239).

2. Right-click and select **Field Setting** from shortcut menu.

3. In the **Name** text box, enter **2003**.

4. Click the **Number** button and select the desired format.

5. Click **OK**.

6. Select cell **C8** and repeat steps 2 through 5, entering **2002** in step 3.

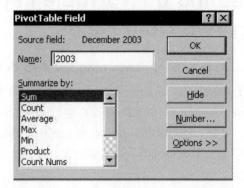

Step 2: Adding Four More Fields to the Data Area in the PivotTable Report

The next step is to add four more data **Fields**, **December 2002** and **December 2003**, to the **Data** area in the **PivotTable** report.

➢ **To add the Data Fields again:**

1. Open the *PivotTable Field List* dialog box (first icon to the right on the **PivotTable** toolbar).

2. From the *PivotTable Field List* dialog box, drag each **Field** two more times to the **Data** area of the **PivotTable** report, as shown.

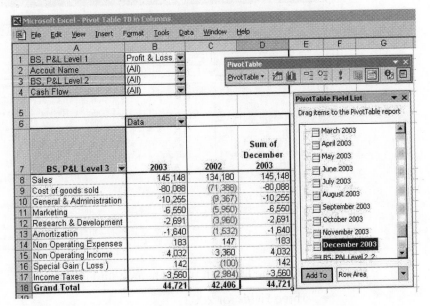

NOTE:

The *PivotTable Field List* dialog box is new in Excel 2002 and later. In Excel 2000, drag a field from the **Fields** buttons at the bottom of the PivotTable toolbar; in Excel 97, drag the field in the *Layout* dialog box in Step 3 of the PivotTable Wizard.

The result is shown below.

	A	B	C	D	E	F	G
	Microsoft Excel - Pivot Table TB in Columns						
	File Edit View Insert Format Tools Data Window Help						
1	BS, P&L Level 1	Profit & Loss ▼					
2	Accout Name	(All) ▼					
3	BS, P&L Level 2	(All) ▼					
4	Cash Flow	(All) ▼					
5							
6		Data ▼					
7	BS, P&L Level 3 ▼	2003	2002	Sum of December 2003	Sum of December 2003 2	Sum of December 2002	Sum of December 2002 2
8	Sales	145,148	134,180	145,148	145148	134180	134180
9	Cost of goods sold	(80,088)	(71,388)	-80,088	-80088	-71388	-71388
10	General & Administration	(10,255)	(9,367)	-10,255	-10255	-9367	-9367
11	Marketing	(6,550)	(5,950)	-6,550	-6550	-5950	-5950
12	Research & Development	(2,691)	(3,960)	-2,691	-2691	-3960	-3960
13	Amortization	(1,640)	(1,532)	-1,640	-1640	-1532	-1532
14	Non Operating Expenses	183	147	183	183	147	147
15	Non Operating Income	4,032	3,360	4,032	4032	3360	3360
16	Special Gain (Loss)	142	(100)	142	142	-100	-100
17	Income Taxes	(3,560)	(2,984)	-3,560	-3560	-2984	-2984
18	**Grand Total**	**44,721**	**42,406**	**44,721**	**44721**	**42406**	**42406**
19							

3. Organize the **Fields** in the **Data** area into two groups:

   ✦ Three **Fields** for 2002

   ✦ Three **Fields** for 2003

   This is done by dragging the **Field** position in the **PivotTable** report.

4. Select the title cell **Field**, for example, cell **D7** in the figure in step 2, and drag the **Field** using the mouse to its new position in the **Data** area.

Step 3: Changing the Calculation Method

In this step, you will change the calculation method of the added **Fields**.

➢ **To change Field 2 to calculate a running balance in years 2002 and 2003:**

1. Select a cell in one of the newly dragged data **Fields**, the **December 2003 Field**.

2. Click **Field Settings** in the **PivotTable** toolbar.

3. In the **PivotTable Field**, in the **Name** box, type **Running Balance 2003**.

4. Click **Options**, and select **Running Total in** from **Show data as**.

5. In **Base Field**, select the **Field** positioned in the **PivotTable** as a row, **BS, P&L Level3**.

6. Repeat steps 1 through 5 and modify the second **December 2002 Field**.

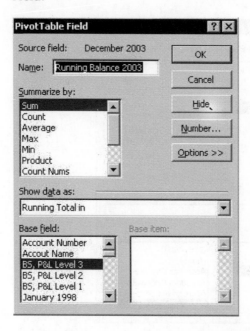

➤ **To change Field 3 to calculate the percentage of December 2002 and December 2003, (that is percentage of the Profit and Loss account types according to sales revenue):**

1. Select a cell in the third dragged data **Field**, the **December 2003 Field**.

2. Click **Field Settings** in the **PivotTable** toolbar.

3. In the **Name** box, type the text **% Of Sales 2003**.

4. In the **PivotTable Field**, select **% Of** from **Show data as**.

5. Select the **BS, P&L Level3 Field** from **Base Field**.

6. Select **Sales** in **Base Items**.

7. Change the percentage formatting, click **Number**, and then select **Custom** from the **Type** box.

8. Type **0.00% ;[RED](0.00) %** (positive percent colored black, negative percent colored red) and click **OK**.

9. Click **OK**.

10. Repeat steps 1 through 9 and format the last **Field** of the **December 2002**.

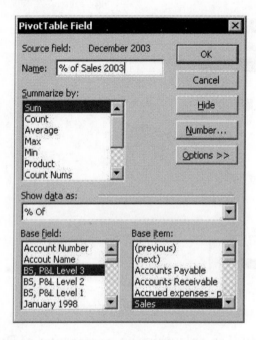

Step 4: Adding Two More Columns for Analysis and Comparison Between Years

In this step, you will learn how to add two more columns for analysis and comparison between years, as shown in columns **H:I** in Figure 13-10.

BS, P&L Level 3	2003	Running Balance 2003	% of Sales 2003	2002	Running Balance 2002	% of Sales 2002	Diff 2002 VS 2003	Diff In % 2002 VS 2003
Sales	145,148	145,148	100.00%	134,180	134,180	100.00%	10,968	7.56%
Cost of goods sold	(80,088)	65,060	(55.18)%	(71,388)	62,792	(53.20)%	(8,700)	10.86%
General & Administration	(10,255)	54,805	(7.07)%	(9,367)	53,425	(6.98)%	(888)	8.66%
Marketing	(6,550)	48,255	(4.51)%	(5,950)	47,475	(4.43)%	(600)	9.16%
Research & Development	(2,691)	45,564	(1.85)%	(3,960)	43,515	(2.95)%	1,269	(47.16)%
Amortization	(1,640)	43,924	(1.13)%	(1,532)	41,983	(1.14)%	(108)	6.59%
Non Operating Expenses	183	44,107	0.13%	147	42,130	0.11%	36	19.67%
Non Operating Income	4,032	48,139	2.78%	3,360	45,490	2.50%	672	16.67%
Special Gain (Loss)	142	48,281	0.10%	(100)	45,390	(0.07)%	242	170.42%
Income Taxes	(3,560)	44,721	(2.45)%	(2,984)	42,406	(2.22)%	(576)	16.18%
Grand Total	**44,721**			**42,406**			**2,315**	**5.18%**

Figure 13-10: PivotTable Report After Adding Two New Analyzing Fields

This is done in two stages:

✦ Adding a new **Field** that calculates the difference between the two years.

✦ Adding a new **Field** that calculates the percentage difference between the two years.

➢ **To add a Field that calculates the difference between the two years:**

1. Select a cell in one of the **PivotTable** report **Data** area.

2. Press **<Alt+P>**,

   OR

   Click the **PivotTable** icon in the **PivotTable** toolbar, select **Formulas**, and the select **Calculated Field**, as shown.

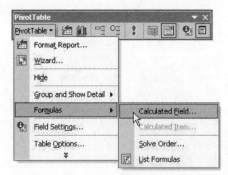

3. In the *Insert Calculated Field* dialog box, in the **Name** text box, enter a name for the formula: **2002 VS 2003**.

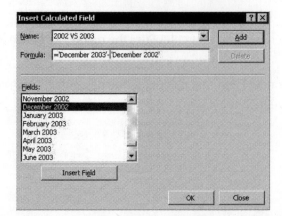

4. In the *Fields* area, select the **December 2003 Field** and click **Insert Field**.

5. Enter a minus (-) sign in the **Formula** box.

6. Select the **Field** name **December 2002** and click **Insert Field**.

7. Click **OK**.

➤ **To add a Field that calculates the percentage difference between the two years:**

NOTE:

To add a **Field** containing a formula that calculates the changes (increase/decrease) in percentage between the years **Fields**, repeat the procedure on the previous page.

1. Type **% off 2002 VS 2003** in the **Name** box as the *Name* for the calculated **Field**.

2. Select the **2002 VS 2003 Field** in the *Fields* dialog box and click the **Insert Field** button.

3. Insert a divider sign (/).

4. Select the **December 2003 Field**, click **Insert Field**, and then click **OK**.

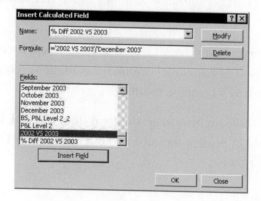

The final result should look like this:

BS, P&L Level 3	2003	Running Balance 2003	% of Sales 2003	2002	Running Balance 2002	% of Sales 2002	Diff 2002 VS 2003	Diff in % 2002 VS 2003
Sales	145,148	145,148	100.00%	134,180	134,180	100.00%	10,968	7.56%
Cost of goods sold	(80,090)	65,060	(55.16)%	(71,388)	62,792	(53.20)%	(8,700)	10.86%
General & Administration	(10,255)	54,805	(7.07)%	(9,367)	53,425	(6.98)%	(888)	8.66%
Marketing	(6,650)	48,255	(4.51)%	(5,950)	47,475	(4.43)%	(600)	9.16%
Research & Development	(2,691)	45,564	(1.85)%	(3,960)	43,515	(2.95)%	1,269	(47.16)%
Amortization	(1,640)	43,924	(1.13)%	(1,532)	41,983	(1.14)%	(108)	6.59%
Non Operating Expenses	183	44,107	0.13%	147	42,130	0.11%	36	19.67%
Non Operating Income	4,032	48,139	2.78%	3,360	45,490	2.50%	672	16.67%
Special Gain (Loss)	142	48,281	0.10%	(100)	45,390	(0.07)%	242	170.42%
Income Taxes	(3,560)	44,721	(2.45)%	(2,984)	42,406	(2.22)%	(576)	16.18%
Grand Total	44,721			42,406			2,315	5.18%

Step 5: Creating a New Field to Present the Subtotals

The **PivotTable** report contains the summary of the **Accounts Types, Level 3**.

There are more important subtotal levels, such as **Gross Income** and **Gross Profit**, as well as additional essential calculations required to analyze the company's business results.

In this step you will learn how to group items from **BS, P&L Level3** to create a new **Field** to present the subtotals of **Profit & Loss Level 1**, as shown in Figure 13-11.

	A	B	C	D	E	F
	Microsoft Excel - Pivot Table TB in Columns1					
	File Edit View Insert Format Tools Data Window Help					
1	BS, P&L Level 1	Profit & Loss ▼				
2	Accout Name	(All) ▼				
3	BS, P&L Level 2	(All) ▼				
4	Cash Flow	(All) ▼				
5						
6			Data ▼			
7	**Profit & Loss Level 1** ▼	**BS, P&L Level 3** ▼	**2003**	**2002**	**Diff 2002 VS 2003**	**Diff in % 2002 VS 2003**
8	Gross Income	Sales	145,148	134,180	10,968	7.56%
9		Cost of goods sold	(80,088)	(71,388)	(8,700)	10.86%
10	**Gross Income Total**		**65,060**	**62,792**	**2,268**	**3.49%**
11	Operating Expenses	General & Administration	(10,255)	(9,367)	(888)	8.66%
12		Marketing	(6,550)	(5,950)	(600)	9.16%
13		Research & Development	(2,691)	(3,960)	1,269	(47.16)%
14		Amortization	(1,640)	(1,532)	(108)	6.59%
15	**Operating Expenses Total**		**(21,136)**	**(20,809)**	**(327)**	**1.55%**
16	Other Income (expenses)	Non Operating Expenses	183	147	36	19.67%
17		Non Operating Income	4,032	3,360	672	16.67%
18		Special Gain (Loss)	142	(100)	242	170.42%
19	**Other Income (expenses) Total**		**4,357**	**3,407**	**950**	**21.80%**
20	Income Taxes	Income Taxes	(3,560)	(2,984)	(576)	16.18%
21	**Income Taxes Total**		**(3,560)**	**(2,984)**	**(576)**	**16.18%**
22	**Net Income (Loss) for the year**		**44,721**	**42,406**	**2,315**	**5.18%**
23						

Figure 13-11: PivotTable Report After Adding New Level 1 Group Field

➢ **To add new group Field:**

1. Copy worksheet *72 — PT Income Statement* by clicking the worksheet tab, pressing **<Ctrl>**, dragging it and then releasing the **<Ctrl>** key and the mouse.

2. Change the worksheet name to *73 — PivotTable PL Group*.

3. Ensure that the **PivotTable** report has only one **Row Field** (the **BS, P&L Level3 Field**), as shown in the figure below (**Row Field** is on the left side of the **Data** area in the **PivotTable** report).

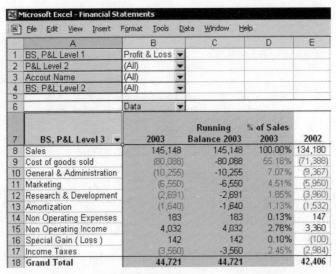

4. Select **Sales** and **Cost of goods sold** from the **BS, P&L Level 3 Field**.

5. Right-click and select **Group and Show Detail**.

6. Choose **Group**.

7. Change the text **Group1** in cell **A7** to **Gross Income** by typing the new text into the cell.

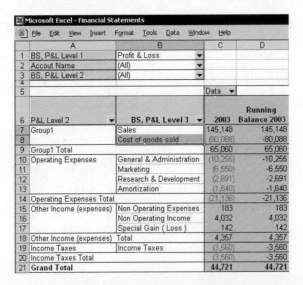

8. Select additional items from the **BS, P&L Level 3 Field** and perform the **Group** action to the group items.

9. Drag the **BS, P&L Level3 Field** to the **Page** area (upper corner above the **PivotTable** report).

The final result should look like this:

Microsoft Excel - Pivot Table TB in Columns1				
File Edit View Insert Format Tools Data Window Help				
	A	B	C	D	E
1	BS, P&L Level 1	Profit & Loss ▼			
2	Accout Name	(All) ▼			
3	BS, P&L Level 3	(All) ▼			
4	BS, P&L Level 2	(All) ▼			
5	Cash Flow	(All) ▼			
6					
7		Data ▼			
8	**Profit & Loss Level 1** ▼	**2003**	**2002**	**Diff 2002 VS 2003**	**Diff in % 2002 VS 2003**
9	Gross Income	65,060	62,792	2,268	3.49%
10	Operating Expenses	(21,136)	(20,809)	(327)	1.55%
11	Other Income (expenses)	4,357	3,407	950	21.80%
12	Income Taxes	(3,560)	(2,984)	(576)	16.18%
13	**Net Income (Loss) for the year**	**44,721**	**42,406**	**2,315**	**5.18%**
14					

Creating Monthly or Quarterly Income Statement Reports

Add a comparison of quarterly Income Statement reports by adding the quarterly month columns **March 2003**, **June 2003**, **September 2003**, and so on, to the **PivotTable** report.

➢ **To create a PivotTable report to compare monthly Income Statement balances figures:**

1. Copy worksheet *73 — PivotTable PL Group* by clicking the worksheet tab, pressing **<Ctrl>**, dragging it and then releasing the **<Ctrl>** key and the mouse.

2. Change the worksheet name to *74 — PivotTable Monthly*.

3. Add the months you want to compare or add the quarterly months (March, June, and so on) from *PivotTable Field List* dialog box to the **Data** area in the **Pivot Table** report. (If the *PivotTable Field List* dialog box is not visible, click the rightmost icon in the **PivotTable** toolbar.)

NOTE:

The *PivotTable Field List* dialog box is new in Excel 2002 and later. In Excel 2000, drag a field from the **Fields** buttons at the bottom of the PivotTable toolbar; in Excel 97, drag the field in the *Layout* dialog box in Step 3 of the PivotTable Wizard.

Microsoft Excel - Financial Statements

File　Edit　View　Insert　Format　Tools　Data　Window　Help

	A	B	C	D	E	F	G	H	I	J
1	Accout Name	(All)								
2	BS, P&L Level 2	(All)								
3	BS, P&L Level 1	Profit & Loss								
4										
5			Data							
6	BS, P&L Level 3 2	BS, P&L Level 3	Q1 2002	Q2 2002	Q3 2002	Q4 2002	Q1 2003	Q2 2003	Q3 2003	Q4 2003
7	Gross Income	Sales	125,954	128,696	131,438	134,180	136,922	139,664	142,406	145,148
8		Cost of goods sold	(64,863)	(67,038)	(69,213)	(71,388)	(73,563)	(75,738)	(77,913)	(80,088)
9	Gross Income Total		61,091	61,658	62,225	62,792	63,359	63,926	64,493	65,060
10	Operating Expenses	General & Administration	(8,701)	(8,923)	(9,145)	(9,367)	(9,589)	(9,811)	(10,033)	(10,255)
11		Marketing	(5,500)	(5,650)	(5,800)	(5,950)	(6,100)	(6,250)	(6,400)	(6,550)
12		Research & Development	(3,365)	(3,564)	(3,762)	(3,960)	(1,719)	(2,043)	(2,367)	(2,691)
13		Amortization	(1,451)	(1,478)	(1,505)	(1,532)	(1,559)	(1,586)	(1,613)	(1,640)
14	Operating Expenses Total		(19,018)	(19,615)	(20,212)	(20,809)	(18,967)	(19,690)	(20,413)	(21,136)
15	Other Operating Income	Non Operating Expenses	120	129	138	147	156	165	174	183
16		Non Operating Income	2,856	3,024	3,192	3,360	3,528	3,696	3,864	4,032
17		Special Gain (Loss)	121	124	127	(100)	133	136	139	142
18	Other Operating Income Total		3,097	3,277	3,457	3,407	3,817	3,997	4,177	4,357
19	Income Taxes	Income Taxes	(2,552)	(2,696)	(2,840)	(2,984)	(3,128)	(3,272)	(3,416)	(3,560)
20	Income Taxes Total		(2,552)	(2,696)	(2,840)	(2,984)	(3,128)	(3,272)	(3,416)	(3,560)
21	Grand Total		42,618	42,624	42,630	42,406	45,081	44,961	44,841	44,721

4. After adding the months you want to compare and analyze, add the calculated **Fields** and format according to the techniques explained in *To format and modify the Field name*, page 240.

Creating a PivotChart Report to Compare Data Between Years

Selecting a cell in the **Data** area of the **PivotTable** report and pressing **<F11>** creates a **PivotChart** report (new in Excel 2000 and later) in a new worksheet of the workbook.

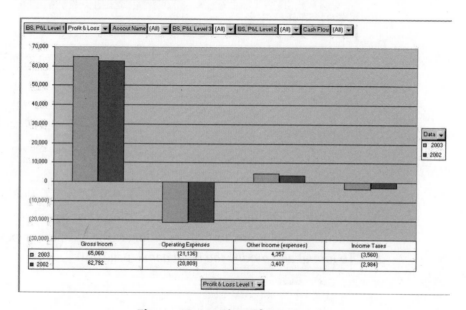

Figure 13-12: PivotChart Report

The **PivotChart** report shown in Figure 13-12 has a Data Table at the bottom. Pressing **<F11>** does not automatically create a Data Table; to add it, follow the procedure below.

➢ **To add the option Show Data Table to the PivotChart report:**

1. From the *Chart* menu, select **Chart Options**.

2. From the *Chart Options* dialog box, select the **Data Table** tab.

3. Select **Show Data Table Option** and click **OK**.

Using PivotTable Reports to Create Common-size Balance Sheets

With the **PivotTable** report technique, you can create a common-size Balance Sheet.

Add two **Fields** to the **Data** area:

- Diff 2002 VS 2003.
- Diff in % 2002 VS 2003.

For details regarding how to add these two **Fields**, refer to *Step 4: Adding Two More Columns for Analysis and Comparison Between Years*, page 245.

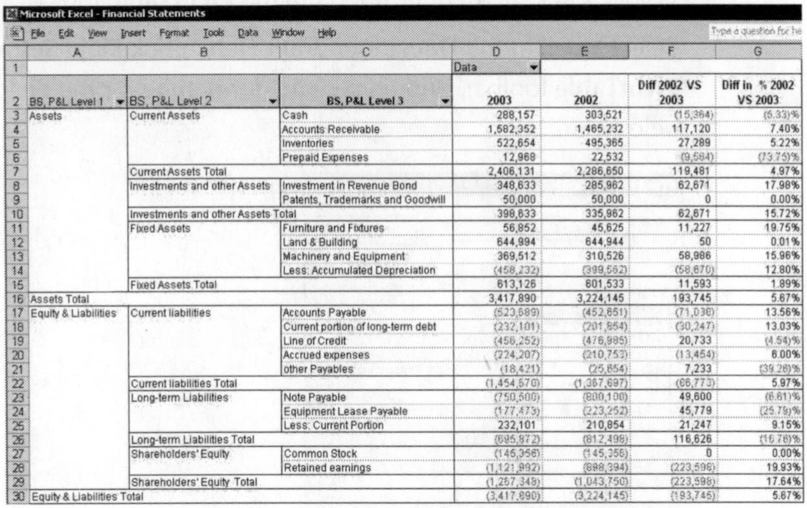

Microsoft Excel - Financial Statements

File Edit View Insert Format Tools Data Window Help

	A	B	C	D	E	F	G
1				Data			
2	BS, P&L Level 1	BS, P&L Level 2	BS, P&L Level 3	2003	2002	Diff 2002 VS 2003	Diff in % 2002 VS 2003
3	Assets	Current Assets	Cash	288,157	303,521	(15,364)	(5.33)%
4			Accounts Receivable	1,582,352	1,465,232	117,120	7.40%
5			Inventories	522,654	495,365	27,289	5.22%
6			Prepaid Expenses	12,968	22,532	(9,564)	(73.75)%
7		Current Assets Total		2,406,131	2,286,650	119,481	4.97%
8		Investments and other Assets	Investment in Revenue Bond	348,633	285,962	62,671	17.98%
9			Patents, Trademarks and Goodwill	50,000	50,000	0	0.00%
10		Investments and other Assets Total		398,633	335,962	62,671	15.72%
11		Fixed Assets	Furniture and Fixtures	56,852	45,625	11,227	19.75%
12			Land & Building	644,994	644,944	50	0.01%
13			Machinery and Equipment	369,512	310,526	58,986	15.96%
14			Less: Accumulated Depreciation	(458,232)	(399,562)	(58,670)	12.80%
15		Fixed Assets Total		613,126	601,533	11,593	1.89%
16	Assets Total			3,417,890	3,224,145	193,745	5.67%
17	Equity & Liabilities	Current liabilities	Accounts Payable	(523,689)	(452,651)	(71,038)	13.56%
18			Current portion of long-term debt	(232,101)	(201,854)	(30,247)	13.03%
19			Line of Credit	(456,252)	(476,985)	20,733	(4.54)%
20			Accrued expenses	(224,207)	(210,753)	(13,454)	6.00%
21			other Payables	(18,421)	(25,654)	7,233	(39.26)%
22		Current liabilities Total		(1,454,670)	(1,367,897)	(86,773)	5.97%
23		Long-term Liabilities	Note Payable	(750,500)	(800,100)	49,600	(6.61)%
24			Equipment Lease Payable	(177,473)	(223,252)	45,779	(25.79)%
25			Less: Current Portion	232,101	210,854	21,247	9.15%
26		Long-term Liabilities Total		(695,872)	(812,498)	116,626	(16.76)%
27		Shareholders' Equity	Common Stock	(145,356)	(145,356)	0	0.00%
28			Retained earnings	(1,121,992)	(898,394)	(223,598)	19.93%
29		Shareholders' Equity Total		(1,267,348)	(1,043,750)	(223,598)	17.64%
30	Equity & Liabilities Total			(3,417,890)	(3,224,145)	(193,745)	5.67%

Figure 13-13: Common-size Balance Sheet

If you check the percentages in cells **G16** and **G30**, you will notice that the percentages of the lines **Assets Total** and **Equity & Liabilities Total** do not equal 100%. The procedure below explains how to get around this problem.

➢ **To add a Field that calculates the subtotals and balance items as a percentage of the total Assets and Equity & Liabilities:**

1. Follow the procedure in *Step 1: Creating a PivotTable Report Containing Two Data Fields*, page 239 and create new PivotTable report in a new worksheet, changing its name to *75 — PivotTable Assets.*

2. Copy worksheet *75 — PivotTable Assets* and change the worksheet name to *76 — PivotTable Liabilities and Equity.*

3. In the first new worksheet, drag the three summary level **Fields** from the **Page** area to the **Row** area, as shown in Figure 13-13.

4. From the *PivotTable Field List* dialog box, drag the **December 2002 Field** and the **December 2003 Field** to the **Data** area in the **PivotTable** report. (If the *PivotTable Field List* dialog box is not visible, click the rightmost icon in the **PivotTable** toolbar.)

5. Select a cell in the **December 2003 Field**, click **Field Settings** (in the **PivotTable** toolbar) and change the formatting for the **Field**, as shown below.

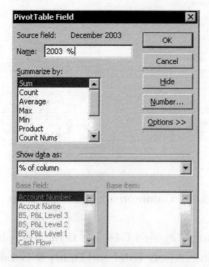

6. Repeat steps 1 through 4 to format the **December 2002 Field**.

7. Repeat the steps above for worksheet *76 — PivotTable Liabilities and Equity.*

The results of this procedure are shown in the following figures.

The **PivotTable** in the first figure contains **Assets** data. The second figure shows **Liabilities & Equity** data.

As can be seen from cells **E16** and **G16** in Figure 13-14 and Figure 13-15, the totals are 100%.

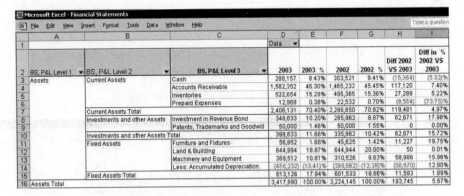

BS, P&L Level 1	BS, P&L Level 2	BS, P&L Level 3	2003	2003 %	2002	2002 %	Diff 2002 VS 2003	Diff in % 2002 VS 2003
Assets	Current Assets	Cash	288,157	8.43%	303,521	9.41%	(15,364)	(5.33)%
		Accounts Receivable	1,582,352	46.30%	1,465,232	45.45%	117,120	7.40%
		Inventories	522,654	15.29%	495,365	15.36%	27,289	5.22%
		Prepaid Expenses	12,968	0.38%	22,532	0.70%	(9,564)	(73.75)%
	Current Assets Total		2,406,131	70.40%	2,286,650	70.92%	119,481	4.97%
	Investments and other Assets	Investment in Revenue Bond	348,633	10.20%	285,962	8.87%	62,671	17.98%
		Patents, Trademarks and Goodwill	50,000	1.46%	50,000	1.55%	0	0.00%
	Investments and other Assets Total		398,633	11.66%	335,962	10.42%	62,671	15.72%
	Fixed Assets	Furniture and Fixtures	56,852	1.66%	45,625	1.42%	11,227	19.75%
		Land & Building	644,994	18.87%	644,944	20.00%	50	0.01%
		Machinery and Equipment	369,512	10.81%	310,526	9.63%	58,986	15.96%
		Less: Accumulated Depreciation	(458,232)	(13.41)%	(399,562)	(12.39)%	(58,670)	12.80%
	Fixed Assets Total		613,126	17.94%	601,533	18.66%	11,593	1.89%
Assets Total			3,417,890	100.00%	3,224,145	100.00%	193,745	5.67%

Figure 13-14: PivotTable Report Showing the Assets Category

BS, P&L Level 1	BS, P&L Level 2	BS, P&L Level 3	2003	2003 %	2002	2002 %	Diff 2002 VS 2003	Diff in % 2002 VS 2003
Liabilities & Equity	Current liabilities	Accounts Payable	(523,689)	15.32%	(452,651)	14.04%	(71,038)	13.56%
		Current portion of long-term debt	(232,101)	6.79%	(201,854)	6.26%	(30,247)	13.03%
		Line of Credit	(456,252)	13.35%	(476,985)	14.79%	20,733	(4.54)%
		Accrued expenses	(224,207)	6.56%	(210,753)	6.54%	(13,454)	6.00%
		other Payables	(18,421)	0.54%	(25,654)	0.80%	7,233	(39.26)%
	Current liabilities Total		(1,454,870)	42.56%	(1,367,897)	42.43%	(86,773)	5.97%
	Long-term Liabilities	Note Payable	(750,500)	21.96%	(800,100)	24.82%	49,600	(6.61)%
		Equipment Lease Payable	(177,473)	5.19%	(223,252)	6.92%	45,779	(25.79)%
		Less: Current Portion	232,101	(6.79)%	210,854	(6.54)%	21,247	9.15%
	Long-term Liabilities Total		(695,872)	20.36%	(812,498)	25.20%	116,626	(16.76)%
	Shareholders' Equity	Common Stock	(145,356)	4.25%	(145,356)	4.51%	0	0.00%
		Retained earnings	(1,121,992)	32.83%	(898,394)	27.86%	(223,598)	19.93%
	Shareholders' Equity Total		(1,267,348)	37.08%	(1,043,750)	32.37%	(223,598)	17.64%
Liabilities & Equity Total			(3,417,890)	100.00%	(3,224,145)	100.00%	(193,745)	5.67%

Figure 13-15: PivotTable Report Showing the Liabilities & Equity Category

Summarizing Accumulated Trial Balance Account Balances Stored in Vertical Sequences in Adjacent Rows

In this section, you will learn to create a **PivotTable** report that uses accumulated balances of the Trial Balances accounts stored in vertical sequences in adjacent rows as its source data.

	Account Number	Accout Name	BS, P&L Level 3	BS, P&L Level 2	BS, P&L Level 1	Month	Sum
2	1011	Checking Account #1	Cash	Current Assets	Assets	January 2002	1,483,475
3	1012	Checking Account #2	Cash	Current Assets	Assets	January 2002	1,637,272
4	1021	Payroll Checking Account	Cash	Current Assets	Assets	January 2002	1,032,983
5	1051	Savings Account #1	Cash	Current Assets	Assets	January 2002	1,816,500
6	1061	Money Market Account #1	Cash	Current Assets	Assets	January 2002	2,119,250
7	1071	Short Term CD's	Cash	Current Assets	Assets	January 2002	908,250
8	1091	Petty Cash	Cash	Current Assets	Assets	January 2002	306,383
9	1111	Accounts Receivable	Accounts Receivable	Current Assets	Assets	January 2002	3,102,582
10	1121	Allowance for doubtful accounts	Accounts Receivable	Current Assets	Assets	January 2002	-302,750
24	1011	Checking Account #1	Cash	Current Assets	Assets	February 2002	1,667,426
25	1012	Checking Account #2	Cash	Current Assets	Assets	February 2002	1,840,294
26	1021	Payroll Checking Account	Cash	Current Assets	Assets	February 2002	1,161,073
27	1051	Savings Account #1	Cash	Current Assets	Assets	February 2002	2,041,746
28	1061	Money Market Account #1	Cash	Current Assets	Assets	February 2002	2,362,037
29	1071	Short Term CD's	Cash	Current Assets	Assets	February 2002	1,020,873
30	1091	Petty Cash	Cash	Current Assets	Assets	February 2002	344,374
31	1111	Accounts Receivable	Accounts Receivable	Current Assets	Assets	February 2002	3,487,302
171	1011	Checking Account #1	Cash	Current Assets	Assets	March 2002	1,668,093
172	1012	Checking Account #2	Cash	Current Assets	Assets	March 2002	1,841,030
173	1021	Payroll Checking Account	Cash	Current Assets	Assets	March 2002	1,161,537
174	1051	Savings Account #1	Cash	Current Assets	Assets	March 2002	2,042,563
175	1061	Money Market Account #1	Cash	Current Assets	Assets	March 2002	2,382,990
176	1071	Short Term CD's	Cash	Current Assets	Assets	March 2002	1,021,281
177	1091	Petty Cash	Cash	Current Assets	Assets	March 2002	344,512
178	1111	Accounts Receivable	Accounts Receivable	Current Assets	Assets	March 2002	3,488,697
179	1121	Allowance for doubtful accounts	Accounts Receivable	Current Assets	Assets	March 2002	-340,427

Figure 13-16: Accumulated Balances of the Trial Balances Accounts in Vertical Sequence in Adjacent Rows

➤ **To store the Accumulated Balances of the Trial Balances accounts in vertical sequences in adjacent rows:**

1. Press **<Shift+F11>** and insert a new worksheet, changing the worksheet name to *22 — TB In Vertical*.

2. Copy the final adjusted Trial Balance (as described in *Chapter 2, Adjusted the Trial Balance*) and paste it into worksheet *22 — TB In Vertical,* as shown below.

	A	B	C	D	E
	Microsoft Excel - Financial Statements				
	File Edit View Insert Format Tools Data Window Help				
1	**Account Number**	**Accout Name**	**Sum**		
2	1011	Checking Account #1	1,483,475		
3	1012	Checking Account #2	1,637,272		
4	1021	Payroll Checking Account	1,032,983		
5	1051	Savings Account #1	1,816,500		
6	1061	Money Market Account #1	2,119,250		
7	1071	Short Term CD's	908,250		
8	1091	Petty Cash	306,383		
9	1111	Accounts Receivable	3,102,582		
10	1121	Allowance for doubtful accounts	-302,750		

3. Insert four columns before column **C** (the column with the title **Sum**).

4. Select worksheet *21 — Trial Balance Data,* and copy cells **C1:E2** (cells **C1:E1** contain the titles and cells **C2:E2** contain the **Validation** list and formulas; for more details, see page 14, *Chapter 1, Introducing Financial Statements.xls Worksheets*).

5. Select the new worksheet you added and paste the copied cells to cells **C1:E2**.

6. Type into cell **F1** the title **Month**.

7. Type into cell **F2** the month-ending date for the final adjusted Trial Balance.

8. Select column **F**, press **<Ctrl+1>**, select the **Number** tab, and then select **Custom**.

9. In the **Type** box, type **mmmm yyyy** and press **OK**.

10. Copy cells **C2:F2** and paste them downwards.

11. Add more previous Trial Balances from worksheet *21 — Trial Balances Data.* When you have finished, the worksheet should look like Figure 13-16, page 259.

After you have stored the accumulated balances of the Trial Balances accounts in vertical sequence in adjacent rows, you are ready to create a **PivotTable** report.

➢ **To create a PivotTable report:**

1. Define a dynamic *Name* for the Trial Balances data, as explained on page 27, *Chapter 2, Adjusting the Trial Balance.*

2. Enter the formula:

    =OFFSET(TB Data In Vertical! $A$1,0,0,COUNTA(TB Data In Vertical!$A:$A),COUNTA(TB Data In Vertical!$1:$1))

    into the **Refers to** box in the *Define Name* dialog box. (The worksheet name **TB_Data** in the formula is the name of the new worksheet.)

3. Create a **PivotTable** report in worksheet *71 — PT Data In Vertical*, as described in *Creating a PivotTable Report,* page 229.

➢ **To analyze the balances for the accounts in the Trial Balances by monthly, quarterly and annual terms:**

NOTE:
This procedure assumes that the calendar year end date is December 31st.

1. Select any cell in the **PivotTable** report and drag the **Month Field** from the **Page** area (left corner) to the **Row** area (left side of the **Data** area).

2. Select one of the cells in the **Month Field**, for example, **A10**.

3. Right-click and select **Group** from **Group and Show Details**.

4. In the *Grouping* dialog box, select **Months**, **Quarters**, and **Years**, as shown, and click **OK**.

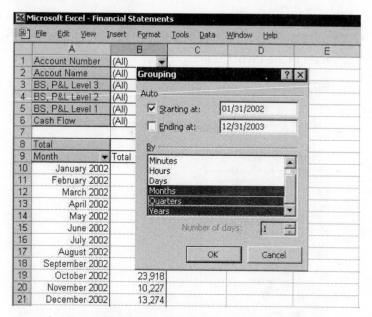

5. Drag the **Years Field** from the **Row** area to the **Column** area (above the Data area) in the **PivotTable** report.

The results are shown in the figure below.

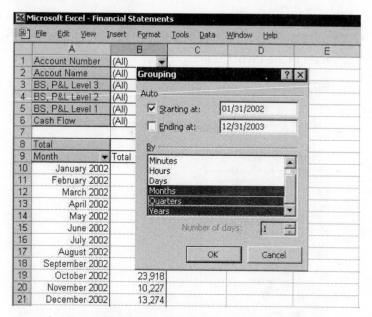

➤ **To add a calculated Field and present the Balances figures in percentages to the PivotTable report:**

1. Drag the **Sum Field** from the *PivotTable Field List* to the **Data** area. (If the *PivotTable Field List* dialog box is not visible, click the rightmost icon in the **PivotTable** toolbar.)

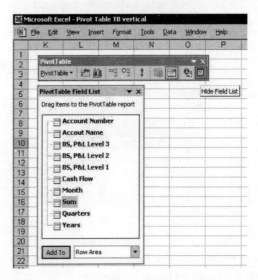

 NOTE:

The *PivotTable Field List* dialog box is new in Excel 2002 and later. In Excel 2000, drag a field from the **Fields** buttons at the bottom of the PivotTable toolbar; in Excel 97, drag the field in the *Layout* dialog box in Step 3 of the PivotTable Wizard.

2. In the **PivotTable Data** area, select a cell from the newly added **SUM Field**.

3. Click **Field Settings** (second from the right) in the **PivotTable** toolbar.

4. In the **Name** text box type %.

5. Select **% of column** from **Show data as**, as shown below.

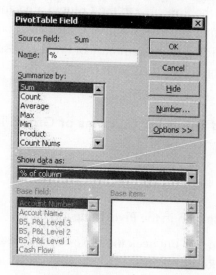

6. From the **BS, P&L Level 1 Field**, filter the data by selecting **Profit & Loss** criteria.

The results are shown in the figure below.

			2002		2003		Total Total	Total %
		Years ▼ Data ▼						
Quarters ▼	**BS, P&L Level 2** ▼		Total	%	Total	%		
Qtr1	Net Sales		96,993	63.16%	156,888	61.57%	253,881	62.17%
	Cost of Sales		(33,331)	(21.71%)	(39,627)	(15.55%)	(72,958)	(17.87%)
	Expenses		(23,922)	(15.58%)	(35,613)	(13.98%)	(59,534)	(14.58%)
	Income Taxes		(9,458)	(6.16%)	(13,316)	(5.23%)	(22,774)	(5.58%)
	Non Operating Expenses		(4,694)	(3.06%)	(12,166)	(4.77%)	(16,860)	(4.13%)
	Non Operating Income		4,831	3.15%	8,645	3.39%	13,476	3.30%
	Special Gain (Loss)		(1,254)	(0.82%)	(524)	(0.21%)	(1,778)	(0.44%)
Qtr1 Total			29,165	18.99%	64,287	25.23%	93,453	22.88%
Qtr2	Net Sales		122,726	79.92%	159,076	62.43%	281,801	69.00%
	Cost of Sales		(33,237)	(21.64%)	(38,739)	(15.20%)	(71,976)	(17.62%)
	Expenses		(24,761)	(16.12%)	(25,718)	(10.09%)	(50,479)	(12.36%)
	Income Taxes		(7,337)	(4.78%)	(14,307)	(5.61%)	(21,644)	(5.30%)
	Non Operating Expenses		(6,950)	(4.53%)	(10,060)	(3.95%)	(17,010)	(4.17%)
	Non Operating Income		10,474	6.82%	4,462	1.75%	14,936	3.66%
	Special Gain (Loss)		2,513	1.64%	2,541	1.00%	5,054	1.24%
Qtr2 Total			63,427	41.30%	77,255	30.32%	140,682	34.45%

You can create numerous other comparative **PivotTable** reports by moving the **Fields** from the **Row** area to the **Column** area and adding item details (by double-clicking any item within the **Row** area, on the left side of the **PivotTable**) according to the summary of Profit & Loss Accounts Groups level or Accounts Types level, and by canceling the **Grand Totals for Rows** or **Columns**.

➢ **To cancel the Grand Totals for Columns or Grand Totals for Rows:**

1. Press **<Alt+P>**,

    OR

    Click the **PivotTable** icon in the **PivotTable** toolbar.

2. Select **Table Option** and uncheck the boxes **Grand total for Columns** or **Grand total for Rows**.

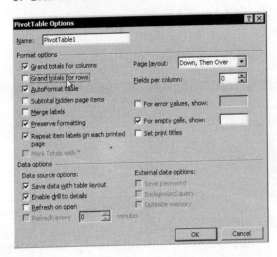

The **PivotTable** report will not display **Grand Total for Rows**, as shown below.

	A	B	C	D	E	F
		Microsoft Excel - Financial Statements				
	File	Edit	View	Insert	Format	Tools	Data	Window	Help
1	Month	(All)				
2	Account Num	(All)				
3	Accout Name	(All)				
4	BS, P&L Leve	(All)				
5	BS, P&L Leve	Profit & Loss				
6	Cash Flow	(All)				
7						
8			Years	Data		
9			2002		2003	
10	Quarters	BS, P&L Level 2	Balance	%	Balance	%
11	Qtr1	Net Sales	96,993	63.16%	156,888	61.57%
12		Cost of Sales	-33,331	-21.71%	-39,627	-15.55%
13		Expenses	-23,922	-15.58%	-35,613	-13.98%
14		Income Taxes	-9,458	-6.16%	-13,316	-5.23%
15		Non Operating Expenses	-4,694	-3.06%	-12,166	-4.77%
16		Non Operating Income	4,831	3.15%	8,645	3.39%
17		Special Gain (Loss)	-1,254	-0.82%	-524	-0.21%
18	Qtr1 Total		29,165	18.99%	64,287	25.23%
19	Qtr2	Net Sales	122,726	79.92%	159,076	62.43%
20		Cost of Sales	-33,237	-21.64%	-38,739	-15.20%
21		Expenses	-24,761	-16.12%	-25,718	-10.09%
22		Income Taxes	-7,337	-4.78%	-14,307	-5.61%
23		Non Operating Expenses	-6,950	-4.53%	-10,060	-3.95%
24		Non Operating Income	10,474	6.82%	4,462	1.75%
25		Special Gain (Loss)	2,513	1.64%	2,541	1.00%
26	Qtr2 Total		63,427	41.30%	77,255	30.32%
27	Qtr3	Net Sales	130,329	84.87%	168,095	65.97%

Adding a Field to a PivotTable Report to Analyze the Balances by Fiscal Year-end Reporting Date

The grouping technique described in the previous section to group dates by months, quarters, and years is only useful when the reporting period is based on a calendar year-end reporting period.

To group dates based on a fiscal year basis, you need to add a new column with a formula that calculates the Quarter numbers on a fiscal year reporting period in worksheet *21 — TB Data In Vertical*. An example of this can be seen in column **H** in the figure below.

	A	B	C	D	E	F	G	H
	Account Number	Account Name	BS, P&L Level 3	BS, P&L Level 2	BS, P&L Level 1	Month	Sum	Quarters by Fiscal Year
2	1011	Checking Account #1	Cash	Current Assets	Assets	January 2003	1,483,475	Q2 / 2003
3	1012	Checking Account #2	Cash	Current Assets	Assets	January 2003	1,637,272	Q2 / 2003
4	1021	Payroll Checking Account	Cash	Current Assets	Assets	January 2003	1,032,983	Q2 / 2003
5	1051	Savings Account #1	Cash	Current Assets	Assets	January 2003	1,816,500	Q2 / 2003
6	1061	Money Market Account #1	Cash	Current Assets	Assets	January 2003	2,119,250	Q2 / 2003
7	1071	Short Term CD's	Cash	Current Assets	Assets	January 2003	908,250	Q2 / 2003
8	1091	Petty Cash	Cash	Current Assets	Assets	January 2003	306,383	Q2 / 2003
9	1111	Accounts Receivable	Accounts Receivable	Current Assets	Assets	January 2003	3,102,582	Q2 / 2003
10	1121	Allowance for doubtful accounts	Accounts Receivable	Current Assets	Assets	January 2003	-302,750	Q2 / 2003

H2 formula: ="Q"&(MOD(CEILING(22+MONTH(F2)-9-1,3)/3,4)+1)&" / "&IF(MONTH(F2)<10,YEAR(F2),YEAR(F2)+1)

Figure 13-17:Formula to Calculate and Present Quarter Numbers for a Fiscal Year Reporting Period

Step 1: Adding a Formula to Calculate the Quarter Number

The first step is adding a formula that will calculate the Quarter number for a fiscal year reporting period in column **H**. In the example, the fiscal year-end reporting date is September 30 of each year.

➤ **To add the formula:**

1. Type the text **Quarters by Fiscal Year** into cell **H1**.

2. Enter the following formula into cell **H2**:

   ="Q"&(MOD(CEILING(22+MONTH(F2)-9-
   1,3)/3,4)+1)&"/"&IF(MONTH(F2)<10,YEAR(F2),YEAR(F2)+1)

   The number **9** in the nested **MONTH** formula is the month number for the fiscal year reporting date.

3. Copy the formula from cell **H2** to all the cells in column **H**, as required.

Step 2: Refreshing the PivotTable Report

The source data used by the **PivotTable** report you created on page 258 is the dynamic range defined as **TB_Data**, which uses the **OFFSET** formula to adjust its size automatically.

In this step you will refresh the **PivotTable** report and add the **Quarters by Fiscal Year Field**.

➤ **To refresh the PivotTable report and add the Field Quarters by Fiscal Year:**

1. Select the worksheet where the **PivotTable** report was created.

2. Select any cell within the **PivotTable** area and click **Refresh Data** in the **PivotTable** toolbar (the red exclamation point).

3. From the *PivotTable Field List* dialog box, drag the **Quarters by Fiscal Year Field** to the **Row** area.

The results are shown in the figure below.

Step 3: Sorting the Quarters in Ascending Order

The next step is to sort the quarters in ascending order. This can be done by dragging the cells one by one in their proper sequence, as shown in column **A** in the figure above.

Step 4: Grouping Quarters by Years

The last step is to group the quarters by years.

➢ **To group quarters by years:**

1. Select the four quarters of the year 2002, right-click and select **Group** from **Group and Show Details**.

2. Select the four next quarters of the year 2003, right-click and select **Group** from **Group and Show Details**.

3. Enter **2002** in cell **A11**, and type **2003** in cell **A16** (as shown below).

4. Enter the text **Years** in the gray button of the **Field** name (cell **A10**).

    The results are shown in the figure below.

Microsoft Excel - Financial Statements		
File Edit View Insert Format Tools Data Window Help		
A	**B**	**C**
1 Month	(All) ▼	
2 Cash Flow	(All) ▼	
3 BS, P&L Level 3	(All) ▼	
4 BS, P&L Level 1	(All) ▼	
5 BS, P&L Level 2	(All) ▼	
6 Accout Name	(All) ▼	
7 Account Number	(All) ▼	
8		
9 Balance		
10 Years ▼	Quarters by Fiscal ▼	Total
11 2002	Q1 / 2002	47,419
12	Q2 / 2002	29,165
13	Q3 / 2002	63,427
14	Q4 / 2002	13,549
15 2002 Total		153,561
16 2003	Q1 / 2003	54,986
17	Q2 / 2003	64,287
18	Q3 / 2003	77,255
19	Q4 / 2003	58,291
20 2003 Total		254,820
21 Grand Total		408,381
22		

5. Use the **PivotTable** report you created to summarize and analyze the balances of the Trial Balance accounts, as desired.

Figure 13-18 shows a comparison balances report that compares the Profit & Loss results between two consecutive years.

	Microsoft Excel - Financial Statements				
	File Edit View Insert Format Tools Data Window Help				
	A	B	C	D	E
1	Quarters by Fiscal Year	(All)			
2	Month	(All)			
3	Cash Flow	(All)			
4	BS, P&L Level 3	(All)			
5	BS, P&L Level 1	Profit & Loss			
6	Accout Name	(All)			
7	Account Number	(All)			
8					
9		Years	Data		
10		2002		2003	
11	BS, P&L Level 2	Balance	%	Balance	%
12	Net Sales	481,129	100.00%	653,069	100.00%
13	Cost of Sales	-145,156	-30.17%	-186,071	-28.49%
14	Expenses	-135,155	-28.09%	-143,706	-22.00%
15	Income Taxes	-38,604	-8.02%	-59,328	-9.08%
16	Non Operating Expenses	-35,258	-7.33%	-39,241	-6.01%
17	Non Operating Income	28,633	5.95%	30,368	4.65%
18	Special Gain (Loss)	-2,028	-0.42%	-272	-0.04%
19	Grand Total	153,561		254,820	

Figure 13-18: Comparison Years PivotTable Report

Figure 13-19 shows a comparison report that compares the Profit & Loss results between consecutives months.

	Microsoft Excel - Financial Statements							
	File Edit View Insert Format Tools Data Window Help							Type a
	A	B	C	D	E	F	G	H
1	Month	(All)						
2	Years	(All)						
3	Cash Flow	(All)						
4	BS, P&L Level 3	(All)						
5	BS, P&L Level 1	Profit & Loss						
6	Accout Name	(All)						
7	Account Number	(All)						
8								
9		Quarters by Fi	Data					
10		Q1 / 2002		Q2 / 2002		Q3 / 2002		Q4 / 2002
11	BS, P&L Level 2	Balance	%	Balance	%	Balance	%	Balance
12	Net Sales	131,081	100.00%	96,993	100.00%	122,726	100.00%	1
13	Cost of Sales	-40,833	-31.15%	-33,331	-34.36%	-33,237	-27.08%	-
14	Expenses	-29,528	-22.53%	-23,922	-24.66%	-24,761	-20.18%	-
15	Income Taxes	-11,770	-8.98%	-9,458	-9.75%	-7,337	-5.98%	-
16	Non Operating Expenses	-11,607	-8.85%	-4,694	-4.84%	-6,950	-5.66%	-
17	Non Operating Income	7,822	5.97%	4,831	4.98%	10,474	8.53%	
18	Special Gain (Loss)	2,254	1.72%	-1,254	-1.29%	2,513	2.05%	
19	Grand Total	47,419		29,165		63,427		

Figure 13-19: Comparison Monthly PivotTable Report

Chapter 14

Analyzing Financial Statements and Calculating the Ratio Analysis

About This Chapter

This chapter introduces techniques for Financial Statement Analysis, and includes the following sections:

✦ **Overview**, page 272, introduces the need for analyzing Financial Statements and calculating the Ratio Analysis.

✦ **Analyzing Financial Reports**, page 272, provides examples of the Two-year Balance Sheet and Two-year Income Statement Comparison Reports.

✦ **Ratio Analysis**, page 277, describes the four different categories of Ratio Analysis, and provides formulas for each ratio included in them.

Overview

Business decision makers at all management levels need to get accurate information. When this information is tied to the stability of the firm — for example, the availability of cash to pay dividends to stockholders, for acquisitions or investments or decisions to close unprofitable departments — the financial analysis information becomes the only way to survive in a competitive business environment.

This chapter discusses various techniques for analyzing Financial Statements, including a comparison of two periods and performing Ratio Analysis.

Analyzing Financial Reports

This section contains examples of comparison Balance Sheet and Income Statement reports. More comparison reports can be found in:

✦ *Chapter 11, Balance Sheet Five-year Comparison Reports*

✦ *Chapter 12, Income Statement Five-year and Quarterly Comparison Reports*

✦ *Chapter 13, Analyzing Financial Statements Using PivotTable and PivotChart Reports.*

Two-year Balance Sheet Comparison Reports

➢ **To create Two-year Balance Sheet Comparison Reports:**

1. Copy worksheet *31 — Balance Sheet*, and rename it to *33 — Two-year Balance Sheet Comparison*.

2. Delete column **B** (the **Notes** number column), and row number **5**.

3. Add titles to range **D7:E7**, and add formulas to columns **D** and **E**, as shown in Figure 14-1.

Column **D** of the comparison Assets report (Figure 14-1) shows the increase or decrease between two years. Column **E** presents this increase/decrease in percentage form.

Assets	2003	2002	Increase (Decrease)	% Increase (Decrease)
Current Assets				
Cash	301,124	318,697	(17,573)	(5.51%)
Accounts Receivable	1,653,558	1,538,494	115,064	7.48%
Inventories	546,173	520,133	26,040	5.01%
Prepaid Expenses	13,552	23,659	(10,107)	(42.72%)
Total Current Assets	2,514,407	2,400,983	113,424	4.72%
Property and Equipment (at Cost)				
Land & Building	674,019	677,191	(3,172)	(0.47%)
Machinery and Equipment	386,140	326,052	60,088	18.43%
Furniture and Fixtures	59,410	47,906	11,504	24.01%
Total Property and Equipment	1,119,569	1,051,150	68,419	6.51%
Less: Accumulated Depreciation	(478,852)	(419,540)	(59,312)	14.14%
Net Book Value	640,717	631,610	9,107	1.44%
Other Assets				
Investment in Revenue Bond	364,321	300,260	64,061	21.34%
Patents, Trademarks and Goodwill	52,250	52,500	(250)	(0.48%)
Total Other Assets	416,571	352,760	63,811	18.09%
Total Assets	3,571,695	3,385,352	186,343	5.50%

Figure 14-1: Assets

You can analyze the increase in Current Assets based on the figures in column **D** and the percentages in column **E**, for example:

✦ Decrease in Cash

✦ Increase in Accounts Receivable

✦ Increase in Inventories

✦ Decrease in Prepaid Expenses

A net increase in the Current Assets could be negative sign when the firm has less cash in its bank accounts, an increase in Accounts Receivable could be a sign of slow collections and/or bad debts, an increase in Inventories might indicate bad inventories and/or customer returns, and so on.

On the other hand, the firm may have recently expanded its business activity, and the firm's directors expect to raise cash from stockholders or the stock market, or possibly raise cash by taking good long-term loans with excellent interest rates while increasing sales and inventories.

As can be seen in Figure 14-2, cell **D47** indicates a decrease in Total Liabilities and cell **D52** an increase in Stockholder Equity.

	A	B	C	D	E
2	December 31, 2003				
31	Liabilities and Stockholder's Equity				
33	Current Liabilities				
34	Line of Credit	476,783	500,834	(24,051)	(4.80%)
35	Current Portion of Long–Term Debt	0	0	0	0.00%
36	Accounts Payable	547,255	475,284	71,971	15.14%
37	Accrued Expenses	234,296	221,291	13,006	5.88%
38	Other Payables	19,250	26,937	(7,687)	(28.54%)
39	Total Current Liabilities	1,277,585	1,224,345	53,239	4.35%
41	Long-Term Liabilities				
42	Note Payable	784,273	840,105	(55,833)	(6.65%)
43	Equipment Leases Payable	185,459	224,965	(39,506)	(17.56%)
44	Less: Current Portion Shown Above	(40,252)	(39,506)	(746)	1.89%
45	Total Long-Term Liabilities	929,480	1,025,564	(96,085)	(9.37%)
47	Total Liabilities	2,207,064	2,249,909	(42,845)	(1.90%)
49	Stockholder's Equity				
50	Capital Stock	151,897	152,623	(726)	(0.48%)
51	Retained Earnings	1,172,482	943,314	229,168	24.29%
52	Total Stockholder's Equity	1,324,379	1,095,937	228,442	20.84%
54	Total Liabilities and Stockholder's Equity	3,531,443	3,345,846	185,597	5.55%

Figure 14-2: Liabilities and Stockholder Equity

Analyzing the decrease in Total Liabilities shows that a decrease in Long-term Liabilities has been adjusted by an increase in Current Liabilities.

An increase in Short-term Liabilities with a concurrent decrease in cash is a very bad sign for the stability of the firm. The firm might find itself in a situation when expensive money (at a high interest rate) is used for paying short-term loans and Accounts Payable, while at the same time the decrease of Long-term Liabilities could mean that it will be difficult to raise money for business activities at low interest rates.

Two-year Income Statement Comparison Report

➤ **To create Two-year Income Statement Comparison Reports:**

1. Copy worksheet *41 — Income Statement,* and rename it to *44 — Two-year Income Statement Comparison.*

2. Insert columns **D** and **E:H**, and add titles and formulas to the cells in the new inserted columns, as shown in Figure 14-3.

When analyzing the Income Statement results over two years, you may notice a substantial increase in the firm's profitability during 2003. This is an increase of over 55% (see cell **H39** in Figure 14-3). The increase in the Net Income is much higher when checking the increase in the Operating Income before income taxes.

Microsoft Excel - Financial Statements

File Edit View Insert Format Tools Data Window Help

December 31, 2003

	A	B	C	D	E	F	G	H
1								
2								
3								
4	XYZ Corporation Inc.							
5	Income Statement							
6	For the year ended December, 31 2003							
7								
8		Notes	2003	%	2002	%	Increase (Decrease)	% Increase (Decrease)
9	**Revenue**	20						
10	Sales		2,920,093	75.35%	2,633,626	78.40%	286,467	10.88%
11	Services		955,214	24.65%	725,458	21.60%	229,756	31.67%
12	**Total Revenue**		3,875,307	100.00%	3,359,084	100.00%	516,223	15.37%
13								
14	**Cost of Goods Sold**							
15	Materials		854,521	22.05%	733,352	21.83%	121,169	16.52%
16	Labor & Subcontractors Costs		602,125	15.54%	536,645	15.98%	65,480	12.20%
17	Other Cost of goods sold		384,521	9.92%	350,241	10.43%	34,280	9.79%
18	Increase / Decrease in Inventories	21	-26,040	(0.67%)	-30,254	(0.90%)	4,214	(13.93%)
19	**Total Cost of Goods Sold**		1,815,127	46.84%	1,589,984	47.33%	225,143	14.16%
20								
21	**Gross Income**		2,060,180	53.16%	1,769,100	52.67%	291,080	16.45%
22								
23	**Operating Expenses**							
24	Selling		480,161	12.39%	441,256	13.14%	38,905	8.82%
25	General & Administrative	22	758,542	19.57%	675,992	20.12%	82,550	12.21%
26	Other Operating Expense	23	275,541	7.11%	260,887	7.77%	14,654	5.62%
27	Depreciation		59,312	1.53%	50,221	1.50%	9,091	18.10%
28	**Total Operating Expenses**		1,573,556	40.60%	1,428,356	42.52%	145,200	10.17%
29								
30	**Net Income before Operations**		486,624	12.56%	340,744	10.14%	145,880	42.81%
31								
32	**Operating Income (Loss)**							
33	Other income (expense)	24	32,512	0.84%	-2,521	(0.08%)	35,033	(1369.65%)
34	Interest expense		75,421	1.95%	62,584	1.86%	12,837	20.51%
35	**Total Operating Income**		107,933	2.79%	60,063	1.79%	47,870	79.70%
36						0.00%		
37	**Income (Loss) Before Income Taxes**		378,691	9.77%	280,681	8.36%	98,010	34.92%
38	Provision (benefit) for income taxes	25	149,523	3.86%	133,251	3.97%	16,272	12.21%
39	**Net Income (Loss) for the year**		229,168	5.91%	147,430	4.39%	81,738	55.44%
40	Retained Earnings beginning of the year	26	943,314	24.34%	795,884	23.69%	147,430	18.52%
41	**Retained Earnings**		1,172,482	30.26%	943,314	28.08%	229,168	24.29%

Figure 14-3: Income Statement Report

Using vertical analysis (that is, checking the percentage in each subtotal in column **H**) gives immediate information about what the reasons are for the dramatic increase in the Net Income — the good news is that the Net Income before Operations jumped impressively.

Ratio Analysis

> ➤ **To create Ratio Analysis Two-year Balance Sheet Comparison Reports:**

1. Copy worksheet *31 — Balance Sheet*, and delete rows **9** and downward.

2. Delete column **B**, and rename it to *34 — Ratio Analysis*.

3. Follow the instructions in this section. The final result should look like Figure 14-6, page 283.

Ratio Analysis provides tools to decision makers, both inside and outside the firm, for analyzing Financial Statements by highlighting the major important parameters that expose the strongest and weakness of the firm business activity results.

In this section, you will learn about twelve Ratios Analysis, which can be bunched into four categories.

✦ Liquidity Ratios, as described on page 278

✦ Asset Management Ratios, as described on page 279

✦ Profitability Ratios, as described on page 280

✦ Leverage Ratios, as described on page 282

	A	B	C	D
	Microsoft Excel - Financial Statements			
	File Edit View Insert Format Tools Data Window Help			Typ
	A	B	C	D
5	XYZ Corporation Inc.			
6				
7		December 31		
8	Financial Ratios	2003	2002	
9				
10	**Liquidity Ratios**			
11	Current Ratio	1.91	1.90	=Current Assets / Current Liabilities
12	Quick Ratio	1.49	1.47	=(Current Assets-Inventories) / Current Liabilities
13				
14	**Assets Management Ratios**			
15	Inventory Turnover	3.32	3.06	=Cost of Goods / Inventories
16	Asset Turnover	1.09	0.99	=Total Sales / Total Assets
17	Receivable turnover Days	156	167	=Accounts Receiveable*365 / Total Credit Sales
18				
19	**Profitability Ratios**			
20	Earnings Per Share	1.51	0.97	=Income Available for common stock / Shares of common stock
21	Return on Assets	13.62%	10.07%	=Net Operating Income / Total Assets
22	Return on Equity	17.30%	13.45%	=Net Income / Shareholder's Equity
23	Return on Sales	5.91%	4.39%	=Net Income / Total Sales
24	Gross Profit Margin	53.16%	52.67%	=Gross Income / Total Sales
25				
26	**Leverage Ratios**			
27	Debt to Equity	169.69%	208.90%	=(Current Liabilities+Long term Liabilities) / Shareholder's Equity
28	Debt Ratio	89.38%	95.35%	=(Current Liabilities+Long term Liabilities) / Current assets

Figure 14-4: Financial Ratios

Category 1: Liquidity Ratios

The ratios in this category indicate the firm's ability to quickly realize its Current Assents as cash and its risk level.

There are two ratios are in this category:

✦ Current Ratio, as described below

✦ Quick Ratio, as described on page 279

The quickest way to turn Current Assets to cash depends mainly on the ability to collect the Accounts Receivable balances, as well as the Inventory quality and level.

Current Ratio

Cell **B11** in Figure 14-5 contains the following formula:

=CurrentAssets/CurrentLiabilities

Cell **C11** contains the following formula:

=OFFSET(CurrentAssets,0,1)/OFFSET(CurrentLiabilities,0,1)

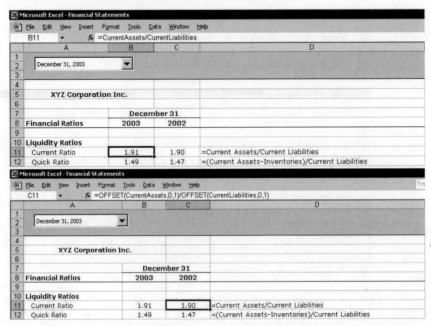

Figure 14-5: Current Ratio — Current Assets/Current Liabilities

The cell range *Names* were defined in worksheet *31 — Balance Sheet.*

Quick Ratio

In this ratio, the Inventories are taken out the Current Assets. The formula for (Current Assets-Inventories/Current Liabilities) is:

=(CurrentAssets-Inventories)/CurrentLiabilities

Category 2: Asset Management Ratios

The ratios in this category indicate the ability to analyze the profitability balances of the Financial Statements.

There are three ratios in this category:

✦ Inventory Turnover Ratio, as described below

✦ Asset Turnover Ratio, as described on page 280

✦ Receivable Turnover Days Ratio, as described on page 280

The firm's profitability depends on the ability to shorten Accounts Receivable balances' collecting time and how fast Inventory can be sold to customers.

Inventory Turnover Ratio

Keeping high levels of inventory increases expenses, including:

✦ Storing expenses

✦ Inventory management

✦ Expensive money invested in Inventory is not available.

The formula for Cost of Goods/Inventories is:

=TotalCOG/Inventories

Asset Turnover Ratio

A high asset turnover ratio indicates that the money available is high, and that Accounts Receivable is being collecting quickly.

The formula for Total Revenue/Total Assets is:

=TotalSales/Assets

Receivable Turnover Days Ratio

As "time is money", the faster you collect Accounts Receivable balances and turn them to cash, the faster you reduce interest expenses and eliminate the possibility of turning uncollectible accounts into bad debts.

The formula for (Accounts Receivable*365/Total Credit Sales) is:

=(AccountsReceivable*365)/TotalSales

Category 3: Profitability Ratios

The ratios in this category indicate the ability to measure management's ability to produce profit.

There are five ratios in this category:

✦ Earnings per Share Ratio, as described on page 281

✦ Return on Assets Ratio, as described on page 281

✦ Return on Equity Ratio, as described on page 281

✦ Return on Sales Ratio, as described on page 281

✦ Gross Profit Margin Ratio, as described on page 281

Investors expect to gain the most profit from investments. Profitability ratios measure how much an investors or potential investors can make on their investments, and reduce the risk level to which they are exposed.

Profitability ratios are very important for long-term investment decisions.

Earnings per Share Ratio

The formula for Income Available for common stock/Shares of common stock is:

=NetIncome/CapitalStock

Return on Assets Ratio

This ratio measures the ability to produce profits from Assets. The formula for Net Operating Income/Total Assets is:

=OperatingIncome/Assets

Return on Equity Ratio

This ratio is also known as the Return on Investments ratio. The formula for Net Income/Shareholders' Equity is:

=NetIncome/StockholdersEquity

Return on Sales Ratio

The formula for Net Income/Total Sales is:

=NetIncome/TotalSales

Gross Profit Margin Ratio

The formula for Gross Income/Total Sales is:

=GrossIncome/TotalSales

Category 4: Leverage Ratios

The ratios in this category indicate the ability to raise funds from out side sources for the business activities.

There are two ratios in this category:

✦ Debt to Equity Ratio, as described below

✦ Debt Ratio, as described below

Leverage means using external sources (both long- and short-term loans) for the business activities.

Debt to Equity Ratio

The formula for Current Liabilities + Long term Liabilities/Shareholders' Equity is:

=(CurrentLiabilities+LongTermLiabilities)/StockholdersEquity

Debt Ratio

The formula for Current Liabilities + Long-term Liabilities/Current Assets is:

=(CurrentLiabilities+LongTermLiabilities)/CurrentAssets

Getting More from the Ratio Analysis

You can use the difference between the Ratio Analyses to get answers to various business questions, such as:

✦ Did working capital improve?

✦ Is there a tendency of investment surplus in Fixed Assets?

✦ Is there an improvement in the profitability measure?

In the model presented here, you can find an evaluation of the changes in the financial relationship between two reporting periods.

	A	B	C	D
1				
2	December 31, 2003 ▼			
3				
4				
5	XYZ Corporation Inc.			
6				
7			December 31	
8	**Financial Ratios**	**2003**	**2002**	**% Increase (Decrease)**
9				
10	**Liquidity Ratios**			
11	Current Ratio	1.91	1.90	0.43%
12	Quick Ratio	1.49	1.47	1.64%
13				
14	**Assets Management Ratios**			
15	Inventory Turnover	3.32	3.06	8.72%
16	Asset Turnover	1.09	0.99	9.35%
17	Receivable turnover Days	156	167	(6.84%)
18				
19	**Profitability Ratios**			
20	Earnings Per Share	1.51	0.97	56.18%
21	Return on Assets	13.62%	10.07%	35.36%
22	Return on Equity	17.30%	13.45%	28.63%
23	Return on Sales	5.91%	4.39%	34.74%
24	Gross Profit Margin	53.16%	52.67%	0.94%
25				
26	**Leverage Ratios**			
27	Debt to Equity	169.69%	208.90%	(18.77%)
28	Debt Ratio	89.38%	95.35%	(6.27%)

Formula bar: D11 ▼ f_x =(B11-C11)/C11

Figure 14-6: Comparing Analysis Ratios Figures Between Two Periods

Getting More from the Ratio Analysis

You can use the difference between the Ratio Analyses to get answers to various business questions, such as:

* Did working capital improve?
* Is there a tendency of investment surplus in Fixed Assets?
* Is there an improvement in the profitability measures?

In the model presented here, you can find an evaluation of the changes in the financial relationship between two reporting periods.

Financial Ratios	2001	2002	% Increase (Decrease)
Liquidity Ratios			
Current Ratio			
Quick Ratio			
Assets Management Ratios			
Inventory Turnover			
Total Asset Turnover			
Profitability Ratios			
Profit Margin			
Return on Assets			
Return on Equity			
Gross Profit Margin			
Leverage Ratios			
Debt to Equity			
Debt Ratio			

Figure 14-6: Comparing Analysis Ratios Figures Between Two Periods

Chapter 15

Analyzing Profit Centers

About This Chapter

This chapter describes how to create the company's **Profit Centers'** Income Statement reports, and includes the following sections:

✦ **Overview**, page 286, introduces the **Profit Center** concept.

✦ **Adding Profit Center Details to the Trial Balances Data Worksheet**, page 287, describes how to add a **Profit Center** details in a new column to the Trial Balances Data.

✦ **Analyzing Profit Centers Using PivotTable Reports**, page 291, describes how to create **PivotTable** reports to analyze **Profit Center** by **Profit Center** while presenting summary balances for Account Name and Account Type.

✦ **Creating an Income Statement to Present Each Profit Center's Results**, page 294, describes how to create **Profit Center** Income Statement reports.

✦ **Printing Profit Center Income Statement Reports**, page 304, describes how to automate the printing of **Profit Center** Income Statement reports.

Overview

Company growth in competitive environments usually requires either expansion into new business areas or varying the existing business activities and broadening product lines.

The first ten chapters of this book showed you how to create a full set of Financial Statements without reference to the specific business areas (that is, dividing business activities into **Profit Centers**) in which the company is involved. In this chapter, you will learn how to analyze the company's **Profit Centers**.

Each **Profit Center** typically requires different management accounting techniques to identify its contribution to the operation as a whole.

This chapter introduces the example fictional company, **XYZ Corporation, Inc.**, with five **Profit Centers** — Constructions, Hotels, Rental, Insurance and General Products.

Adding Profit Center Details to the Trial Balances Data Worksheet

➤ **To add Profit Centers' names in a new column:**

1. Press **<Shift+F11>** to add new worksheet, and rename it to *81 — TB ProfitCenters*.

2. In worksheet *21 — Trial Balances Data*, copy all worksheet cells by pressing **<Ctrl+A>** and then **<Ctrl+C>**.

3. In worksheet *81 — TB ProfitCenters*, select cell **A1** and press **<Enter>** to paste.

4. Delete all the rows where the **Accounts Number** (in column **A** starting from cell **A2**) is less than 4000.

5. Add a new column (column **F** below), and enter the **Profit Centers'** names into the appropriate cells using the **INDEX** formula, as described later in this section.

In each **Account Number** in column **A**, the last digit indicates the **Profit Center** name, for example, 1 is for *Construction*, 2 for *Hotels* and so on.

As shown in Figure 15-1, the **INDEX** formula calculates and returns the **Profit Center** name to each cell in column **F**.

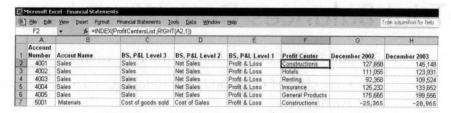

Figure 15-1: Return Profit Center Name Formula

The following formula will return the **Profit Center** name to cell **F2** in column **F**:

=INDEX(ProfitCentersList,RIGHT(A2,1))

✦ The **RIGHT** formula (nested within the **INDEX** formula) returns the last digit of the account number in cell **A2**.

✦ In worksheet *13 — Parameters & Calculations*, range **A20:A25** includes the **Profit Centers** List. The *Name* defined for the range is **ProfitCentersList**, as shown below.

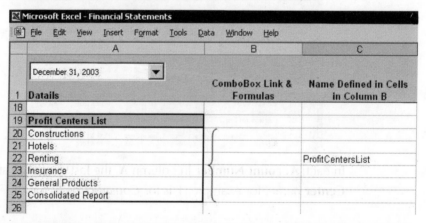

✦ The **INDEX** formula returns the **Profit Center** name from the defined range *Name* **ProfitCentersList**.

Defining a Name for the Trial Balances Data in Worksheet 81 – TB ProfitCenters

➢ **To define a dynamic range Name for the Trial Balances data in worksheet 81 – TB ProfitCenters:**

1. Select worksheet *81 — TB ProfitCenters.*

2. Select any cell in the data area and press **<Ctrl+Shift+*>**. (When using Excel 2003, you can also press **<Ctrl+A>**.)

3. Press **<Ctrl+F3>** and enter **TB_PC_Data** in the **Names in Workbook** box (TB for Trial Balances, PC for Profit Centers).

4. Enter the following formula in the **Refers To** box:

   =OFFSET(81- TB ProfitCenters'!$A$1,0,0,COUNTA(81- TB ProfitCenters '!$A:$A),COUNTA(81- TB ProfitCenters'!$1:$1))

5. Click **OK**.

To learn more regarding defining dynamic range *Names* and the **OFFSET** formula, refer to page 27, *Chapter 2, Adjusting the Trial Balance.*

Saving Filtering Profit Centers Criteria Using Custom Views

To enable easy and immediate filtering of the data stored in the cells in worksheet *81 — TB ProfitCenters* (shown on page 287), save the filtering criteria in a **Custom View** (which enables you to filter for a **Profit Center**) from any worksheet in the **Financial Statements.xls** workbook (for more details, refer to page 129, *Chapter 8, Customizing the Financial Statements.xls Workbook and Presenting Information*, and page 179, *Chapter 10, Printing and Mailing Financial Statements Reports*).

➤ **To save the Profit Center filter criteria:**

1. From the *Data* menu, select **Filter** and then **AutoFilter**.

2. From the drop-down list at the top of column **F**, choose the first **Profit Center** name.

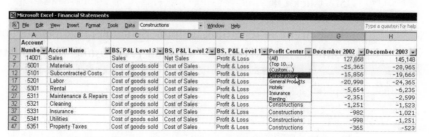

3. In the **Custom View** box (described on page 130, *Chapter 8, Customizing the Financial Statemenrs.xls Workbook and Presenting Information*), type the name of the **Profit Center** and click **OK** twice.

4. Repeat steps 2 and 3 for all of the filtering criteria and save each one in **Custom View**, and then save **Financial Statements.xls** workbook. Your results should look like this:

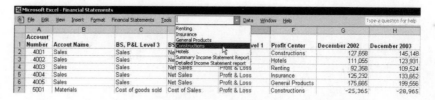

Analyzing Profit Centers Using PivotTable Reports

The following **PivotTable** report presents the balances for the **Accounts Name** summarized by **Profit Centers**. Two comparison periods are provided — Year To Date (YTD) for December 2003 and YTD for December 2002.

Account Name	Constructions YTD December 2003	YTD December 2002	General Products YTD December 2003	YTD December 2002	Hotels YTD December 2003	YTD December 2002	Insurance YTD December 2003	YTD December 2002	Renting YTD December 2003	YTD December 2002	Total YTD December 2003	Total YTD December 2002
Accounting Fees	-2,956	-2,253	-4,998	-4,577	-6,500	-5,652	-3,654	-3,326	-3,755	-3,265	-21,863	-19,073
Advertising	-2,025	-1,855	-9,856	-7,785	-6,585	-4,485	-9,985	-8,858	-3,962	-2,995	-32,413	-25,976
Attorney Fees	-5,695	-3,325	-4,583	-5,012	-3,025	-2,532	-3,996	-4,452	-3,985	-3,025	-21,284	-18,346
Building Maintenance	-965	-854	0	0			-3,268	-3,325	0	0	-4,233	-4,179
Cleaning	-1,523	-1,251	0	0	-4,464	-3,720	0	0	-5,585	-4,568	-11,552	-9,539
Computer Software & Services	-3,458	-2,658	-5,998	-4,859	-4,002	-3,552	-13,252	-10,225	-5,223	-4,458	-31,933	-25,752
Depreciation	-3,002	-2,856	-1,445	-1,254	-5,002	-4,526	-1,662	-1,252	-7,758	-6,985	-18,869	-16,873
Equip Maint. & Repairs	-354	-232	0	0	-2,691	-3,960	0	0	-1,254	-1,114	-4,299	-5,306
Equipment Lease	-2,624	-2,221	0	0	-2,441	-2,532	-4,256	-3,265	-2,691	-2,125	-12,012	-10,143
Insurance	-1,021	-982	-1,552	-1,253	-4,536	-3,780	0	0	-4,536	-3,780	-11,645	-9,795
Labor	-24,365	-20,998	-5,623	-4,562	-32,634	-29,855	0	0	-12,554	-9,985	-75,176	-65,400
Maintenance & Repairs	-2,599	-2,351	-3,452	-2,235	-7,586	-6,658	0	0	-17,552	-15,223	-31,189	-26,467
Materials	-28,965	-25,365	-155,023	-132,522	0	0	0	0	0	0	-183,988	-157,887
Promotional Events					-4,485	-6,523					-4,485	-6,523
Property Taxes	-523	-365	0	0	-4,680	-3,900	0	0	-4,441	-3,359	-9,644	-7,624
Rental	-6,235	-5,654	-4,125	-3,325	-12,546	-10,526	0	0	-1,558	-1,125	-24,464	-20,630
Subcontracted Costs	-19,665	-15,856	0	0	0	0	0	0	0	0	-19,665	-15,856
Telephone	-858	-758	-3,265	-2,254	-2,691	-3,960	-6,523	-5,652	-2,691	-2,665	-16,026	-15,289
Travel	-199	-251	-3,665	-2,256	-2,665	-2,352	-7,859	-6,658	-1,456	-1,251	-15,844	-12,768
Utilities	-1,251	-998	0	0	-4,608	-3,840	0	0	-4,955	-4,598	-10,814	-9,436
Commissions	-4,252	-3,332	-6,205	-4,589	-3,022	-2,225	0	0	-3,988	-4,412	-17,467	-14,558
Salary & Wages	-10,225	-9,582	-11,252	-9,956	-5,295	-4,458	-35,821	-32,562	0	0	-62,393	-56,558
Sales	145,148	127,658	199,556	175,665	123,931	111,055	133,652	125,232	109,524	92,358	711,811	631,968
Utilities	-567	-459	-3,488	-2,258	-3,002	-2,232	-3,226	-2,258	-6,584	-4,445	-16,867	-11,652
Commissions Insurance							-29,956	-26,595			-29,956	-26,595
Increase (Decrease) in Inventory			22,023	15,223							22,023	15,223
Grand Total	21,803	23,202	-2,951	2,191	1,471	-213	10,394	16,806	15,016	12,980	45,733	54,966

Figure 15-2: PivotTable Report Presenting the Account Name Balances Summarized by Profit Centers

BS, P&L Level 3	Constructions Balance December 2003	Balance December 2002	General Products Balance December 2003	Balance December 2002	Hotels Balance December 2003	Balance December 2002	Insurance Balance December 2003	Balance December 2002	Renting Balance December 2003	Balance December 2002	Total Balance December 2003	Total Balance December 2002
Sales	145,148	127,658	199,556	175,665	123,931	111,055	133,652	125,232	109,524	92,358	711,811	631,968
Cost of goods sold	-86,147	-73,820	-147,752	-128,674	-71,054	-62,279	0	0	-51,161	-42,638	-356,114	-307,411
Amortization	-3,002	-2,856	-1,445	-1,254	-5,002	-4,526	-1,662	-1,252	-7,758	-6,985	-18,869	-16,873
General Expenses	-27,919	-22,593	-37,249	-31,172	-32,312	-31,230	-81,655	-71,723	-27,639	-22,348	-206,774	-179,066
Marketing	-6,277	-5,187	-16,061	-12,374	-14,092	-13,233	-39,941	-35,451	-7,950	-7,407	-84,321	-73,652
Grand Total	21,803	23,202	-2,951	2,191	1,471	-213	10,394	16,806	15,016	12,980	45,733	54,966

Figure 15-3: PivotTable Report Presenting the Account Type Balances Summarized by Profit Centers

To learn how to create **PivotTable** report, refer to *Chapter 13, Analyzing Financial Statements Using PivotTable and PivotChart Reports.*

The **PivotTable** data source for the two **PivotTable** reports presented in the two previous figures is **TB_PC_Data**, which is the *Name* defined for the Trial Balances data, as described in *Defining a Name for the Trial Balances Data in Worksheet 81 — TB ProfitCenters*, page 289.

➢ **To create two PivotTable reports that use the source of the range:**

1. Add new worksheet, rename it to *82 — PT Account Name*, and then create a **PivotTable** report.

2. Add new worksheet, and rename it to *83 — PT AccountType*.

3. In worksheet *82 — PT Account Name*, select a cell inside the **PivotTable** you just created, press **<Ctrl+Shift+*>** to select it and press **<Ctrl+C>** to copy it.

4. In worksheet *83 — PT AccountType*, paste it by pressing **<Enter>**.

5. Modify one **PivotTable** report to summarize the data from the source data (which is **TB_PC_Data** based on **Account Name**, as shown in Figure 15-2, page 291) and the second **PivotTable** report based on **Account Type** (as in Figure 15-3, page 291).

Why Use Two PivotTable Reports?

Excel's powerful and innovative **PivotTable** report feature greatly facilitates data analysis. It quickly and easily summarizes the data from the data source, and the results are updated by refreshing.

However, you will need more than one **PivotTable** report to present summarized data in a different subtotals levels. To do this you will have to duplicate the **PivotTable** report as many times as required by copying the **PivotTable** report to a new worksheet and changing the **Field** structures to present a new **PivotTable** report.

The next step in creating an Income Statement report for each **Profit Center** is to define *Names* in the two worksheets where the **PivotTable** reports created.

Defining Names

➤ **To define range Names in worksheet 82 – PT AccountName:**

1. Define the *Name* **PT_PC_AccountName** for worksheet *82 — PT AccountName* by pressing **<Ctrl+A>** to select all cells in the worksheet. (In Excel 2003, press **<Ctrl+A+A>** from a selected cell in the data area.)

2. Press **<Ctrl+F3>** and type the *Name* into the **Names in Workbook** box.

3. Define the *Name* **PT_Titles_AccountName** to row **2** of the worksheet (the title line).

4. Define the *Name* **PT_ColA_AccountName** to column **A** of the worksheet.

➤ **To define range Names in worksheet 83 – PT AccountType:**

1. Define the *Name* **PT_PC_AccountType** for worksheet *83 — PT AccountType* by pressing **<Ctrl+A>** to select all cells in the worksheet. (In Excel 2003, press **<Ctrl+A+A>** from a selected cell in the data area.)

2. Press **<Ctrl+F3>** and type the *Name* into the **Names in Workbook** box.

3. Define the *Name* **PT_Titles_AccountType** to row **2** in the worksheet (the title line).

4. Define the *Name* **PT_ColA_AccountType** to column **A** of the worksheet.

Creating an Income Statement to Present Each Profit Center's Results

This section explains how to create an Income Statement that uses two **Combo Boxes**.

✦ One **Combo Box** enables you to select the **Profit Center** name.

✦ The second **Combo Box** enables you to select the reporting month.

The figure below shows a summary Income Statement report for the **Constructions Profit Center**.

		A	B	C	D	E
	1					
	2	Constructions ▼	December 31, 2003 ▼			
	3					
	4	XYZ Corporation Inc.				
	5	Income Statement				
	6	For the year ended December, 31 2003				
	7					
	8	Constructions	2003	%	2002	%
	9					
	10	Gross Income				
	11	Sales	145,148	100.00%	127,658	100.00%
+	23	Cost of Goods Sold	86,147	59.35%	73,820	50.86%
	24	Gross Income	59,001	40.65%	53,838	37.09%
	25					
	26	Operating Expenses				
+	30	Marketing	6,277	4.32%	5,187	3.57%
	31	Amortization	3,002	2.07%	2,856	1.97%
+	38	General Expenses	27,919	19.23%	22,593	15.57%
	39	Operating Expenses	37,198	25.63%	30,636	21.11%
	40					
	41	Net Income From Operations	21,803	15.02%	23,202	15.99%
	42					

Figure 15-4: Summary Income Statement for a Profit Center

Refer to *Chapter 5, Income Statement* for information about how to create Income Statements. The worksheet *41 — Income Statement* is used as the base for adding and modifying **Profit Centers** Income Statement reports.

➤ **To add a second Combo Box and Profit Center name:**

1. Add a new worksheet, and rename it to *84 — IS ProfitCenters*.

2. In worksheet *41 — Income Statement,* copy rows **1:9**.

3. In worksheet *84 — IS ProfitCenters,* press **<Enter>** to paste.

4. Add two columns and insert formulas to return the percentage calculation, **Sales=100%** (see columns **C** and **E** in Figure 15-4, page 294).

5. Select worksheet *13 — Parameters & Calculations.*

6. In cells **20** to **25** in column **A**, type the names of all **Profit Centers** included in the Consolidation Report, select the list range and define the *Name* **ProfitCentersList** (as described on page 288, and shown in the figure below).

7. Select cell **B16** and define the *Name* **PC_Number** (the cell link to the new **Combo Box**).

8. Select cell **B17** and define the *Name* **PC_Name**.

9. Enter the following formula into cell **B17**:

   =INDEX(ProfitCentersList,PC_Number)

   The formula will return the **Profit Center** name from the **Profit Center list** in cells **A20** to **A25**.

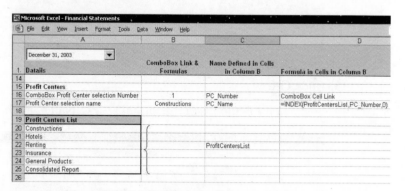

10. Select worksheet *84 — IS ProfitCenters.*

11. Copy the **Combo Box** containing the month's list and paste it aside.

12. Select the copied **Combo Box**, then right-click and select **Format Control** from shortcut menu.

13. Select the **Control** tab.

14. In the **Input Range** box, replace the **MonthsList** reference with **ProfitCentersList**. In the **Cell Link** box, replace the **MonthSelectionNumber** reference with **PC_Number**, as shown.

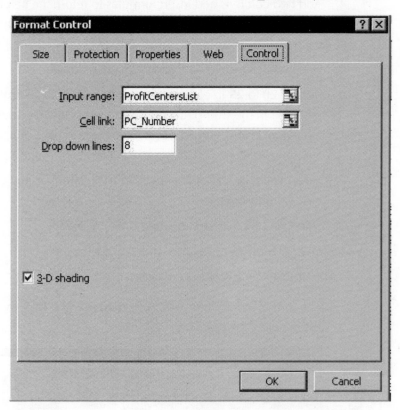

15. Click **OK**.

16. Select cell **A8** and insert the formula = **PC_Name**, as shown below.

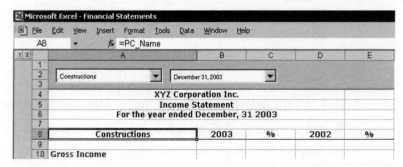

Creating Summary and Detailed Profit Center Income Statement Reports

➢ **To create two types of Profit Center Income Statement reports, a Summary report and a Detailed report:**

1. Add **Accounts Types** items to the white cells in column **A** — cells **A11, A23, A30:A31, A38**) and **Accounts Name** items to the gray cells in column **A**.

Microsoft Excel - Financial Statements

File   Edit   View   Insert   Format   Tools   Data   Window   Help

Constructions ▼   December 31, 2003 ▼

	A	B	C	D	E
1					
2					
3					
4	XYZ Corporation Inc.				
5	Income Statement				
6	For the year ended December, 31 2003				
7					
8	**Constructions**	**2003**	**%**	**2002**	**%**
9					
10	**Gross Income**				
11	Sales	145,148	100.00%	127,658	100.00%
12	Materials	28,965	19.96%	25,365	17.48%
13	Labor	24,365	16.79%	20,998	14.47%
14	Subcontracted Costs	19,665	13.55%	15,856	10.92%
15	Rental	6,235	4.30%	5,654	3.90%
16	Maintenance & Repairs	2,599	1.79%	2,351	1.62%
17	Cleaning	1,523	1.05%	1,251	0.86%
18	Insurance	1,021	0.70%	982	0.68%
19	Property Taxes	523	0.36%	365	0.25%
20	Commissions Insurance	0	0.00%	0	0.00%
21	Utilities	587	0.40%	459	0.32%
22	Increase (Decrease) in Inventory	0	0.00%	0	0.00%
23	Cost of Goods Sold	86,147	59.35%	73,820	50.86%
24	**Gross Income**	**59,001**	**40.65%**	**53,838**	**37.09%**
25					
26	**Operating Expenses**				
27	Advertising	2,025	1.40%	1,855	1.28%
28	Promotional Events	0	0.00%	0	0.00%
29	Commissions	4,252	2.93%	3,332	2.30%
30	Marketing	6,277	4.32%	5,187	3.57%
31	Amortization	3,002	2.07%	2,856	1.97%
32	Salary & Wages	10,225	7.04%	9,582	6.60%
33	Accounting Fees	2,956	2.04%	2,253	1.55%
34	Attorney Fees	5,695	3.92%	3,325	2.29%
35	Computer Software & Services	3,458	2.38%	2,658	1.83%
36	Telephone	856	0.59%	758	0.52%
37	Travel	199	0.14%	251	0.17%
38	General Expenses	27,919	19.23%	22,593	15.57%
39	**Operating Expenses**	**37,198**	**25.63%**	**30,636**	**21.11%**
40					
41	**Net Income From Operations**	**21,803**	**15.02%**	**23,202**	**15.99%**
42					

2. Use the **Group** and **Outline** symbols, as follows:

   ✦ Select rows **12-22** (as shown in the previous step).

   ✦ From the *Data* menu, choose **Group and Outline** and select **Group**.

   ✦ Repeat twice, and group Marketing expenses by selecting rows **27:29**, and General expenses by selecting rows **32:37**.

3. Insert the formulas that return summary balances from the **PivotTable** report, as follows:

   ✦ Into cells in columns **B** and **D**, insert the formulas that return the summary balances from the **PivotTables** report, according to the **Account Types** and **Account Name** you entered to cells in column **A**.

      ❖ The first formula returns the summary balances to the **Account Types** from the **PivotTable** report in worksheet *83 — PT AccountType* (see Figure 15-3).

      ❖ The second formula returns the summary balances to **Accounts Name** from the **PivotTable** report in worksheet *82 — PT AccountName* (see Figure 15-2).

The formula in cell **B11**, and in all cells in the **Accounts Type** level, is as follows:

=IF(PC_Number=6, INDEX(PC_PT_AccountType,MATCH(A11,PT_ColA_
AccountType,0),12),INDEX(PC_PT_AccountType,MATCH(A11,PT_ColA_
AccountType,0),MATCH(PC_Name,PT_Titles_AccountType,0)))

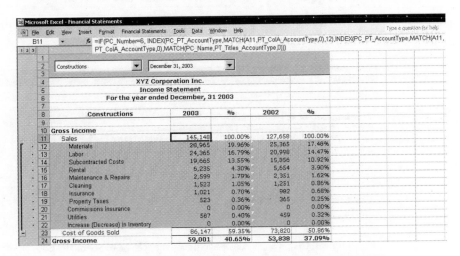

Figure 15-5: Formula for Account Type Level

Building the Formula Step-by-Step

The following sections break up the **IF** formula to simplify understanding how it is created.

First Argument in the IF Formula

Enter **PC_Number=6** into the **Logical_test** argument of the **IF** function, as shown:

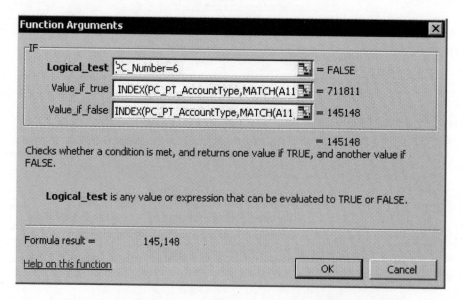

Figure 15-6: If Function with Two Nested INDEX Formulas

Six items in the **Profit Centers** list (shown on page 288), five **Profit Centers** plus one that will display the total balances to the whole five, the Consolidated Report.

Selecting one of the first five items from the **Combo Box** list (which is the **Profit Centers** list), causes the formula in the **Logical test** to calculate and return the result from the third argument in the **IF** formula.

Selecting **Consolidated Report**, number 6 in the **Combo Box Profit Center** list, will return the summarized balances from the second argument in the **IF** formula, that is, column **L** (column **12**) in the **PivotTable** report (shown below).

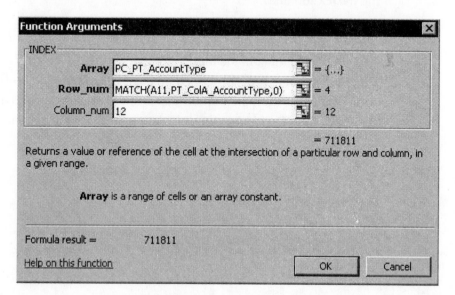

BS, P&L Level 3 ▼	Constructions		General Products		Hotels		Insurance		Renting		Total Balance December 2003	Total Balance December 2002
	Balance December 2003	Balance December 2002	Balance December 2003	Balance December 2002	Balance December 2003	Balance December 2002	Balance December 2003	Balance December 2002	Balance December 2003	Balance December 2002		
Sales	145,148	127,858	199,556	175,665	123,931	111,055	133,852	125,232	109,524	92,358	711,811	631,968
Cost of goods sold	-86,147	-73,820	-147,752	-128,674	-71,054	-62,279	0	0	-51,161	-42,638	-356,114	-307,411
Amortization	-3,002	-2,856	-1,445	-1,254	-5,002	-4,526	-1,662	-1,252	-7,758	-6,985	-18,869	-16,873
General Expenses	-27,919	-22,593	-37,249	-31,172	-32,312	-31,230	-81,655	-71,723	-27,639	-22,348	-208,774	-179,066
Marketing	-6,277	-5,187	-16,061	-12,374	-14,092	-13,233	-39,941	-35,451	-7,950	-7,407	-84,321	-73,652
Grand Total	21,803	23,202	-2,951	2,191	1,471	-213	10,394	16,806	15,016	12,980	45,733	54,966

Figure 15-7: PivotTable Report Presenting the Account Type Balances Summarized by Profit Centers

Second Argument in the IF Formula, the INDEX Formula

Insert the **INDEX** formula to the **Value_if_true** argument of the **IF** formula:

=INDEX(PT_PC_AccountType,MATCH(A11,PT_ColA_AccountType,0),12)

Figure 15-8: INDEX Formula in the Second Argument of the IF Formula

✦ **Array** (first argument in Figure 15-7): The *Name* defined for the worksheet that contains the **PivotTable** report (described on page 293), as shown in Figure 15-3, page 291.

✦ **Row_num** (second argument): Returns the row number in column **A** for the **Account Type** in cell **A11**, in this example, for **Sales**.

✦ **Column_Num** (third argument): Enter the column number, which is column **L** (column **12** in the worksheet; in the formulas in the cells in column **D**, change the number to **13**) in the **PivotTable** report worksheet, as shown in Figure 15-3, page 291.

Third Argument in the IF Formula

Enter the **INDEX** formula to the **Value_if_false** argument of the **IF** formula:

=INDEX(PC_PT_AccountType,MATCH(A11,PT_ColA_AccountType,0),
MATCH(PC_Name,PT_Titles_AccountType,0))

The formula is similar to the formula in the second argument in the **IF** formula. The difference between the two is within the third argument of the **INDEX** formula:

= MATCH(PC_Name,PT_Titles_AccountType,0)

The **MATCH** formula in the third argument returns the column number in **PT_Titles_AccountType** (described on page 293) where the **Profit Center** name you chose from the **Combo Box** is found (in the formulas in the cells in column **D**, add 1 to the calculation result for the column number).

Formula in Cell B12 and All Accounts Name Level Cells

The formula that will be entered to all cells in the **Account Name** level (see Figure 15-9) is the same form as that entered to cell **B11**. The differences are that the *Names* defined to the **PivotTable** report contain summaries of the **Account Name** (for more details, see *Defining Names*, page 293):

✦ *Name* defined for worksheet *82 — PT AccountName*: **PT_PC_AccountName**

✦ *Name* defined for column **A**: **PT_ColA_AccountName**

✦ *Name* defined for row **2**, the title's row: **PT_Titles_AccountName**

The formula in cell B12:

=IF(PC_Number=6,INDEX(PT_PC_AccountName,MATCH(A12,PT_ColA_AccountName,0),12)*- 1,INDEX(PT_PC_AccountName,MATCH(A12,PT_ColA_AccountName,0),MATCH(PC_Name,PT_Titles_AccountName,0))*-1)

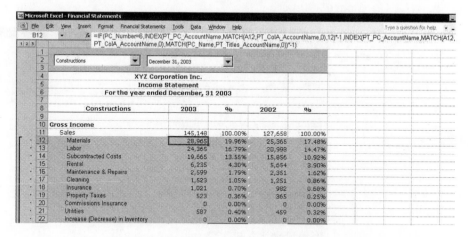

Figure 15-9: Formula That Returns Summarized Balances for Account Name

Printing Profit Center Income Statement Reports

This section describes how to print all **Profit Center** Income Statement reports, as well as how to automate printing in either Summary or Detailed mode, using macros added to the **Custom Menu**.

➢ **To add a Custom View for the Summary Income Statement report:**

1. Hide the detailed rows by clicking button **1** from the three **Group and Outline** level buttons (numbered 1, 2, 3).

2. Select and set the print area.

3. Add a **Custom View**, as shown in the figure below. (For more details, refer to *Saving Filtering Profit Centers Criteria Using Custom Views*, page 290.)

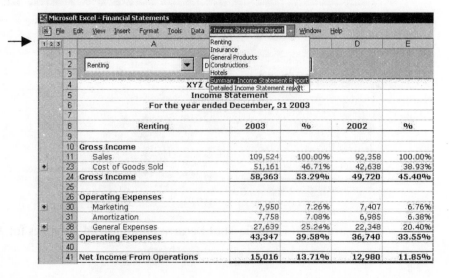

> **To add a Custom View for the Detailed Income Statement report:**

1. Unhide the detailed rows by clicking **3** from the three **Group and Outline** level numbers.

2. Select and set the print area.

3. Add a **Custom View**, as shown in the figure below. (For more details, refer to *Saving Filtering Profit Centers Criteria Using Custom Views*, page 290.)

Automating the Printing of Profit Center Reports

The printing of **Profit Center** reports can be automated by adding two macros to a regular module:

✦ The first macro (see below) prints Summary **Profit Center** reports, including the **Consolidation** report.

```
Sub Print_PC_IS_SummaryReports()

Dim NumberPages  As Integer, I As Integer
Application.ScreenUpdating = False

ActiveWorkbook.CustomViews("Summary Income Statement Report").Show
NumberPages = Range("ProfitCentersList").Cells.Count

For I = 1 To NumberPages
Range("PC_Number").Value = I

With ActiveSheet.PageSetup
    .CenterFooter = I
    .LeftFooter = ActiveWorkbook.FullName & "&A &T &D"
End With
ActiveSheet.PrintOut
Next I

Application.ScreenUpdating = True
End Sub
```

✦ The second macro (see below) prints Detailed **Profit Center** reports, including the **Consolidation** report.

```
Sub Print_PC_IS_DetailedReports()
Dim NumberPages  As Integer, I As Integer
Application.ScreenUpdating = False

ActiveWorkbook.CustomViews("Detailed Income Statement report").Show
NumberPages = Range("ProfitCentersList").Cells.Count

For I = 1 To NumberPages
Range("PC_Number").Value = I

With ActiveSheet.PageSetup
    .CenterFooter = I
    .LeftFooter = ActiveWorkbook.FullName & "&A &T &D"
End With
ActiveSheet.PrintOut
Next I

Application.ScreenUpdating = True
End Sub
```

Operate the macros from the **Custom Menu** you created, according to the instructions on page 119, *Chapter 8, Customizing the Financial Statements.xls Workbook and Presenting Information.*

NOTE:

The macro VBA code lines can be copied from http://www.excelforum.com/f96-s, the macro is also available in Chapter15.xls workbook at the companion CD-ROM

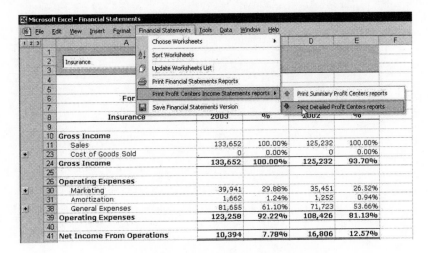

Figure 15-10: Custom Menu

Index

We'd Like to Hear from You!

Our goal is to publish a book that will help you to get the most out of Excel, upgrade your working level, and bring to your desk the best solutions needed for everyday tasks.

I would appreciate it if you could find a few moments and share with us your thoughts, comments, suggestions, ideas, tips, areas to cover, helpful solutions that other Excel users might need, and how we can improve and make this book better.

Looking forward to hear from you,

Joseph Rubin, CPA

Author

jrubin@exceltip.com

www.exceltip.com

Joseph Rubin's Excel books:

> *F1 Get the Most out of Excel! The Ultimate Excel Help Tip Guide* (print & e-Book)
>
> *Financial Statements.xls* (print & e-Book)

For more information and ordering: www.exceltip.com

Notes

Notes